© Sir Stirling Moss and Philip Porter

All rights reserved. No part of this publication may be reproduced,
stored in a retrieval system or transmitted, in any form or by
any means, electronic, mechanical, photocopying, recording or
otherwise, without prior permission in writing from
the publisher

First published in May 2006

ISBN 0-9550068-2-1
ISBN 0-9550068-3-X (Leather-bound edition)

Published by
Porter Press International
an imprint of Porter & Porter Ltd.

PO Box 2, Tenbury Wells,
WR15 8XX, UK.
Tel: +44 (0)1584 781588
Fax: +44 (0)1584 781630
sales@stirlingmoss.com
www.stirlingmoss.com

Designed by Grafx Resource
Printed and bound by World Print Limited in China

COPYRIGHT
We have made every effort to trace and acknowledge copyright holders and we apologise in advance for any unintentional omission. We would be pleased to insert the appropriate acknowledgement in any subsequent edition. We wish to thank the Editors and publishers of the named publications, which we have managed to trace, for their kind permission to reproduce the cuttings and/or photographs. Without their co-operation, this publication would not have been possible.

PHOTO CREDITS
The following have been extremely helpful in providing or allowing use of photographs: Stirling Moss Archive, Doug Nye, The Zagari/Spitzley Collection, The GP Library, Paul Vestey, Matt & Di Spitzley, Ted Walker/Ferret Fotographics, The Klemantaski Collection and Bernard Cahier.

Stirling Moss Scrapbook 1961

To Luke, go for it!
Stirling Moss

Stirling Moss & Philip Porter

Design by Andrew Garman

Porter Press International

INTRODUCTION

In the first of this series of books, I wrote in my introduction what a thrill it was to be producing a book with my great childhood hero. Since then I have had the privilege of getting to know Stirling and Susie even better and I still cannot quite believe it is all happening. I don't give a damn about sounding naïve - why shouldn't we have heroes? In my opinion, it is a very healthy thing in an increasingly unhealthy age.

As I get to know Stirling better and better, my admiration and respect grow apace. The adulation that has surrounded him for more than five decades is not based on PR hype but real achievement, courage, character, inordinate skill and sportsmanship. If the young today looked up to, and were influenced by, such as Stirling what a better place the world would be.

Why have I chosen 1961 as the edition following 1955? Well, I chose 1955 to launch the series because we published on the 50th anniversary but, more importantly, it was a pivotal year for the aspiring young racing driver. That year he proved himself to be one of the greats in the traditional front-engined era. By 1961 motor racing was looking very different, a complete contrast to 1955. This was one reason for choosing 1961.

The most compelling reasons, though, were twofold - Monaco and Nűrburgring. The stage was set for the British under-dog. In equal cars Stirling could beat his competitors too easily. He needed handicapping and through such handicapping would demonstrate his brilliance and pre-eminence. In 1961, the Ferraris had significantly more power than the British Grand Prix cars. The stage was set.

His two victories at circuits where skill was paramount and power was secondary sealed his greatness.

In boxing and tennis (singles), for example, you have just one rival. In team sports, such as soccer, football, cricket, baseball, rugby and hockey, you share the challenge and lean on your team mates. In athletics, success is largely based on strength and fitness.

In these two Grands Prix, Stirling Moss was one man pitted against three worthy rivals equipped with greatly superior machinery. He did not knock out one man, he knocked out three, and it was not brawn which brought victory. It was sheer skill, intelligence, fitness, daring, strength of character and courageous determination.

Add to all this, his seventh Tourist Trophy win in one of the most charismatic Ferraris of all time, umpteen wins in single-seaters and sports racers, plus a year when he continued to fill the newspapers as the Beckham of his era, a year when he went out with a vast selection of stunning ladies, dashed around the world and lived life flat out, and it is a heady mix.

This, then, is a behind-the-scenes, period look at that heady mix, narrated by Stirling's own diaries, his own scrapbooks of cuttings and photos from around the world and his many memories and forthright comments. I hope you will enjoy our second offering as much as people seem to have enjoyed the first.

The 1955 edition was very generously reviewed and set the scene for the series. If the critics are kind once again and you, the reader, do indeed enjoy this latest edition, we are well on our way to sharing every one of Stirling's wonderful, fascinating scrapbooks that have never before seen the light of day.

Philip Porter
Knighton-on-Teme, Worcestershire.

ACKNOWLEDGEMENTS

I would like to thank Doug Nye, Ted Walker, Simon Taylor, Ann & Penny Malone, Eoin Young, Graeme Hurst, Mike Monk, Lucia Ercolani, Peter Sachs, John Brierley, Claire Bryan, Eric Jackson, Ray Barker, Robin Puplett, Dermot Bambridge, the late-Geoff Williams, John Elmgreen, Terry McGrath, Lionel Higginson, Jeremy Wade, Pat Moss Carlsson and Stirling's old friend Herb Jones. We are honoured to have been able to include paintings by two of the world's pre-eminent motoring painters, Alan Fearnley and Michael Turner. Clive Beecham went so far as to entrust me with his irreplaceable albums on his fabulous ex-Walker/Wilkins Ferrari 250 GT SWB. Mary Fulford-Talbot, my PA, has laboured long and hard on the copyright jungle and given an enormous amount of other assistance with great good humour, as have other colleagues in our office - Louise, Annelise, Christine, Lara and Leanne, plus remote colleague and distinguished author Jonathan Wood.

Mark Holman has given me exceptional support with proof-reading and wise comments and, thanks to the wonders of the internet, it has made not a jot of difference that he is in New Zealand! Mrs Betty Walker, widow of that wonderful gentleman Rob Walker, Stirling's friend and entrant, gave crucial and extremely kind help with photographs and her memories, both of which have improved this book no end. Betty's daughter, Dauvergne Morgan, has also been most kind and helpful. As with the 1955 book, Stirling's best friend, David Haynes, and former secretary/assistant, Val Pirie, have given very valuable assistance with stories and memories.

I would like to thank my wife, and colleague, Julie for her terrific support and invaluable input. Once again, our designer Andy Garman has worked very hard, overcoming many challenges and difficulties, and always with good humour, great patience and wonderful loyalty. Working with old material of varying and sometimes dubious quality has meant that Andy's role has been far more than merely conventional design work.

Finally, Stirling himself and his remarkable wife, Susie. What can one say? Without them, it would not have happened. Incontrovertibly true, but I can say a lot more! They have been unbelievably supportive and kind, totally believing in the concept, generously giving their time, being incredibly patient and being infectiously enthusiastic. A great lady and a very great man.

THE STORY SO FAR - THE PRELUDE TO 1961.

Born on September 17 1929, it is not too surprising that Stirling Moss should have a career in motor racing as both his parents had competed in forms of motor sport. His father, Alfred, had raced at Indianapolis and his mother, Aileen, had tackled trials and rallies. As a child he was taken to such events and thus breathed the cut and thrust from an early age.

An Austin Seven to drive around the family farm was his first car. During the war he had a motorbike and his father, who was a highly successful dentist, bought him a three-wheeler Morgan when Stirling was 15. Yearning for four wheels, he acquired an MG TB. When father bought a BMW 328, he was persuaded to let his son do a few competitive events with it. In parallel, Stirling had been very successfully competing in horse-jumping events, a sport in which his sister Pat was to excel in future years before turning to international rallying.

These successes on four-legged creatures brought modest winnings and, supplemented by an indulgent father, for his 18th birthday Stirling was able to buy one of the new Cooper 500cc racing jobs to compete in the low-cost formula that had been created by a bunch of Bristol enthusiasts after the war.

Immediately, he tasted success in hillclimbs and races, ending his first season with 11 wins from 15 starts. He was already being noticed by the press and for 1949 he graduated to a Mark III Cooper and now had the option of running a 1,000cc twin and competing in the larger class as well. Another fruitful season included his international début at Lake Garda in Italy where he won his class by four minutes, victory in the 500cc race at the British GP and Fastest Time of Day (ftd) at Shelsley Walsh. Already, stars such as the great Nuvolari were tipping him for greatness.

For 1950 the 20-year-old joined the HWM team. Though this British team was always short of funding and the engines lacked power, it was good experience for Stirling with plenty of racing against established stars in mainland Europe. He continued to race the 500 and in September had a big break. The Tourist Trophy was Britain's classic sports car race and Stirling approached a number of the works teams. However, they thought this young man was going a bit too fast and did not want him to kill himself in one of their cars!

In spite of this, he managed to persuade motoring journalist Tommy Wisdom to lend him his works-prepared Jaguar XK 120. In foul conditions, Stirling drove the socks off the rest and took a brilliant victory. That evening William Lyons, the renowned Jaguar MD, asked him to lead the new works team in 1951, a fine 21st birthday present.

During 1951 Moss raced the Formula Two HWM, the new Kieft 500 and the new Jaguar C-types. The HWMs continued to be out-classed and unreliable but again brought experience. By slip-streaming the Ferraris at Monza, he finished a brilliant third. The Kieft was a very advanced design and the combination was pretty dominant throughout the season. For Le Mans, Jaguar gave Stirling, who was paired with reliable Jack Fairman, the job of breaking the opposition by setting a cracking pace. He did and, although his car and another in the team, succumbed to a minor but terminal problem, the third C-type was able to back off as the competition was gone and take a seminal victory. This win did more to establish Jaguar worldwide than any other single factor.

Later in the season Stirling added a second victory in the TT to his growing list of achievements. However, a week earlier Enzo Ferrari had seriously offended him. The fiery Italian had invited Moss to Bari to drive one of his cars. When Stirling arrived, he found the drive had been given to Taruffi. Stirling would never forget this treatment and would never drive for Ferrari, though relations greatly improved in 1961.

As a full-time professional racing driver (probably the only one in Britain), Stirling needed to keep earning in the off-season and so this led him into the rallying world in the winter. In 1952 he tackled the Monte Carlo Rally, in a works Sunbeam-Talbot, and missed outright victory by just four seconds.

In these formative years, Stirling desperately wanted to persevere with British cars but this worthy patriotism adversely affected his career. It did him, however, no harm with the British public who increasingly adored this knight in shining armour going out to do battle in foreign lands.

Stirling's early career was built on his great success in the tiny 'half pint' racers, the motorcycle-engined racers that were so popular after the War. Here he is seen making his international debut in the Cooper-JAP 1,000 at Lake Garda in 1949

For 1952 he was offered, and not surprisingly turned down, a Ferrari contract. He also turned down Raymond Mays's advances because, although the B.R.M. was British, it was a joke during this period. Britain was still a good few years away from being pre-eminent in GP racing. Stirling was persuaded to race the Bristol-engined G-type ERA but it was a major mistake being utterly unreliable and too slow. Meanwhile, he was enjoying some success with the Kieft-Norton 500 but productively changed stables mid-season, returning to the Cooper fold. In winning the Reims sports car race with a C-type Jaguar, he recorded the first-ever victory by a disc-braked car in an international event.

Still persisting with British cars, he became involved with the Cooper-Alta Special project for 1953. It was another disaster and mid-season he changed to a more conventional Cooper powered by the Alta engine. It was marginally better but his career was suffering and would stall, he reluctantly realised, if he did not drive a foreign car.

In 1954 Mercedes-Benz, who had been so successful pre-war, returned to GP racing. They signed 1951 World Champion, Juan Manuel Fangio to lead the team and Stirling's manager Ken Gregory approached M-B team manager, Alfred Neubauer. The German recognised the young Englishman's talents in sports car but pointed out that he had not really

The Vanwall was the first effective British Grand Prix car and enabled Stirling to satisfy his patriotism. The irony of his 1958 season was that three GP wins to Mike Hawthorn's one were not sufficient to bring Stirling the World Championship by a single point from his compatriot. Hawthorn's Ferrari was more reliable and he consistently scored points, while Stirling had the frustration of retiring from five races

proved himself yet in Grand Prix racing. He suggested Stirling should purchase a suitable car, race it in 1954 and then speak to him again at the end of the year.

Thus a Maserati 250F was purchased for Stirling and he set out to prove himself in one of the great GP cars of all time. Though dogged by bad luck, a Moss characteristic, he did sufficient to be drafted into the works Maserati team and now there was no questioning his ability. Meanwhile, he was still leading the Jaguar works team and had finished second at Le Mans in '53, having broken the opposition again. Though delayed by mechanical maladies, he and Peter Walker followed their team mates, Rolt and Hamilton, home for another momentous team triumph. In 1954 Jaguar débuted the fabulous D-types but Moss's season was ruined by unreliability.

For 1955 both Maserati and Mercedes offered him a contract. He chose the German team and was to enjoy a quite extraordinary season. In the GP cars, he and Fangio became known as 'the train' because the pupil shadowed the master in almost every race bar one which was the British GP. Stirling finished ahead by a whisker, taking his first GP win. In sports cars he was in a class of his own, bar not even Fangio. He won the Mille Miglia (probably his most famous triumph of all time), the Targa Florio and the TT. All were truly heroic performances. If Mercedes had not withdrawn from the Le Mans race, following the awful accident, he would likely have taken the Grand Slam of classic sports car races. All was looking fantastic and then Mercedes dropped a bombshell. They withdrew from racing.

Having weighed up the British options of B.R.M., Vanwall and Connaught, Stirling signed up with Maserati as Team Leader for 1956. However, he somewhat assuaged his patriotism by joining the Aston Martin team for sports car events. It was a season of promise but not consistent results. Highlights included wins in the Monaco and Italian Grands Prix and seconds at Le Mans and in the German GP.

In '55 Stirling had been tempted to join Vanwall, masterminded by the forceful Tony Vandervell. With Colin Chapman and Frank Costin behind the design of the second generation Vanwall, and the financial backing to do the job properly, here was an emerging British team to be taken seriously. For 1957 Stirling threw in his lot with Vanwall and it was to prove a good decision.

The first half of the season was frustrating but then team mate Tony Brooks and Stirling shared a car to win the British GP, the first time it had been won by a British car and driver combination. Fine wins followed in the Pescara and Italian GPs and, for the third season, Stirling finished second to Fangio in the World Championship.

For 1958 Moss was to continue with Vanwall but the team did not travel to Argentina for the season-opening GP and so Stirling drove Rob Walker's little Cooper-Climax. He won and recorded Cooper's first ever GP win and the first for a rear-engined car since the Auto Unions in 1939. It was to be a foretaste of things to come.

The 1958 season was one of utter frustration with Stirling so nearly winning the Championship. Fangio had now retired and Stirling's great rival for honours that year was his compatriot Mike Hawthorn who was driving for Ferrari. Though Hawthorn only took one win, he had consistency on his side. In addition to Argentina, Stirling won the Dutch, Portuguese and Moroccan Grands Prix for Vanwall but retired from five others. He had the consolation of winning his fourth TT and took a load of more minor victories in a variety of cars during the year.

Overall success was to elude Stirling again in 1959, though he did help Aston Martin win the World Sports Car Championship with wins at the Nürburgring (his third in four years) and the TT. In Formula One, Stirling was to drive Rob Walker's Coopers but gearbox problems blighted the car's early season promise. A brief flirtation with a BRM P25, while the gearbox problems were assailed, was not the answer. After the gearbox problems with the Cooper had lost him three GPs, he won the Portuguese and Italian races. The Championship was again to be decided in the final GP, at Sebring, this time between Moss and Jack Brabham in the works Cooper. Stirling needed to win and make fastest lap. He lead until the transmission broke on the sixth lap!

For 1960, it appeared that a Lotus 18 was the car to have and Rob Walker obliged. At that stage, though, Lotuses were fast but fragile. The Coopers were less sophisticated but strong. Though the Lotus was only delivered days before the Monaco GP, Stirling took a great win which was a maiden GP victory for the Lotus marque. At the Dutch Grand Prix, Stirling was playing a waiting game, shadowing Brabham in the lead. Bad luck manifested itself yet again, when the Australian's Cooper clipped a kerb and threw up a lump of concrete which punctured Stirling's front tyre and wrecked the wheel. After pitting, Stirling was 12th but drove brilliantly to carve through the field and finish fourth, a second behind Graham Hill.

In practice for the Belgian GP at Spa, Stirling experienced the worst of Lotus when the axle shaft broke in practice. With a wheel adrift at 140mph, the result was a massive accident. He broke both legs and his nose, and crushed three spinal vertebrae. Absolutely remarkably, he was testing again a month later and racing just seven weeks after this colossal shunt. Another frustrating season ended, at least, on a high note with a win in the United States Grand Prix at Riverside in California.

As usual the versatile Moss had raced a rash of other cars and enjoyed much success. He had a productive season with the Formula Two Porsche, won his 6th TT in Rob Walker's 250 GT Ferrari, enjoyed the spoils in late season with a Lotus 19 sports racer and, in a Birdcage Maserati, won the Nűrburgring 1,000kms yet again.

There then occurred a change in Formula One regulations which, initially, was to prove a disaster for the British teams. The President of the CSI, one Augustin Perouse, championed a change from 2½ litre capacity engines to a maximum of 1½ litres. The Brits were not keen and lost vital time vainly arguing against the change. They proposed a new 3-litre 'InterContinental' formula but then Coventry-Climax did not help that cause when they refused to build such an engine. A series of InterContinental races would be run in 1961 but they had little real status.

While the British teams of BRM, Cooper and Lotus had been prevaricating, Ferrari had pressed ahead with designing, building and developing a 1,500cc V6 in good time for the 1961 season. When the British teams finally had to accept that they could not influence the intransigent ruling body, in spite of threats of a boycott, there was insufficient time for Coventry-Climax or BRM to develop new engines. It was to prove disastrous for their cause.

Coventry-Climax began work on a new V8 engine but it would not be used in anger until at least mid-season and was then dogged with development problems. BRM were also working on a new V8 but were forced to become Climax customers for '61. All the Coventry firm could do was dig out what was now an ageing design. Their FPF in 2½-litre form, when allied with the advantages of the Cooper and Lotus mid-engined chassis designs, had been good enough to win the 1959 Championship, but an updated 1½-lire version was another matter when the old four-cylinder was up against a brand new multi-cylinder power unit from the Italians.

Meanwhile, Colin Chapman whose Lotus was said to be the finest chassis design in 1960, was hard at work refining the concept and producing an improved version for 1961. By dispensing with the saddle fuel tank over the driver's legs and adopting two side pannier tanks instead, he lowered the centre of gravity. The rear axle shaft that had broken so disastrously for Stirling at Spa was now spared the sole responsibility of retaining the wheels as double wishbones were added at the rear. Front suspension was now by rocker arms with inboard springs. As for transmission, the Lotus 'queerbox', as it was sarcastically known, was replaced by one from ZF and the brakes were moved outboard to aid cooling. Frontal area was reduced and air penetration thus improved by Chapman refining the boxy Lotus 18 to become the slimmer, more svelte Lotus 21. To help achieve this, the driver was now even more reclined.

However, as Stirling explains later in this book, Chapman would not, or could not, sell a Lotus 21 to Stirling's entrant Rob Walker. The prospects for the man who was now unquestionably the world's finest racing driver did not look good for 1961. He would be racing last year's car with an engine producing 152bhp, as against the Ferrari's 190bhp.

He relished a challenge, though, and the stage was set for heroic performances.

To complete the scene-setting, we should mention that Stirling had married Katie Molson in 1957 but unfortunately the racing lifestyle had not been conducive to married life and they had separated in 1960. During that year, quite ludicrously Stirling had been banned from driving for a year for changing lanes in the Mersey Tunnel and thus was not on the road in the first months of 1961. During the year he began the designs and preparation work for the building of his high-tech house in London's Mayfair. This was, very sadly, to be Stirling's last full season in motor racing at the highest level.

GLOSSARY	
Alf	Alf Francis (long-term Chief Mechanic)
BARC	British Automobile Racing Club
CN	Caroline Nuttall
DH	David Haynes (Stirling's best friend)
Ftd	Fastest Time of Day
JC	Judy Carne
KG	Ken Gregory (long-term Manager)
KM	Katie Moss (Stirling's first wife)
LAP	London Airport (Heathrow today)
Nym	Ken Gregory's wife
Rob	Rob Walker (Entrant)
SA	Shirlee Adams
36	Stirling's home in Shepherd St. in 1961
VP	Valerie (Val) Pirie (Secretary/Assistant in 1961)
!X!	signifies disgust or a strong reaction!
G = good, F = fair, EX = excellent, NG = no good, etc., usually in relation to films	
The 'Wheel'	The Steering Wheel Club, a motor racing bar and restaurant for members, located just off Shepherds Market, London.

1961

World News:

Yuri Gagarin, a Soviet test pilot, took Russia to victory over America in the space race when he orbited the earth in the Vostok 1 spacecraft. The flight capsule, measuring only 2.58 metres in diameter, was launched from Baikonur cosmodrome in Kazakhstan, and landed 108 minutes later at Saratov. John F. Kennedy became the youngest President of the United States of America and the first Roman Catholic to hold that office. 'Appeal for Amnesty' (now known as Amnesty International) was launched by British lawyer Peter Benenson, in a climate in which abuses of human rights were becoming widely condemned. Following abduction from his hiding place in Buenos Aires by Israeli intelligence in 1960, former SS officer Adolf Eichmann was found guilty of war crimes against the Jews, and sentenced to death. Tensions between Russia and the USA culminated in an attempt by 1,500 Cuban exiles, trained and supported by the CIA, to overthrow the Castro Government. Landing at the 'Bay of Pigs', the rebels were quickly overcome by Castro's Russian-supplied MiG fighters and armaments. Following the white referendum which led to South Africa leaving the British Commonwealth and South Africa becoming a republic, black leaders made it clear they would not tolerate apartheid and would, if necessary, use force. The post-World War II Alliance was broken by Russia with the overnight erection of the 'Berlin Wall', 28 miles (45km) long and 15 feet (4.5m) high, dividing Berlin in two. It was an effort to halt the flow of East Germans who had chosen to flee to West Berlin, and was policed by East German armed forces. The first US aircraft was hijacked when Puerto Rican-born Antuilo Ramierez Ortiz forced at gunpoint a National Airlines plane to fly to Havana, Cuba, where he was given asylum. The USSR detonated a 50 megaton hydrogen bomb, the largest man-made explosion ever. OPEC (Organisation of Petrol Exporting Countries) was formally constituted.

Television:

TV Shows Worldwide:
I love Lucy
The Dick Van Dyke Show
The Flinstones
Alfred Hitchcock Presents
Perry Mason

Top UK TV Shows:
No Hiding Place
Bootsie and Snudge
Take Your Pick
The Army Game
Emergency Ward 10
Sunday Night at the London Palladium
The Dickie Henderson Show
Double Your Money
Armchair Theatre

Trivia:

Scalextric was the third best-selling toy in 1961, just beaten by Noddy
Coronation Street, the world's longest running soap, went nationwide in 1961
The Morecombe and Wise Show first appeared on ATV in 1961
Miss World was won by the UK contestant (Rosemarie Frankland) for the first time
The Avengers arrived in 1961, a year before the first official Bond movie
'Dord' was a non-existent word that appeared in the 1961 edition of Webster's New international dictionary by mistake

Movies:

Breakfast at Tiffany's, Audrey Hepburn & George Peppard
Jules et Jim, Jeanne Moreau
Guns of Navarone, David Niven, Gregory Peck, Anthony Quinn, Stanley Baker, Anthony Quayle, James Darren, Richard Harris, Bryan Forbes, James Robertson Justice
The Hustler, Paul Newman
The Innocents, Deborah Kerr, Michael Redgrave, Peter Wyngarde
Judgment at Nuremberg, Spencer Tracey, Burt Lancaster, Marlene Dietrich, Maximilian Schell
The Misfits, Clark Gable & Marilyn Monroe
One-Eyed Jacks, Marlon Brando
101 Dalmatians (Disney)
One, Two, Three, James Cagney & Horst Buchholz
Splendor in the Grass, Natalie Wood & Warren Beatty
West Side Story, Natalie Wood, Rita Moreno, Russ Tamblyn, George Chakiris
Two Women, Sophia Loren
The Roman Spring of Mrs Stone, Vivian Leigh & Warren Beatty

The Oscars
Best Film: *West Side Story*
Best Actor: Maximilian Schell, *Judgment at Nuremberg*
Best Actress: Sophia Loren, *Two Women*

Sport:

Tennis - Angela Mortimer defeated Christine Truman at Wimbledon and Rod Laver defeated Chuck McKinley to win Men's title
World Series - NY Yankees beat Cincinnati 4-1
Cricket - Hampshire won Country Championship
Golf - Arnold Palmer won his first British Open when he beat Dai Rees by a stroke at Royal Birkdale
Boxing - Floyd Patterson knocked out Ingemar Johansson to retain the World Heavyweight title
Rowing - Cambridge won the Boat Race
Soccer – FA Cup Final – Tottenham Hotspur 2, Leicester 0
Racing – The Grand National was won by 28-1 outsider Nicolaus Silver, ridden by Bobby Beasley and trained by Fred Rimell (Sir William Lyons's younger daughter, Mary, married Rimell's son in 1961)

Music:

Hits of 1961:

I Fall To Pieces, Patsy Cline
Tossin' and Turnin', Bobby Lewis
Cryin', Roy Orbison
Take Good Car Of My Baby, Bobby Vee
Running Scared, Roy Orbison
Hit The Road Jack, Ray Charles
The Boll Weevil Song, Brook Benton
Who Put The Bomp, Barry Mann
Hello Mary Lou, Ricky Nelson
It's Gonna Work Out Fine, Ike and Tina Turner

UK No. 1s:

Johnny Tillotson	Poetry in Motion	Jan 12
Elvis Presley	Are You Lonesome Tonight	Jan 26
Petula Clark	Sailor	Feb 23
Everly Brothers	Walk Right Back	Mar 2
Elvis Presley	Wooden Heart	Mar 23
The Marcels	Blue Moon	May 4
Floyd Cramer	On The Rebound	May 18
The Temperance Seven	You're Driving Me Crazy	May 25
Elvis Presley	Surrender	Jun 1
Del Shannon	Runaway	Jun 29
Everly Brothers	Temptation	Jul 20
Eden Kane	Well I Ask You	Aug 3
Helen Shapiro	You Don't Know	Aug 10
John Leyton	Johnny Remember Me	Aug 31
Shirley Bassey	Reach for the Stars/ Climb Every Mountain	Sep 21
The Shadows	Kon Tiki	Oct 5
The Highwaymen	Michael	Oct 12
Helen Shapiro	Walkin' Back To Happiness	Oct 19
Elvis Presley	His Latest Flame	Nov 9
Frankie Vaughan	Tower Of Strength	Dec 7
Danny Williams	Moon River	Dec 28

Fashion:

The innocence of the 1950s was still apparent in the early '60s look. Shapely bodices and full skirts hung on until 1962. In 1961 Mary Quant opened her second Bazaar boutique, this time in Knightsbridge, and within two years she would revolutionise fashion in the High Street. At the beginning of the decade, Paris still led the fashion world. In January 1961 Yves St Laurent, who had left Christian Dior, showed his first collection under his own name. As to women's hairstyles, the beehive of the '50s, achieved through hair lacquer and backcombing, was superseded in the 1960s by a sleeker look.

Money:

Exchange Rates per One British Pound

	U.S. $	German Marks	Japanese Yen	French Francs	Italian Lira	Canadian $	Australian $
1961	2.80	11.30	1008	13.82	1750	2.84	2.50
2006	1.77	2.83*	207	9.50*	2803*	2.04	2.36

* 2003 (pre-Euro)

Motoring:

In the fifties, customers demanded solid virtues, such as interior space, comparative economy and dependability, rather than excitement. Saloon car performance was pretty feeble, the steering soggy and handling questionable, especially in the wet. If the average car could carry sufficient persons and their luggage, the average driver would be satisfied and never explore the limits because he drove so slowly. This was the age of gentlemanly motoring magazines writing charitably of all cars including, on occasions, absolute dross. A Morris Oxford saloon could manage just 80mph and the revolutionary new Minis (£448) ran out of steam at 72mph. Even the popular sports cars had a top speed of only around 100mph, or less. Of the seriously fast sports cars, the Mercedes-Benz 300SL cost over £4500 and the Ferrari 250 GT cost almost £6000. It is hardly surprising the Jaguar E-type, launched in early 1961, made such an impact when it offered 150mph performance, independent rear suspension, stunning looks and a price tag of a shade over £2000.

0-60mph Acceleration Times (seconds)

Mini-Minor 850 de luxe saloon	28.7
Morris Oxford	24.1
Holden Special Sedan	19.6
Ford Galaxie	13.6
Lotus Elite	11.4
Aston Martin DB4 Saloon	9.3
Ferrari 250 GT California Spyder	7.2
Jaguar E-type Fixed Head Coupe	6.9
Ferrari 250 GT SWB Berlinetta	6.8

Books:

Catch-22, Joseph Heller
A Severed Head, Iris Murdoch
A House for Mr Biswas, V S Naipaul
Call for the Dead, John Le Carré
The Prime of Miss Jean Brodie, Muriel Spark
The Agony & the Ecstasy, Irving Stone
Tropic of Cancer, Henry Miller
New English Bible published

1961

JANUARY

Calendar

7	New Zealand GP, Ardmore – 1st in heat, ret'd in final in 2.5 Lotus-Climax 18
21	Lady Wigram Trophy, Christchurch, NZ – 2nd in 2.5 Lotus-Climax 18
29	Australian GP (Inter-Continental race), Warwick Farm, Sydney - 1st in 2.5 Lotus-Climax 18

In spite of it being New Year's Day and a Sunday, Stirling was in his office in the morning before departing with Ken Gregory, and his wife Nym, and friend Helen for London Airport. Together with Jack Brabham, he was en route to Auckland in New Zealand. Testing even the famous Moss stamina, he failed to go to bed that night or the next as he was on an aircraft on January 2 and most of January 3, stopping only for a haircut in Sydney!

Arriving at Auckland at 9.30pm, he saw a friend called Shalima and did not retire until 3.30am.

Woken by excessive noise and the telephone, he was up five hours later and headed for the circuit to practice. "Loose stones," he noted in his diary. "Got about 140mph with 40/37 gear, 6,600 [rpm]. Engine fair only. Hotel and to cinema with Shalima. Food and chatted till late. Bed at 12.45am."

Up late next day, he again went to the circuit. "Car feels pretty good. I got 6,800 [rpm] (146mph)… Later home and called Geoff Sykes re race at Warwick Farm. £1,500 and expenses. BP cocktails and then Shalima cooked me a fab Chinese/Indian meal. Bed at 3am."

SM	1.20.2
Jack [Brabham]	1.20.4
Dan [Gurney]	1.20.7
[Graham] Hill	1.20.8
[John] Surtees	1.21.4
Jo [Bonnier]	1.21.8
Innes [Ireland]	1.21.8

Stirling was a great film-goer and on Friday, January 6 he went to see *Pollyanna* which he rated as excellent (Ex). After eating at Shalima's friend's, he attended a Drivers' Meeting and went to bed at 9.45pm, an unheard-of hour for Moss.

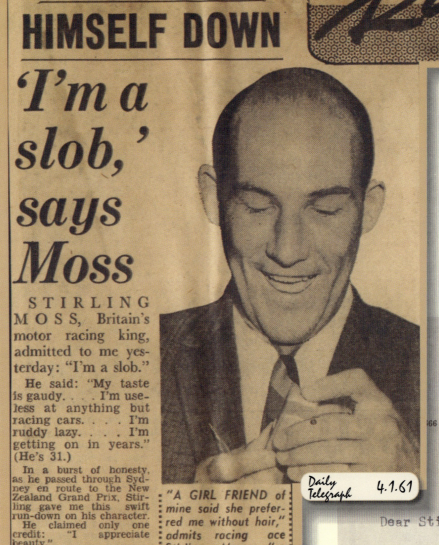

SHALIMA

"Shalima was a half-Indian, half-Maori girl that I knew from New Zealand; a very interesting person, but quite a thinker, not just a flirt, but quite deep."

Daily Telegraph, 4.1.61

January

Stirling Moss Scrapbook

Shalima was a friend in New Zealand

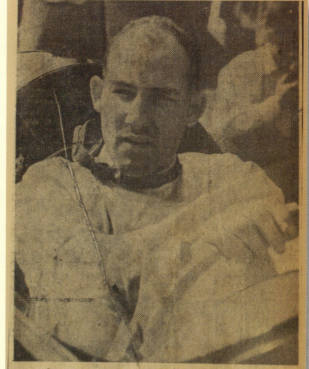

MOSS FAVOURS WORLD TITLE RACES HERE

SYDNEY, Tuesday: Stirling Moss, world famous motor racing driver and top rival to Jack Brabham for the world's speed crown, said in Sydney today he knew of no reason why races counting for the world's title and championship should not be raced in Australia.

Brabham, who is accompanying Moss to New Zealand to race in the International Grand Prix at Auckland next Saturday, is looking forward to driving on the Warwick Farm circuit on January 30.

Moss expressed disapproval of the decision to reduce the formula one engine capacity from 2,500 to 1,500 c.c.

He said that it meant that top drivers would be driving dead-beat cars and it appeared that the F.I.A., the controlling automobile body, made rules without asking the views of top drivers.

Canberra Times 4.1.61

England's champion racing driver Stirling Moss is the subject of Face To Face on ABN 2 at 9.40 on Wednesday night.

MOSS is interviewed by John Freeman in the 30-minute program.

The famed racing ace is questioned about his career since the time as an 11-year-old he drove an old Austin around a rough farm track.

Moss, now 30, has been the British champion seven times and was the first Englishman to win the Italian Mille Miglia.

He has made two trips to Australia to compete in Australian Grand Prix events in Melbourne.

A film of his life story is now being made in England.

One of John Freeman's questions to Stirling Moss in Face to Face is, "What is the difference between an amateur racing driver and a professional?" Moss replies, "Professionals go faster."

Sydney Morn Herald 2.1.61

Stirling Moss

Busy Stirling Moss flew back to Britain from winning a race in South Africa, went to a party in London ("A long way to go for a party, I thought") and caught a plane the next day for New Zealand — 11,000 miles altogether.

On arrival here last night he sighed for the spacious days of piston-engined aircraft in which sleepers were provided, rather than the cramped accommodation of jets, and said he was looking forward to "a bit of a rest" in New Zealand as well as competing at Ardmore and Christchurch.

What was he going to do? "Get lost, if possible," replied Moss with a quick smile.

Auckland Star 4.1.61

Stirling and Pat in same race

FOR the first time, Stirling Moss and his sister Pat are to compete in the same race.

Rally driver Mr. John Sprinzel announced yesterday that he has signed them to drive Healey-Sprites at Sebring, Florida, in America's round of the world sports car championship, next March.

Sporting Life 5.1.61

N.Z. Herald 5.1.61

FROM CARS TO CAMERAS

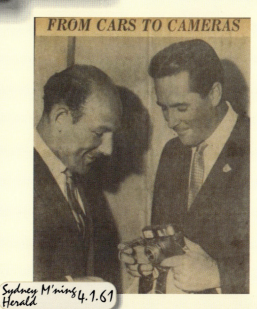

Sydney M'ning Herald 4.1.61

A keen photographer, Australia's world champion racing driver, Jack Brabham (right), discusses his new camera with one of his closest rivals, Stirling Moss, of Britain, at Kingsford Smith Airport yesterday. They arrived by B.O.A.C. from England and later left for New Zealand to compete in the Grand Prix at Ardmore next Sunday. Brabham and several other international drivers will return to Sydney later this month to race at Warwick Farm.

Such unusual behaviour was explained by him rising at an ungodly hour. "Up at 5am! Out to circuit at 7.30 + Shalima, Herb [Jones] and Yvonne. 1st heat won by 3.8secs from Bruce [McLaren]. Ftd. 1.19.6. Car feels good. Race and I had a good start using high 1st. Followed Jack and took him when he lifted for fast left. Pulled out 16+ secs at 45 mins and then tubular drive shaft sheared. Safety wire held wheel! Jack 1st @ 1 sec Bruce. My car felt good. Home and tea and bath and letters. To official 'do'. On to Club and bed at 6am." That was more like the Moss routine!

Some four hours later Stirling was up, packing his bags and heading for the airport. His destination was Fiji for a few days' holiday before going on to Australia. Unfortunately, it rained all the next day but he swam and wrote a dozen letters before partying in the evening and meeting Denise Allan. "Drank Carva [sic], awful!"

More swimming followed next day and some fishing. "Caught two Walahou. Met Shalima at 10.30 after seeing *Tiger Bay* (G). Bed at 2am."

After a similarly relaxing day, Stirling was on the move again that evening, flying to Tahiti. "Airport and off T.I.A. [airline] DC10 at 11.30pm. No sleep, no bed. Gained a day due to date line. Arrived 9.00 local time (7am) Hotel Tahitian and Chalet 17. Fab (1775fr for two. 88fr = $1. 245 = £1. Food and nap. Later rented Vespa. Danced and met Pu-Ku. Bed at 3am."

Dissatisfied with his Vespa scooter, Stirling swopped it for another and headed off round the island but unfortunately it was a rather dull and wet day, as was the next one. It was clearly no fun on a scooter in these conditions, so he hired a Renault from Hertz instead.

"Drove round island in rain. Later shopped. Bath and food at La Chapiteau. Saw Brando and a pretty blue-eyed Tahitian! Hotel and danced. Met Gerard Picot (?) and Micheau. On to La Fayette and bed at 3am."

The miserable weather continued and Stirling packed and moved hotels. He later met Micheau. "Had a fabulous dinner, lights out at 9.30 due to shut-down of generators and bed at 11pm."

Next morning was devoted to a little painting and then he visited Papeete, the capital of Tahiti, and indulged in another favourite pastime, namely, shopping. Later he dined with Micheau before flying back to Fiji at 12.15am. "Just as we were leaving a little waitress (Michelle) came up and gave us each a lei! [flower garland] I did a Tamaran. No bed.

"Tue 17 Jan: NO DAY. Lost due to dateline."

On Wednesday January 18, Stirling arrived back at the Nadi Hotel in Fiji at 6am. After breakfast, he flew to Auckland, arriving at 2.30pm. An hour and a

This golden hare emblem on a chequered background has been adopted for the racing team which the United Dominions Trust is backing this year through their Laystall subsidiary. The U.D.T./Laystall team will race Lotus cars exclusively. Drivers in the team include Stirling Moss, Cliff Allison and Henry Taylor

The Sphere 14.1.61

Herb Jones in a Jaguar XK 120. He and Stirling are still great friends

Aerial view of Warwick Farm circuit

New Zealand Grand Prix

The condition of the Ardmore circuit was a major concern for organisers and drivers alike. Stirling was quoted as saying that he had only driven on a rougher circuit once before – Ardmore two years previously! Attempts at patching up the surface before the event left a scattering of small stones everywhere.

Two 50-mile heats determined the grid order for the 150-mile non-Championship Grand Prix. Stirling easily won the first and set up a new lap record, putting him on pole for the GP. Bruce McLaren led initially but Stirling took the lead after five laps and Brabham passed McLaren for second. Stirling built a gap of 20 seconds but, on the 30th lap, was forced to retire with transmission problems.

Thereafter only McLaren posed any threat to Brabham and they finished in that order with Graham Hill in a sick BRM third.

Herb Jones

"My interest in motors and motor racing had stemmed from my father who was an official at the Indianapolis Motor Speedway. He managed to get me in to see all of the practice and qualifying events. I even had a metal pit pass to go anywhere at the circuit. My first sporting car was a 1941 Ford convertible with full race-tuned '48 Ford Mercury engine. It was fantastic in a straight line – corners were another matter! The MG TC started me off on British sports cars, and next came the love of the Jaguar, a car that was capturing the hearts of many Americans in the early 1950s.

"This was following Jaguar's Le Mans wins, and the Jaguar XK 120 was the kind of car that movie stars drove. It was one of the best-looking cars going. Whether it went fast or not, it looked like it was the fastest, even just sitting in front of the best hotels in Beverly Hills. It was well-received, well-engineered, well-appointed and I never heard a bad word about it."

Herb acquired a rather tired 120 and entered a few races. His friendly local dealer then ordered a new C-type-engined 120 for Herb to drive. "The dealer had a neat sense of humour and he said that they had lightened the car ready for the first race. When I got in, I found that they had drilled holes in the key!"

Herb was now competing against and becoming friends with people like Phil Hill and Ritchie Ginther. Another he raced with and swopped cars with after they had become great friends was film star James Dean.

"At Palm Springs, California, I was under the car trying to tighten the manifold. After a few tries, a voice from above asked if he could help by holding the spanner [from the top] while I tightened from under the manifold. When I crawled from under the Jag, whom did I encounter but none other than Clark Gable!"

Herb and Stirling became great friends in the fifties and saw a lot of each other in 1961. During the year, Herb became 'godfather' to Damon Hill.

"Nearly 30 years ago, I was on a motoring programme called 'Wheelbase' with Stirling and was asked by the interviewer why I, as an American, liked British sports cars. My answer was that although American cars had more power, they should never deviate from a straight line!"

1961

half later, he was in the air but, "Diverted from Wellington to Palmerston N by 5.10pm. Delay announced until 7.30.(Into town and had food because NAC [airline] gave us [only] a cup of tea and two biscuits at 4.30pm). Back at 7.15 and told delay until 7.45! Waited, no refreshments. Off at 7.50. Flew and returned to P.N. at 9.15pm! Sat around until 10.30 odd when we were taken to Grand Hotel. Still no food. Bed at 11.30pm."

The misery continued. "Called at 5.45! With tea and two biscuits (NAC b'fast and dinner!). By bus for 96 miles to Wellington @ 11am. B'fast. DC3 to Christchurch. Met and to Warners Hotel. Saw film. Jag cocktail 'do'. Food with Joe and Marianne. Bed at 12pm."

Next morning he was up early and went to the Wigram circuit where it was wet. "Car felt fairly good." He was reaching 145mph and pulling 6,500rpm in top. "Later cancelled due to waterlogged track. Heard Lotus broke three more cars at Levin! Town, bath and saw *Shane* (G). Food at Malando's.

Up at 7.00 and qualifying. Six cars had a shunt on 1st lap. I did not try hard and was 5th! Town and packed and to circuit again. Race. I was hit rear and front at 1st corner. Bent track rod and cracked wheel. Car was very difficult to handle! I lay 8th, later moved up to 2nd. Jack 1.33.0, SM 1.33.2. About 15 laps from end (race 47 laps not 71 due to rain) Number 49 turned into me, mounted the car and bent my radius arms and broke carb bells. Car then missed. Later off at 8.00 and Auckland at 11.30. SM met me and to Jock's and Mimi's. Called at Cat and Griddle. Bed at 5.30am."

On Sunday Shalima and her mother saw Stirling off on the JVO (a ship - see page 14) Next day he saw the *League of Gentlemen* (G) on board. However, "Sea rough. Decided to fly due to no fun on JVO." The boat docked next day some five hours late at 11am. He met Lorraine and went to her mother's for lunch. That afternoon, he flew to Sydney.

He was awoken early next morning, "due to windows expanding and making a noise! To Bondi [Beach] 9 – 2pm, sun and I surfed on a board. Later met about four press guys and BP men. Took Jan Lindsay out to see *North to Alaska* (F) and food. Home at 5am."

On Thursday 26, he went water skiing with friends before visiting the TV studios for 'Meet the Press' with David McNicoll of the Consolidated Press. Afterwards he dined with Jan and was in bed at 3am. Next morning he went to the beach with Virginia. Ironically Stirling's and Jack Brabham's cars had not yet arrived and were still on board the

EVENT 6 — 3.10 p.m.
INTERNATIONAL "100" RACE
(45 Laps — 101.25 miles)

No.	Entrant and Driver	Car	c.c.	Colour
1	A. G. Mildren Pty. Ltd. (Drv. A. G. Mildren)	Cooper Maserati	2489	Green
2	Capitol Motors (Drv. A. Glass)	Cooper Maserati	2489	Green/White
3	B. S. Stillwell (Drv. T.B.N.)	Aston Martin DBR1/300	2996	Green
4	A. N. Davison	Aston Martin DBR1/300	2996	Green
5	Owen Racing Organisation (Drv. G. Hill)	B.R.M.	2495	Green
6	Owen Racing Organisation (Drv. D. Gurney)	B.R.M.	2495	Green
7	R.R.C. Walker (Drv. S. Moss)	Lotus	2490	Blue
8	Team Lotus (Drv. I. Ireland)	Lotus	2494	Green
9	Bill Patterson Motors (Drv. G. W. Patterson)	Cooper Climax	2496	White/Blue
10	R. Flockhart	Cooper Climax	2460	Green
11	J. Brabham	Cooper Climax	2496	Green
12	Stan Jones Motors (Drv. S. Jones)	Cooper Climax	2200	Blue
14	Superior Cars Pty. Ltd. (Drv. A. Miller)	Cooper Climax	2200	Yellow
15	Ecurie Hall (Drv. N. Hall)	Cooper Climax	2180	Green
16	B. S. Stillwell	Cooper Climax	2496	Red
17	B. S. Stillwell (Drv. T.B.N.)	Cooper Climax	2200	Red
18	J. Roxburgh	Cooper Climax	1960	Red/White

Sidelight on NZ GP

A local Press report suggested that a mechanic from Auckland had noticed that the half-shaft on Stirling's Lotus was bent and pointed this out to him, saying it would not last half the race. "Moss agreed the shaft was bent," the mechanic was quoted as saying, "but decided to carry on and take the risk. The risk didn't come off."

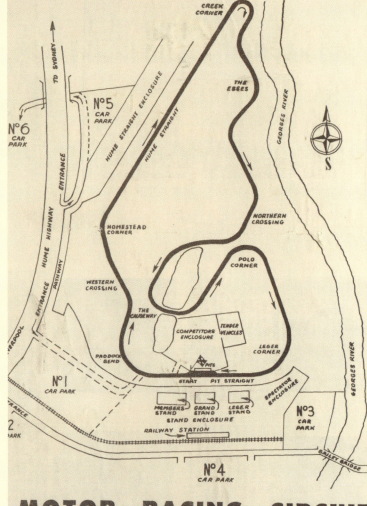

WARWICK FARM MOTOR RACING CIRCUIT

Another Win for Mr. Moss

Cape Times Woman Reporter

"WOMEN?— They're wonderful."

Stirling Moss, the man who has been photographed with the world's most beautiful women, and whose name has almost as high box-office appeal as Elvis, made this short and snappy reply to my question when I asked his opinion of women.

He qualified his remark with a shrug of his shoulders and a gleam in his eye by saying: "Where would we be without them?"

I went to the Press conference at the D. F. Malan Airport last night determined not to be impressed by this legendary lady killer.

But as I sat next to him while he answered questions fired at me, I felt myself thawing, unwillingly — but distinctly thawing.

This uncrowned king of the racing track is short, slightly built and losing his hair. But he is fascinating.

He is a man who obviously pays attention to fashion, but would probably not be included among the "10 Best Dressed Men".

Somehow his charcoal stovepipe trousers, narrow-striped jacket, black moccasins and black socks did not look ostentatious.

They fit him perfectly and on him looked perfect.

He wore a fashionable collar held together with a gold tie pin, a gold signet ring, and a gold wrist chain. A most unusual watch strap completed his ensemble.

"I believe you have some lovely girls in the Cape?", Moss asked.

"Yes", piped up half a dozen eager men. "You should see them at Clifton."

"But isn't the water very cold there?"

"Who worries about the water."

Painting

"He started painting with Mrs Rob Walker (Betty) down in Frome (where they lived in Somerset) one weekend and did one still life of fruit, if my memory serves me correctly," states Val Pirie. "I didn't know he did a Van Gogh in Tahiti – or was it Cezanne or somebody else? He might have thought of trying but there couldn't have been any birds that afternoon and he got bored and tried his hand at it again but we never saw a lovely sunset!"

"He and Katie had split up," recalls Betty Walker, "and he was terribly, terribly low and I said, 'I tell you what, I'll show you how to paint'. We covered our canvases first and did it all properly. He was absolutely marvellous; he copied exactly. He turned out a damn good picture of some fruit in a bowl. Soon afterwards it appeared on the third page in the Daily Express! It was almost half a page!"

Jill Stevenson

```
LIVERPOOL
8 15 AM
8 JAN
1962
S.O.

S.Moss Esq,
44 Shepherd St,
LONDON. W.1
```

18th January.1961.

S.Moss Esq,
44 Shepherd St,
LONDON. W.1

Dear Sir,

It is my earnest wish and insistence that you have no further contact or communication with my daughter Miss Diana Jones, whatsoever.

I must also inform you she is still a MINOR, being 19 years of age.

Further communication on either side is unnecessary.

Yours Respectfully,

T. Jones. (Mr)

Stirling Moss ...

PAINTING

"Betty Walker was a very fine painter. She was always saying I should try it but I never had time. Then after one of my accidents, I went down to their house and she said, 'Come on, we'll have a day painting'. I had a go at a still-life with some fruit and a bottle of Benedictine. I did this painting and they printed it in, I think, the Daily Express. The Benedictine monks actually sent me a bottle of the stuff, with their compliments, which I thought was rather nice," recalls Stirling with a chuckle.

"What I liked about painting was that you had to really concentrate and seek out a colour. It isn't just the colour you immediately see, but there is far more depth to colour, and the light makes objects take on different colours. Betty explained all this to me.

"I must say it was very rewarding. I didn't go anywhere with it but it was interesting. I still have the original picture somewhere."

Levin

Stirling is referring to the Hudson Trophy Race at Levin in New Zealand which was won by Joakim Bonnier in a Yeoman Credit Cooper-Climax from Jim Clark in a works Lotus and local man Denny Hulme in another Cooper.

"Me marry Stirling? — No, with a capital N"

Jill is angry

JILL STEVENSON, 22-year-old Cape Town model, is incensed at rumours that link her name with that of top racing driver Stirling Moss, simply because she went to East London to watch him race and was seen around town with him there.

Her trip to see the S.A. friends to watch him drive at East London.

"Stirling left Cape Town on Wednesday after winning the Cape race and I followed with my friends two days later.

"The three of us went everywhere and did everything together. We had a wonderful time. I made two friends for life—but that is all there is to it.

"I have not even had a letter from Stirling yet although he did promise to write. I am planning an overseas trip soon but I don't expect to see him again until he comes back to the Union at the end of this year."

She described Stirling Moss as a "wonderful, modest and kind person." Did he ask her to marry him? "No, with a big N. Anyway, how could he when he is not divorced yet from his Canadian wife Katie?"

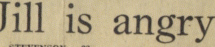

Jo'berg Sunday Times 8.1.61

1961

JVO being transported from NZ. As a consequence, SM borrowed a car for the first practice session.

Later circuit and practiced with new FJ Lotus. …only used 7,400 and car isn't set up properly. 1.45.6." This time was mighty impressive compared with his rivals in their F1 cars - Gurney 1.40.8, Ireland 1.40.8 and Hill 1.41.2.

Saturday saw Stirling on the beach before heading for the circuit and practice in the company of Virginia and Jill Huey. His Lotus 18 had finally arrived at 7am. All was not well, for the car was wrongly geared and "understeers except on throttle". In spite of this, Stirling was quickest, beating Gurney in the BRM by a whisker and was 2½ seconds faster than Brabham.

Sunday dawned and was seriously hot. "Up at 9.30 Hot 108°! Circuit + Jan. Race. I had a good start and led till end. Nine drivers stopped and nearly all due to heat. 148° on the track. I was burnt on the fuel tank! Gears excellent except 5th one tooth too high. Get 6,450 rpm Ftd. Innes 2nd just on two laps back. Bath and airport. Delayed till 12pm so took Virginia to food and watched 'Meet the Press' on TV (my recording). No Bed.

TV Question – Why does SM have more publicity than JB. [Answer] Due to his exemplary private life?!"

JB is, of course, Jack Brabham, the local hero and double World Champion.

The flight was delayed in Darwin for eight hours and Stirling then travelled on, via Manila, to Hong Kong. Next morning he went to town and shopped. "Ordered shirts and suits. Radio and tape. Home and party and bed at 2am."

Drivers

Moss on: JACK BRABHAM

"Jack Brabham was quite a tough competitor. A good hard racer. I mean fast. He would fight right into the corner and you could never completely discount him. You could never reckon that, you'd passed him, that he would give up. He would hang in there.

"He was one of the few real racers. When the Ferraris were missing, it was generally between us in single-seaters that season. He was usually my main competitor."

Moss is fastest in blinding rain

STIRLING MOSS lapped at 88 m.p.h. in steady rain in to-day's training runs for to-morrow's seventh international Lady Wigram Trophy race at Christchurch, New Zealand. Moss, whose goggles constantly misted over with rain, described conditions as "miserable."

Driving Rob Walker's Lotus, he returned an unofficial time of 1min. 26.5sec. for the 2.16 mile circuit. Cooper works' drivers, world champion Jack Brabham and New Zealander Bruce McLaren, lapped at 83.7 m.p.h.

M'chester Eve News 20.1.61

MOSS LEADS N. ZEALAND PRACTICE

STIRLING MOSS, lapping at 88 m.p.h. in steady rain, was the only driver to do serious training for tomorrow's 7th international Lady Wigram Trophy race at Christchurch, New Zealand.

Driving Rob Walker's Lotus, he returned an unofficial time of 1min. 26.5secs. for the 2.16 mile circuit, while the Cooper works drivers, world champion Jack Brabham and the New Zealander Bruce McLaren, were content to tour round at 83.7 m.p.h.

The track is in excellent condition, but Moss, whose goggles were constantly misted over with rain, described the conditions as "miserable."

Coventry Eve Telegraph 20.1.61

The Lady Wigram Trophy Race

Heavy rain during Friday's practice forced the organisers to abandon the day and re-schedule qualifying for early next morning before the race. In fact, it was wetter still and the course was said to resemble a lake more than a motor racing circuit!

Practice was something of a lottery and Clark handled the conditions best to take pole. However, the session was more farce than motor racing. Future World Champion Denny Hulme spun off. Then someone shunted Johnnie Mansel's Tec-Mec which pushed him off and he capsized into a ditch. He was thrown clear and was just regaining his feet when Bob Smith's Ferrari flew over his head, knocking Mansel to the ground once more. He was about to make another attempt to stand when Brian Blackburn's Maserati emulated the Ferrari and both nose-dived into the ditch. Miraculously, they all escaped serious injury, which is more than can be said for their machinery.

In view of the conditions, the race was shortened by about 50 miles. Clark led initially but was taken by Brabham and Bonnier. McLaren had inadvertently shunted Stirling in the first corner, Autosport stating that the Lotus "became a brute to handle". Both Bonnier and then Clark spun off the main straight while trying to pass Brabham. Meanwhile, Stirling was inheriting places as cars fell off the track or expired. Then someone attacked him again making a sick motor car sicker and he did extremely well to nurse the car into second place at the finish and record a lap just 0.2 secs slower than Brabham's fastest.

A recumbent Moss is tended to by Shalima

Sydney Sun 26.1.61

SUNBATH (above) for English racing car driver Stirling Moss on Sydney's Bondi beach. LEFT: His sleep disturbed by the photographer, Moss poses for his picture. He is in Sydney for the Warwick Farm International 100 to-

Stirling Moss ...

THE AUSSIE GIRLS

"Jan Lindsay was an Australian lady who was in banking and Virginia Turner was another Australian who I recall was a Catholic."

Stirling in what became his trademark crash hat

JVO

The Johan Van Oldenbarnavelt was actually a Dutch ship which operated a regular service to and from New Zealand and Australia between 1950 and 1963. Named after a Dutch hero (1547-1619), it was not too surprisingly abbreviated to JVO. Launched in 1929, at the age of 33 it was sold and became a Greek cruise liner named the Lakonia which caught fire on December 22 1963 and sunk a few days later with the loss of 128 lives.

1961

Australian Grand Prix

Heat was going to be a major factor in this race. "If the weather was hot for practice, race day was infernal," was how Autosport expressed it. Stirling's crew had made the effort, in spite of the conditions, to change his gear ratios. "A giant crowd of 65,000 broiled slowly in the stands, on every available tree, tower and tin roof, and around the boundary," wrote the weekly motor racing 'bible'. Stirling had removed the side panels of his Lotus 18, something he would memorably do later in the year, for extra cooling.

Ron Flockhart momentarily led from the third row but soon Stirling was at the head of the field and began lapping backmarkers as early as the sixth circuit. Behind were the BRMs of Graham Hill and Dan Gurney. Then Hill retired with a fuel tank burst by the heat. A succession of cars followed him into retirement with the heat accounting for either the drivers or the cars. Maladies included boiling fuel, overheating oil and every other form of overheating. Brabham stopped for iced water for himself and his car. During the pit stop, one of his mechanics collapsed.

Of the seven still running, Stirling led from Gurney and Ireland in the works Lotus. Then Gurney's fuel pump packed up and Innes finished second though his friend was way ahead. Just four cars were running at the end.

"When Moss crossed the line an easy winner," wrote Autosport, "the crowd cheered just as it would have cheered the closest finish in racing history. No one needed persuasion to realise Moss had won a great battle, not with any other man but with himself and the elements. When, seemingly as fresh as a daisy, he made his joyful circuit of honour in an official Sunbeam Alpine the multitude's open admiration knew no bounds. The whistles and catcalls came from everywhere, along with the thunder of applause."

Daily Tel, Australia 30.1.61

Quite Frankly with FRANK BROWNE

MOSS LEFT IMPRESSION

To be quite honest I went to Warwick Farm on Sunday hoping to see Jack Brabham give Stirling Moss his dust.

Seeing that the world championship had eluded Moss while Brabham had secured it twice, I was inclined to think that we might be indulging in the grand old Australian habit of selling our own champs short and boosting the men from overseas.

I know better now. Brabham may chalk up more world titles, and Moss may pass into retirement without one, but there's not much doubt that the balding, colorful, English driver will leave a larger impression on crowds than Brabham.

ABOVE: Stirling Moss with the side panels of his Lotus removed to beat the heat in which the International "100" was run yesterday. BELOW: Weather observer Dennis Shields taking the temperature reading at 2.30 p.m. yesterday when it was 106.9 degrees—the hottest of the year.

Daily Tel, Australia 30.1.61

January

● Moss hurtles to victory on a 148 deg. track in the International 100 at Warwick Farm, Sydney.

● Victor's laurels for Moss, above. But in the pits, below, before the race, he was stripped for action while he watched preparations to beat the heat.

Moss triumphs

IN searing heat, ace British racing car driver Stirling Moss beat some of the world's best drivers to win the "International 100" at Warwick Farm, Sydney, on January 29. It was Sydney's first international car race.

Moss used BP 100 octane aviation gasoline and Energol oil, containing the same viscosity index improver as normal Vistco-Static, in his Lotus.

Driving superbly, Moss led from start to finish, lapping every other car.

He had the race to himself after his main rivals fell victims of mechanical troubles, mostly brought on by the heat.

Moss covered the 45 laps of the 100-mile race in 76 min. 33.9 sec., at an average speed of 79.26 mph.

It was a triumphant performance by driver, car, and BP fuel and lubricants!

Drivers and spectators sweltered in Sydney's hottest day for a year. Shade temperature reached 107 deg.

A foot above the bitumen track, the thermometer reading was 148 deg.

The crowd of 65,000 was disappointed that the expected duel between Moss and world champion Jack Brabham did not occur.

Brabham, who was never better than third, was forced to withdraw after 30 laps when the fuel in his Cooper-Climax boiled. He had made two pit stops in an attempt to cure the trouble by having the fuel pump and lines splashed with water.

Several drivers collapsed with heat exhaustion. Of the 14 starters, nine failed to finish.

Before the race, Moss was hosed with cold water. His mechanic, Tony Claverley, removed the side panels of the car to allow cooling draughts of air to stream through the cockpit.

The Lotus ran faultlessly. It gained the fastest lap time of 1 min. 40.3 sec. of the 2¼-mile course — an average of 80.6 mph.

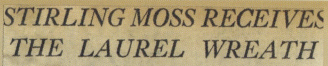

STIRLING MOSS RECEIVES THE LAUREL WREATH

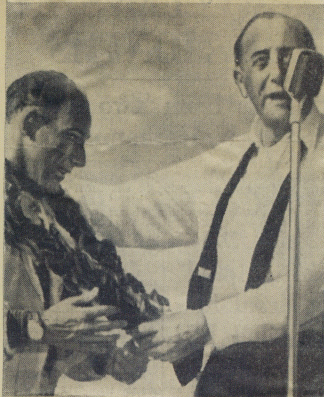

Lord Baillieu, president of the Dunlop Rubber Co., presents the laurel wreath to Stirling Moss for winning the 101-mile international road race at Sydney. [Picture by radio and wire.]

101-MILE RACE 114 Deg.

Ron Flockhart, of Scotland, pushed his Cooper Climax across the finishing line to take fifth place.

Several drivers were overcome by the heat. Miller, who finished fourth, collapsed after crossing the finishing line and fell from the cockpit of his car.

Ambulance men treated hundreds of spectators in the huge crowd for heat exhaustion and sunburn.

Moss appeared unaffected by the heat. He led from start to finish, gaining a commanding lead in the opening laps. He had the fastest lap time of 1min. 40.3sec., speeding round the circuit...

...works Lotus car in temperatay, won easily the 101-mile Sydney.

Birmingham Post 30.1.61

Rob Walker on the Warwick Farm race

Rob Walker, writing many years later in Classic Cars magazine, vividly recalled the race. The venue, which was a horse racing course near Sydney, was owned by Sam Hordern, a cousin of Walker's, and Hordern had the idea of a doing 'an Aintree', i.e. creating a motor racing circuit around it. Walker put Hordern in touch with Geoff Sykes, who had been responsible for the British track, and he master-minded the project and would become 'Mr. Motor Racing' in Australia.

Walker comments that SM was fastest by just a thousandth of a second, the first time he had ever known timing to thousandths. "My head mechanic, Tony Cleverly, removed some side panels on the Lotus so that Stirling could get a flow of air through the cockpit. He also set the engine up for petrol, which has a much higher boiling point than the alcohol mixtures used by most of the cars. Every other car made at least one pitstop, either to cool vaporising fuel or to pour buckets of iced water over the drivers. Stirling was the sole exception; he ran non-stop throughout.

At the finish Moss was the only man capable of stepping out of his car. Innes was lifted out of his and drenched with water and ice. Miller, another finisher, fell from his cockpit and lay unconscious beside the car.

Stirling told me that he only forced himself to get out of the car and walk up to receive his cup as he knew that psychologically it underlined his superiority."

Stirling Moss Scrapbook

February

1961 Calendar

No racing events this month

Stirling spent the first three days of the month shopping in Hong Kong and two more shopping in Tokyo. On the second day in Hong Kong he was taken to the Thieves' Market by a friend called Paul Braga – "bought some excellent curios". He flew with Japan Airlines ("excellent") to Tokyo and checked into the Imperial Hotel and had a "look at nice life". Appropriately, he saw *The World of Suzie Wong* (G). "Later food with Eko Mori and then to Club 88. Bed at 3.45am." Next day he was shopping again. "Shops are open till 9pm including the large stores. Saw *Oceans 11* (G). Chinese food and saw shows. Bed at 1.30am."

Before heading for the airport on Monday 6, Stirling purchased "30 yds of lavender raw silk and 12 yds of brown linen. Also grass paper and an automatic dialing device! To airport and off at 3pm. No bed. 2 hrs sleep. Crossed date line."

On Tuesday, February 7, "Up at God knows when! S. Francisco at 8.30 and on to L.A. Rented a Corvair and to motel. Looked around. Later saw Ruth and then Dan, Lance [Reventlow], Bruce & Co. Home and bed at 2am."

"Wed 8 Feb (This is yesterday!) Up very late. Haircut and down town. Called on Lance. Later food with Dan and Shirlee Adams. Home, packed. Bed at 2am.

"Thurs 9 Feb (This is the 8th). Up at 6am! Couldn't sleep. TWA to NY at 1pm. Checked in St. Moritz. Food solo at Sardi's. Bed at 2am.

"Stopped by a cop in LA for jumping STOP, passing on ramp to Freeway and right turn. He said he wished he could drive like me and let me go!"

On the actual Thursday, Stirling went to the Jaguar offices and had lunch with John Gordon Benett. He later "met Shirlee Adams and went to the Little Club. Bed at 4am." Next day, "Up and looked around SCCA Car show. Lunch with John Benett. Later met Uncle Ilia and Shelley Ripley (of Jags) and danced etc. Bed at 4am." Shelley Ripley worked in the advertising department at Jaguar.

On the Saturday he lunched with Cam and Jean Argetsinger and Bill Millikin. He went on to a SCCA (Sports Car Club of America) reception with Shelley. He later joined up with "Denise and Co and bed at 5am". He was up again after just two hours sleep and off to fly Pan-Am back to London, where he was met by secretary Val Pirie, Herb Jones, Ken Gregory and Nym. They went to the Lotus House and he hit the sack at five again!

After 12 hours sleep, he did some work and then took Judy Carne to the Candlelight Room, which was in the

Stirling Moss ...

SHOPPING

PP: "You seemed to do a lot of shopping. It was obviously something you enjoyed which is quite unusual for a chap."

SM: "You see I am always looking for different things, that is the point. I always liked to go to Hong Kong because you could get things made there very quickly, you know. For example, I'd get a shoulder bag made with positions for a lot of my things, my razor there, and the aftershave there and the toothbrush there, those sort of things. I have always been a frustrated designer."

Immortality bestowed. Moss and Brabham join the Madame Tussauds line-up of wax figures

Autocar 3.2.61

February

Stirling Moss Scrapbook

Sardi's

In the heart of the Theatre District at 234 west 44th street, New York City, Sardi's has been the "Toast of Broadway" for over 80 years. It was most unusual for Stirling to dine alone as he much preferred to be in company.

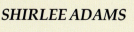

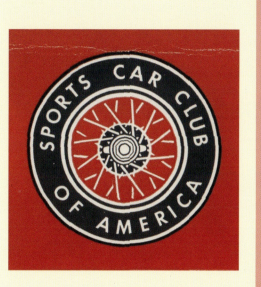

£1,500 EACH

Jack Brabham and Stirling Moss didn't race for peanuts at Warwick Farm on Sunday. They got £1,500 each.

That's a lot of money for a little over an hour's driving but don't run away with the idea that the £1,500 is all profit.

This motor racing is a very expensive business. Moss and Brabham had to pay the transport of their cars to Australia, their hotel bills, fares, mechanics and smaller items which generally run into a hundred pounds.

Still, after they do all that there is still a fair amount of change left out of the £1,500.

Add to that a few minor individual advertising perks and they would finish up with plenty.

Naturally, the more countries they visit and the more appearances they make, the more cash in the bank.

Moss reckons that winning grand prix are all very nice, but when it comes to making money there is nothing like flitting from country to country.

"I won 19 races during the year and that is plenty of hay," he said.

He wants to come back to Australia and if there is ever another international he'll be here.

In the meantime, the Warwick Farm chiefs are thinking of bigger and better things.

Their plans envisage a Grand Prix in Australia in about two years, the Australian race following closely on the United States Grand Prix in December, the New Zealand Grand Prix early in January.

In the meantime, the track will be altered to enable greater speeds and accommodation for the public will be improved with more covered seats and better parking facilities.

The Sun 1.2.61

SOME MAY LOSE £10,000 A YEAR

By TOM WISDOM

THE world's top racing drivers, who can earn more than £30,000 a year, may have their salaries cut by a third next season.

Promoters of international races and racing car makers decided in Monte Carlo recently to scale down starting money for world championship events.

And this month the accessory firms—who pay drivers to use their products—will meet in secret to make an agreement to cut "retainers."

Some firms making products like oil, fuel and tyres have been paying up to £10,000 a season to teams and £8,000 to individual drivers.

COMPETITION

There has been tremendous competition to sign up the stars. Three firms have been paying the top money, and half a dozen firms a little less.

Stirling Moss—reckoned to be the world's best driver though he has never won the world championship—is said to have been earning more than £30,000 a year.

And Australian Jack Brabham, in his second year as champion, is believed to be earning more than Moss at present.

The accessory firms are expected to decide also to cut down drastically on grand prix racing. They feel the motoring public are more influenced by touring-car events and rallies.

But a grand prix race like the European championship, to be held in Germany, can still be worth more than £10,000 to the winning driver and maker.

Daily Herald 2.2.61

Stirling has always liked clothes and always dressed well

COUNTING PROFIT

They proved that Australians know how to run a big meeting. The races started right on the tick of time and cars which broke down during the races were hauled to the pits without any interruption to the following event.

True the big race was a washout. But you couldn't blame the drivers or the cars. The heat was so intense on the track—145 degrees—that of the 18 starters only one—Stirling Moss—completed the full 45 laps.

And while Moss was shielding his eyes Jack Brabham was bathing a badly blistered left foot. He got the blisters from an almost red hot clutch pedal and still was suffering when he left Sydney yesterday for England.

That is why he wore sandals. He hadn't put a shoe on since the race.

They are still counting the profits from Sunday. Final figures won't be known for a few more days, but you can bet your boots that Warwick Farm car racing is here to stay.

the other over his eyes. affair.

The Sun 1.2.61

Stirling Moss ...

SHIRLEE ADAMS

"She was a girl I met on an airline; she worked for American Airlines. A very attractive girl, I chatted her up. She came to Monaco and my mother said what a nice girl she was because, every time I would go past, she clapped. In fact, I met Peter Fonda not long ago and, of course, she is his stepmother, because she married Henry Fonda."

Henry Fonda and Shirlee Adams married in 1965, and he died in 1982.

The Thieves' Market

The so-called Thieves' Market was apparently a bunch of antique shops in Hollywood Road, Hong Kong. "Paul Braga knew a lot about Chinese art."

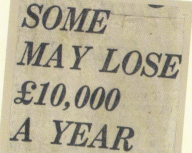

1961

Stirling Moss Scrapbook

basement of the Mayfair Hotel, just round the corner from Stirling's home. Going to bed at 3am, he was up two hours later and worked all day before meeting "Marion and Francis and food. Bed at 2am".

The second half of February consisted mainly of working in the office at his home in Shepherd Street in Mayfair. Work was interspersed with interviews. One evening he picked up Judy and went to Woolwich for a "Brains Trust 'do' + Bruce McLaren, Surtees, [John] Sprinzel and Co."

On Friday 17 he did a radio programme with Raymond Baxter and then met Caroline Nuttall and took her to the Colony Club before meeting up with Herb and going to the Astor. Next day he lunched with Marion, saw Chet Flynn, a General Motors executive who raced Ferraris and suchlike, and took Judy to dinner at the White Elephant.

In the next few days he had an anti-tetanus injection and two fillings done by his dentist father. He went to the RAC for a BRDC (British Racing Drivers' Club) dinner, worked on a book, saw Caroline several times, gave a talk at an Institute of Petroleum event and took part in a Press photographic session with sister Pat.

On February 23 he flew from London up to "Manchester by BEA to Opera House and saw Judy in her show. VG." After the show, he ate with Judy, David Haynes and Pat. After retiring at 2am, he was up at eight, went to the theatre and then flew back to London where he was met by the Press. He returned to the office to work, did an interview, saw Les Leston "and then Caroline came and cooked me roast pork. Bed at 2.30am." Next day, Stirling, who was almost fanatical about cleanliness, "Cleaned house and later Marie-Claude, a fan, called. At 6.30 Herb, Maria and Sylvia Collins came and off to Dorchester for Variety Club 'do'. Home and danced, etc. Bed at 5am."

In spite of the late night, Stirling was up at 8.30am next morning and flew to Italy where he "Tested Maser sports Type 60. Engine bad. 5,800 (should be 6,300) 1.48 at Monza. Type 63 1 lap and axle broke. Engine good. Car feels difficult. Steering from car and not driver. Could get 6,200 – 6,300. Same axle. Orsi agreed loan of car for season. Home and Val met me. Food at Herb's and bed at 12.30."

Monday saw Stirling spending time with a charity organisation called 'Youth Ventures'. Later he took Caroline to see *Never on a Sunday* (F). They ate at the Beachcomber.

On the last day of the month, Stirling took Raymond Baxter to lunch, saw Pat, did an interview, Beverley called round and, together with friends, he went to the *Talk of the Town* where he saw Max Bygraves.

The Brains Trust

The Brains Trust was a series of programmes broadcast on radio from the early forties by the BBC. Consisting of questions put to an eminent trio of intellectuals, the first series was broadcast for 84 episodes without a break and when broadcast on Sunday afternoons was listened to by 29% of the UK population. Members of the team included Sir Malcolm Sargent, Anna Neagle, Kenneth Clark and Will Hay. It was created during the Second World War by the Variety Dept of the BBC but became hugely influential. Designed as entertainment, it became educational as first-class brains discussed topical subjects. It was often copied and applied to specialist subjects with a panel of experts from that field.

Sprite for Sebring

In its February 10 issue Autosport reported that the Sebring Sprite, which Stirling was to drive in the 4-Hour event of that name in March, was to be fitted with a fully modified Formula Junior single-seater motor with a very special BMC gearbox incorporating needle-roller bearings. They speculated that Pat Moss, who was also entered in a Sprite, might not drive after all, in which case her place would be taken by rising star Paul Hawkins "of the John Sprinzel organisation".

---

the hot seat of an Aston Martin):

Our Motoring Editor, Mr. David McKay, offered the first words of cheer.

"Don't be too frightened by the noise, which is hellish," he said. "And if you brace your feet against the floor boards, the chances are you won't be flung out going around the bends at 90."

Next to put me at ease was A.A.R.C. director Mr. Brian Martin. "You'll have no windscreen, of course," he said. "But don't worry. You'll soon get used to copping a 100-mile-an-hour gale full in the face."

Fortified by these reassurances, I was perfectly nonchalant when the time came for me to meet my Jehu. "Mr. Mirling Stoss, I presume," I said, shaking him warmly by the scarf, "well now, and which is our vuh-vuh-vuh-vehicle?"

Mr. Moss, a slender, impassive man, pointed. "That dark green Aston Martin."

I limped over and got in.

"No, no," said Mr. Moss, "not the Ford Prefect—that other one, with the same dark green color as your complexion."

With the aid of a shoehorn I slipped into the passenger's seat of this superannuated sardine tin. Then, suddenly, everything went black.

"Who sandbagged me!" I bellowed. "Turn on the lights!"

"Tilt his crash helmet out of his eyes," said a voice. Someone dealt me a stunning blow on the back of the neck, and daylight reappeared. Next, someone else smacked a sweaty pair of goggles across my nose, while Mr. Moss, cursing gently to himself, proceeded to garrot me with a leather strap.

"Just one thing," said Mr. Moss, "shut your mouth."

"I never said a word!" I protested, indignantly.

"I mean, don't open your mouth once we start. The wind, you know. You mightn't be able to shut it again."

"Mpf," I said, clamping my jaws. I had no desire to whirl around the track looking like Al Jolson singing "Mammy."

Mr. Moss climbed behind the wheel. "Now, hang on to something," he said.

The only thing I could see to hang on to was Mr. Moss, so I reached around and seized him affectionately by the backbone.

"Don't tickle me, dammit!" he exclaimed. "Hold the side of the car! Brace the feet and arch the back."

By now, all I needed was a prayer wheel to look the spitting image of a Yogi adept in the convolutions of the Lotus Position.

"We'll take the first lap slowly," said Mr. Moss.

Whooooosh!

I badly wanted to ask Mr. M. two questions: A, would he mind driving back to retrieve my stomach, and, B, if this was slow, how fast was fast? However, I remembered what he said about keeping the trap shut, and merely glared at him.

Whoooooosh!

By dint of mumbling such passages as I could remember from the Book of Common Prayer, I got around the first lap without once leaving the car.

Whooooooosh!

Now I caught on. So this was fast, eh? Between clutching the back of the head (to keep it from blowing off) in the straight, and grabbing the side of the car around the corners, I was too distracted to admire the scenery of the second lap.

Whoooooooosh!

Mr. Moss now was making upward gestures at me with his thumb. If he wanted to trade insults at a time like this, then I was his man. I hastily made a few gestures back.

A foolish mistake. It appears that he was only inquiring if I were still alive. I should have ignored him and pretended I was dead.

Whoooooooooooosh!

"Slow old bus," said Mr. Moss, as they were coming on to the tarmac, "sorry I couldn't manage a faster run for you."

"Think nothing of it," I said, politely. "Tell you what—in return for your hospitality I'd like you to join me at a little party at Prince's tonight."

"That's very nice of you," said Mr. Moss.

"Then, later, at about 2 a.m., I'll drive you home in my Morris Minor," I said. Mr. Moss went the color of the Aston Martin. "I—I just remembered—I've got a previous engagement," he said.

SQUIB!
—Alexander Macdonald

Sunday Tel., Sydney 5.2.61

Sunday Tel., Sydney 5.2.61

SUNDAY TELEGRAPH columnist Alexander Macdonald braces himself and prepares for the worst as he takes a spin round the Warwick Farm circuit this week with British speed king Stirling Moss. READ HIS STORY ON THE BACK PAGE—"TRAPPED LIKE A RAT IN THE HOT SEAT OF AN ASTON MARTIN)."

John Gordon Benett

John Gordon Benett was born in the Channel Islands and competed in the Jersey road races of 1947 and '48 before moving to the States and working for BMC. He was a works driver for Cunningham in the early fifties and was right-hand man to the infamous Max Hoffman, the Jaguar, VW and later Mercedes distributor. In the late fifties, Benett joined Jaguar as General Sales Manager. He later became Sales Vice-President and remained with the company until the British Leyland fiasco of the late sixties.

February

Stirling Moss Scrapbook

> *Stirling Moss ...*
>
> *...US COPS*
>
> *"That was pretty nice. That is unusual, to be let off over there. They were very tough over there, the cops. He must have been a racing fan. It sounds as though I was a naughty boy!"*

Pay cut for top racing drivers
Daily Herald Thursday February 2 1961

Moss to try new Maserati

STIRLING MOSS will fly to Milan on Sunday to test the new Maserati 2,800 sports car at the Monza track, it was announced in Milan yesterday.

He may drive the car in the Sebring 12-hour sports car race in Florida this year.

Sporting Life 23.2.61

Cam Argestsinger

Cam Argetsinger began organising racing in 1948 with a road race through the streets of his home town, Watkins Glen. Those taking part included Briggs Cunningham and the Collier brothers, Miles and Sam both driving super-charged MGs. By 1950 some 100,000 spectators converged on the small town for the race meeting but an accident two years later resulted in a child being killed and this was the end of the Watkins Glen street circuit. Initially, it was moved to the nearby town of Dix and then 550 acres were purchased to create a purpose-built circuit incorporating something of the flavour of the original course. The stature of the circuit grew and in 1961, with Argetsinger as executive director of the Grand Prix Corporation, as the organising body was known, applied to hold an American Grand Prix at Watkins Glen.

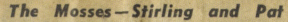

The Mosses — Stirling and Pat

Evening Standard 24.2.61

Racing driver Stirling Moss and his sister Pat leave London Airport on a "short-hop" flight to Manchester. They were off to visit friends before Stirling leaves next week to race in America.

STATLER HILTON — **28th YEAR** — **host** — WEEKLY GUIDE TO NEW YORK

The first National Sports Car Show is at the Statler Hilton through February 13th. Here's British driver Stirling Moss.

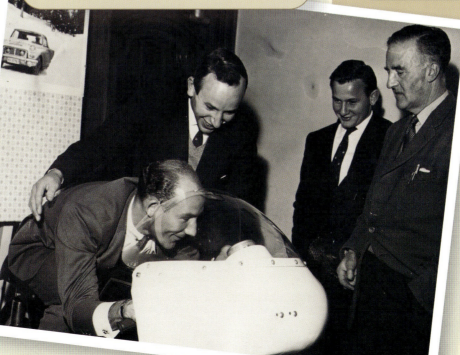

Stirling, seen here with John Surtees and Bruce McLaren, took part in a motoring forum at Woolwich Town Hall, organised by the Woolwich Road Safety Committee!

1961

Stirling's father, Alfred

Stirling Moss …

THE 1961 LADIES

PP: *"You seemed to go out with a few ladies quite a lot in 1961 and loads of others you just saw once or twice."*
SM: *"I was having about five serious relationships, I think, and quite a lot of other ones which weren't so serious. These were ships that passed in the night … without dropping anchor!"*
PP: *"One of them was Judy Carne. She had an extraordinary life?"*
SM: *"I met her at the White Elephant. She was a very pert, very cute girl and a very amusing person."*
PP: *"Were they aware of each other?"*
SM: *"They all knew that they weren't the only ones, yes. I wouldn't say who the others were."*
PP: *"You always seemed to stay on good terms?"*
SM: *"Yes, because I never misled anybody. I always told them that I was, you know, a free agent, and so I didn't want to get too deeply involved with anybody. It wasn't me. I remember being quite keen on people, up to a point, but I wasn't looking to get married, that was the thing."*

Moss won't talk about dancer from Northampton

RACING driver Stirling Moss flew from London to Manchester last night for a "date" with Northampton dancer Judith Carne, who is appearing in a show there.

To-day he stalked angrily from a lounge at Manchester airport to board a plane home, and refused to comment on his friendship with Miss Carne.

He said: "I am very annoyed by this talk. I came here for a private visit and I don't think anyone has the right to make a drama out of it."

But he happily autographed a national newspaper photograph of himself and Miss Carne for a 12-year-old boy.

"CLOSE FRIENDS"

Then to a reporter he said: "It does not matter how many questions you ask me I am not saying anything more."

But in her dressing [room at the] Manchester Opera Ho[use] she is appearing in "[The Boy Friend]" On the Brighter S[ide] confirmed to-day tha[t she and] Stirling were "close [friends]. "We met before Ch[ristmas] recently. Stirling telephoned me from Hong Kong," she said.

"I have been to meet his parents and he has also met my parents. My parents like him very much."

DINNER AT CLUB

Judy Carne—real name Joyce Botterill—is the 21-year-old daughter of Mr. and Mrs. Harold Botterill, of 7, Foxgrove-avenue, Northampton. She has toured in "The Boy Friend" and is frequently seen on ITV and B.B.C. TV.

Last night she dined with Moss at a Cheshire club.

Northants Clarion 24.2.61

Our manufacturers are more concerned with cutting costs than improving their models says STIRLING MOSS

Aberdeen Journal 25.2.61

Porsche Not Able To Afford Moss

Kenneth Cole writing in Autosport in a rather pompous and patronising article stated that Porsche, who would be entering Formula One for the 1961 season as the formula had changed to 1½ litres, a size of engine that the German concern had been building for some years, had a very restricted budget. "…Porsche cannot afford DM.100,000 to put a driver of the very highest class under contract. This, of course, rules out Stirling Moss."

He went on to pontificate that skill could only be acquired by practice and that, as Hans Herrmann (one of Porsche's drivers) had only limited experience this would compromise their performance. Herrmann had, of course, been racing for many years and was a member of the post-war Mercedes-Benz team.

Stirling responded in the next issue – see March.

Stirling Moss …

ADDRESSES IN 1961

PP: *"Where were you living in 1961? There is a mention of 36 and possibly 51. Were you living in this road, prior to here?"*
SM: *"I was living at 36 Shepherd Street. I bought it in the very late 50s. It was one of the ones built since the war, having been a bomb site. I did quite a lot of things to it to make it better. I put in all sorts of various gadgetry and stuff and then I managed to buy my present address a few doors away, which was also a bomb site.*

"I did the design for this house during 1960 and 1961 and actually started to build around the time of my crash in '62."
PP: *"Where was your office then?"*
SM: *"It was in my home at 36. I have lived with my office for a phenomenal time. I have lived with my office for most of my life. At one time, my father had a place in William IV Street, by Trafalgar Square, and I had it there. Apart from that, I have always had it nearby because it is very difficult to separate one's ordinary life from the other. There is a tremendous amount of overlap."*

Even today you can call on Stirling and Susie and they will be working, at almost any hour, in their respective offices.

Judy Carne

Judy Carne, the actress and entertainer, was born Joyce Botterill in 1939. Originally training as a dancer, she entered the theatre in the late fifties. In 1961 she appeared in the popular BBC sit-com, 'The Rag Trade'.

Judy would be very much an incarnation of the era known as the 'Swinging Sixties', a stylish chick who was pretty outrageous. She had relationships with Vidal Sassoon (who created her short, kinky haircut), Stirling, Burt Reynolds, Steve McQueen and Anthony Newley. She met Reynolds in 1962 on a flight to Miami and they married in 1963. The marriage lasted two years before ending in a bitter divorce.

During the sixties she appeared in a few obscure movies and some well-known TV dramas but her big break came in 1968 when she became one of the regular team on Rowan & Martin's Laugh-In. She achieved considerable fame with her stock phrase, "Sock it to me". Another member of the team was Goldie Hawn.

Whereas Goldie Hawn's career has endured, Judy Carne's went into steep decline. Sadly drug addiction ruined her life for many years and a serious car accident, in which she broke her neck, in 1978 nearly took her life. For a while she had to wear a heavy steel halo cage screwed into her skull as support. Seven years later, her autobiography, 'Laughing on the Outside, Crying on the Inside', was published. Having lived for years in the USA, she moved back to her native Northampton.

SHOWGIRL—AFTER SAYING GOOD-BYE

Judy Carne at Manchester Opera House to-day after saying good-bye to Stirling Moss. With her is her Yorkshire terrier, Kiltie.

JUDY SAYS: I JUST ADORE STIRLING

Manchester Eve News 24.2.61

Judy Carne with her other companion

MOSS 'MORE THAN FRIEND,' SAYS JUDY

RED-HAIRED actress Judy Carne told The Star in Manchester this afternoon: "Stirling Moss and I are more than just good friends. It would be silly to say otherwise. We are very fond of each other."

Judy said she and the racing car ace had been meeting since last November when they were introduced at a Curzon Street, London, restaurant.

Judy, who comes from Northampton, said: "Somehow, Stirling found my telephone number and began to ring me."

She added that with his sister Pat, Stirling — estranged from his wife Katie — flew to Manchester so he could see her this week.

"I don't know anything about cars," she said.

"I can't even drive. But now I will certainly take an interest in motor racing. And Stirling is fascinated by the theatre."

"I love show business. But I am not over-ambitious and if the right man came along, I would give it up."

Stirling, who accompanied his sister, flew from Manchester Airport for London later today, said: "I am very annoyed. I don't want to answer any questions."

Sheffield Star 24.2.61

Caroline Nuttall

"She was a debutante friend of Dauvergne Walker's," recalls Stirling.

"Caroline Nuttall was a very great friend," states Dauvergne Morgan, as Rob and Betty Walker's daughter is today. "Later, she was a godmother to my eldest daughter. She was absolutely gorgeous and had very deep chestnut hair. She was the Silvikrin girl, I think. She did various ads in America at the beginning of television advertising. In one, she would be in a fast car with her hair streaking out behind her.

"Her family lived in the Bahamas and her aunt was the famous Wimbledon champion, Betty Nuttall. Caroline, in an unbelievable tragedy, committed suicide with her mother about 20 years ago."

MARCH

1961 Calendar

- 24   Sebring 4-Hours, Florida, USA – 4th in Austin-Healey Sprite
- 25   Florida International 12-Hour GP of Endurance, Sebring – ret'd in Maserati T 61 (sharing with Graham Hill), took over & ret'd in Maserati T 63 (sharing with Masten Gregory)

On March 1 Stirling and his secretary Val Pirie drove up to Coventry to view and discuss what SM termed in his diary 'Project 99'. This was the all-new secret Ferguson four-wheel-drive Grand Prix car which would be designated the P99. Back in London he went to the Steering Wheel Club, which was just round the corner from his home in Shepherd's Market, and "met the lads".

Next day he and Peter Garnier, Sports Editor and later Editor of Autocar, went down to Byfleet for the opening of Tony Brooks's new garage. Brooks had a sparkling turnout of chums which would have been impressive on any GP grid. After the ceremony, SM, Reg Parnell, Colin Chapman, Graham Hill, Henry Taylor and Bruce McLaren had a meeting to discuss Formula One for 1961 and the 'alternative' Inter-Continental formula. Returning to town, he worked till 9pm and then Herb cooked him a meal.

After a series of meetings on Friday, he dined at the Candlelight and then went on to Edmondo Ros's club in Mayfair. He was in bed at 5am. The whole of the next day was spent cleaning the flat and in the evening he took Ken and Nym to see *Pepe* (G). He was in bed at the same hour again.

Sunday was spent at his parents' home at Tring with Val and Caroline Nuttall (CN). Monday saw him visiting the Ideal Home Exhibition, no doubt looking for 'gadgets'. "At 7 to Queens and ice skating + VP and Dauvergne. Food and bed at 2am."

On Tuesday Stirling went to see *Oliver* with Herb, Francis and Caroline. At 1.30pm next day, he "flew to Edinburgh in 'Caribbean'. To North British Hotel and met Jim Clark. Saw Judy's show and food. Had a fight with a cameraman. Bed at 3am." He flew home

Stirling's relationship with actress Judy Carne was a long-running one by his standards and would endure until she moved to Hollywood at the end of the year

Cars

FERGUSON P99

The Ferguson P99 was a four-wheel drive Grand Prix car which was designed to test out and publicise the Ferguson four-wheel drive system for possible application in road-going production cars. It was the baby of Harry Ferguson of tractor fame and master-minded by Tony Rolt and colleagues. The conventional Coventry-Climax engine was mounted at an angle in front of the multi-tubular frame chassis. Transfer gears took the drive to the five-speed transmission and Ferguson differential and subsequently further front and rear differentials. Suspension was all-independent and, during testing, the Maxaret aircraft anti-locking brake device was tried.

Zoom!

STIRLING MOSS is to take on the intensive training of three potential driving aces.

And one of them, 25-year-old Park-lane car salesman Keith Taffs, hasn't even got a car.

With a Belgian and a Dutchman Keith qualified for the Moss treatment at a private race meeting at Silverstone yesterday.

Now the prospect of schooling by Moss fills Keith with a mixture of fear and excitement.

"I've never met him," he told us yesterday. Keith will be a dedicated pupil. He has no girl friend. Racing is his only love.

Daily Sketch 3.3.61

Stirling enjoyed going to movie premieres

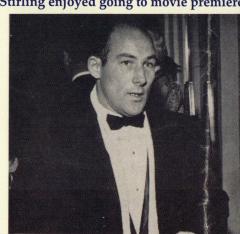

KINEMATOGRAPH WEEKLY: MARCH 16, 1961

RANK FD PREMIERES 'GRASS IS GREENER

Stirling sees Judy —then he slips away

Express Staff Reporter

STIRLING MOSS turned up unexpectedly in Edinburgh last night to see his girl friend and gave a startling demonstration — on foot — of his celebrated racing start.

He went to the King's Theatre to see his actress friend, Judy Carne, in the Stanley Baxter revue, "On the Brighter Side."

HE HAILED A TAXI

And after the show, while the fair-haired Miss Carne took refuge backstage, Stirling hurried to the front door to make sure he could leave unnoticed.

Then Miss Carne hurried from a side door and slipped quickly into a friend's car.

Stirling and Judy last night.

Stirling's Reply

In reply to Kenneth Cole's article in Autosport (see February), the magazine published this letter from Stirling.

"Regarding the interesting contribution from Mr. Kenneth Cole on 'A Comeback for German Racing Cars?' I feel that I would like to clear up one point that has been touched upon in the article, namely, the fact that because they have not got 100,000 Deutschmarks available Porsche could not afford to have me driving for them.

"I was asked by Hushke von Hanstein, on behalf of Porsche, to drive for them during the 1961 season. The reason that I didn't accept this had absolutely no bearing on the money side at all. There are two reasons why I turned it down, one was that I have been very happy driving for Rob Walker, and the other is that I particularly want to drive a British car in the Number 1 formula.

"In closing I would like to say I do feel Porsche are going to be the people to beat and if I had to forecast the World Championship for 1961 I would put my money on Joe Bonnier."

Edmondo Ros

Edmondo Ros was born in Port of Spain, Trinidad in 1910, moving to London in 1937. Within three years, he was leading his own Latin American band and became a regular on BBC radio before he retired to Jávea in Spain in 1975. In 1991 the then 89-year-old Latin American music pioneer received an OBE and recalls bumping into Stirling at the Palace.

"Stirling was a very frequent visitor to my nightclub, the Bagatelle, and was always the last to leave. He loved dancing."

Hounded by the press, Judy looks like a scared rabbit caught in the firing line of the photographers' lenses

1961

next morning, did some work and took CN to the "premiere of *The Grass is Greener* G. Entered separately. Food and bed at 1.30am."

Friday: "Up early and to Silverstone with Val and Dauvergne. Tested new DB4 and two Healeys. Cooper 2½. Got 6,600 but car's steering doesn't feel too good. Lots of castor. Oversteer also. Not too accurate. Lotus with wishbones at rear has too much rear steering. Like an oversteer. To town and 'Wheel' where they were given my Motor Sportsman of the Year award by Martini Rosso, throu' me. On to Paul's party. VG Bed at 2am."

On the same diary page are written the following lap times: Lotus 2½ 1.34.8, Cooper 2½ 1.34.1, DB4 1.49.6, Rally Healey 1.57.8.

Even though it was a Saturday, Stirling worked all day before meeting David Haynes and going successively to the "31 Room, L'Enfant Terrible, L'Exile, etc." Sunday was spent cleaning in the morning before lunch at Sue's, where he won 4/- [20p] at cards. Following this he worked on a book, before taking Dory for food.

On Monday Stirling and Ken set off for Goodwood. "Tested Inter-Continental Lotus and Cooper and F1 Cooper and Elite. Cooper is lousy. Henry did 1 lap and said 'undrivable'. Lotus with wishbones rear is not too good, it has a roll oversteer. Elite and BRP F1 fabulous. Lotus was faster than Cooper. Town and work. At 7.00 joined others and went ice-skating. Drinks and food and bed at Ken's at 1.15am."

Tuesday 14 March: "Up at 9. Work and LAP at 2.00. Off TWA at 2.15 to IDL. Belmont Plaza. Met Shirlee and food. Bed at 5am." Translated, this means Stirling took off from London Airport and flew with Trans World Airlines to New York where he met Shirlee Adams. IDL was the former code for JFK and was based on the name of the field (Idlewild) upon which the airport was built.

Next day he flew on by BOAC to Nassau. There he met up with wife Katie and others. He went out to eat, gambled and "Won £150!"

He went water skiing next morning before collecting Beverley from Oakes field. "Hired boat and skied, etc. Later food and danced. Bev is fab and was A. Murray instructress. Bed at 4am."

As Bev flew off, Stirling indulged in a favourite pastime of teaching water skiing and then "did turnarounds!" Later he met a girl called Gia. Next day he and friend Norman Solomon went to see *Carry on Nurse* (EX). With Shirley Eaton. Fab. Food at White Gates (F) and then dancing with Penny Hansen. Bed at 4.15am."

On Sunday March 19 he had lunch with his in-

Stirling Moss ...

NORMAN SOLOMON

"Norman Soloman was a very good friend of mine from Nassau. He owned a shop called Mademoiselle and he was quite a retailer in Nassau. He had his own Porsche and was a competent amateur; he was one guy that I always felt, if he had really put his mind to it, could have been a very good racing driver."

Judy Carne on Stirling

The following quotes from Judy Carne's autobiography, 'Laughing on the Outside, Crying on the Inside', published in 1985, give a fascinating insight into Stirling's character and lifestyle in 1961.

"The White Elephant," she wrote, "continued to be the hub of my social activity. It was there that I met Stirling Moss, Britain's top race-car driver, and somewhat of a national hero. He seemed too warm and gentle a man to be engaged in such a dangerous sport, and surprisingly humble as well. He was interested in my career, going out of his way to see as many of my performances as he could. We started seeing each other regularly and it became a comfortable romance in which I learned something new about the world every time I saw him. That's how he was – tuned into the latest happenings on 'any' subject."

Judy went on to say that "Stirling's eccentric wit is legend". Another of Judy's friends was top hair stylist Vidal Sassoon, who had a modern penthouse on Curzon Place, around the corner from Stirling's Mayfair house. "If Vidal Sassoon was ahead of his time in terms of décor, Stirling was equally advanced in the electronic automation of his home. He had a button for everything..." The panel beside his bed, she wrote, was like the controls of an aircraft, able to lower a TV from the ceiling, open his garage doors, run a bath to a desired temperature and control the stereo.

"His concern was the efficient use of space, and in that way, he was revolutionary in his concept of interior design."

Judy stated that the bathroom had 'his and hers' facilities for everything with sunken bathtubs and the water controlled by steering wheels. Famously, the toilet seat was heated!

She commented that he was very disciplined, planning every day in advance and starting with exercise. "We even had pet names for each: he was 'Stan' and I was 'Doreen', don't ask me why." When arch motor racing enthusiast Steve McQueen, who was keen on Judy's flatmate Janet, came over to London "to pick up pointers from the master", the four of them went out together in the evenings. "Like Stirling, he was very humble about his profession, even to the point of insecurity. He seemed unaware of his stature."

Judy said how much she loved going motor racing and wearing her treasured racing jacket with her hero's name emblazoned on the back. During the day she was filming the 'Rag Trade' for BBC TV and continuing to appear in the revue 'On the Brighter Side' in the evenings, recording a single which made the charts. Work would mean they would see less of each other and then Judy landed a TV role in Hollywood.

"The press made Stirling out to be a notorious womanizer, which made him seem callous. In truth, he is simply a great lover of women."

Stirling Moss ...

THE PRESS & THE LIMELIGHT

PP: *"Was the press intrusion annoying?"*
SM: *"No it goes with the territory. He must have annoyed me or something. But in principle, no, it's just one of those things you have to take."*
PP: *"After your retirement, did you miss it when it disappeared?"*
SM: *"No! The only thing I miss nowadays is that I don't get invitations to the first nights of these good shows. I mean, I haven't been a judge for Miss World or Miss Universe for a long time! Those were the perks that go with the territory. It is a life that is easy to get into.*

"I don't know why I was avoiding the publicity on this occasion. I suppose it was because I didn't want too much to appear in the press about Judy because it would upset the others."

Ice Skating

Queens Court was built in 1930 in London's Bayswater at 17 Queensway by A.O. Edwards, Chairman of the Grosvenor House Hotel in Park Lane. Queens has been the only permanent ice rink in central London for more than 70 years. Park Lane is a stone's throw from SM's home in Mayfair and Queensway is about a mile way.

"Dauvergne is Rob Walker's daughter," states Val Pirie. "We went skating on Monday evenings. In those days, Mondays was the Hooray Henry night there and SM asked me to go along with him (because he is basically very shy) so he wouldn't be on his own and so he could look at the talent. We went on as many Mondays in the winter as he was here."

Stirling Moss ...

BEVERLEY

"Beverley Wheeler, was a girl I met, I think, on Cunard Air. She was an airline stewardess. A lot of the girls I knew were airline stewardesses because they could get around." Arthur Murray dance studios are spread throughout the US and claim to have taught over 40m people to dance.

GETTING DOWN TO IT

STIRLING MOSS nips about the Silverstone test area yesterday on his new Trobike. This small machine has a hinged frame so that when folded it can be carried in the boot of a car and used as a personal runabout.

Northants Chronical 3.3.61

1961

laws, Mr. and Mrs Molson of the Canadian brewing family and then went on to Babbie's (Babbie Holt was Katie's aunt), finally going to bed at 3am after a chat with Margot (Katie's best friend who married Sir Gawaine Baillie). Bev was back on Monday and they skied, ate at North Beach Lodge and danced.

After his relaxing few days in Nassau, Stirling flew to Miami and was not amused when he arrived as there was no-one to meet him. "Hired car thanks to Casner's inefficiency. To Bas' for party and two press men. On to Lake Placid. Tower motel. Bed at 1am."

Wednesday 22: "Up at 8am and practised Sprite. Axle too high. 4.2 needs 4.55 Got 6,000 and 6,200 Car feels good. Did in/out lap. 4.07 odd. Then Maser. Car is awfulish. Arrived 1½ hrs late for practice. Too high geared. Bad engine/brakes; too hard. No flying lap (3.25) Ferrari (3.16). Motel and bath. Cinema + Pat [Moss] and Co. Food and bed at 1.15am."

Thursday: "Up at 9. Practice. I did 3.55.3 with the Sprite! Now we have the 4.2 axle. I need three new tyres! Later Maser. Car does not feel good. Need ALL gears. Get 6,000 only. Brakes fair, understeer and oversteer, oil surge, etc. Off at 3.45 and collected Bev from St. Petersburg by 6.15. Track and no night practice due to broken exhaust system! Outfit is awful. Food and motel and bed at 12.15."

The Sebring 4-Hours took place on the Friday with the main event on Saturday. Stirling was up at 7.30 and off to the circuit. He had to race the number two Sprite as the number one car had a "duff clutch. Good start. Diced with Bruce and Walt. Get 103mph. Valve bounce at 6,700. Could go to 7,100. Handles well. 3.58. To 2nd and then clutch slip. Drifted and finished 5th. Pat's motel and swim. Later to Tampa and collected Joan Morris at airport. Motel and bed at 12.00."

Saturday was to be a day of farcical frustration for Stirling. "Up at 8am and circuit. Start. The car wouldn't start. 15 mins before I had asked the mechanic (Bobby) if it was OK, he said 'Yes'. Off 6 mins late! Made up to within 4 mins odd. Get 6,100 odd. Use 1st - 5th. 2nd/3rd should be higher. Overall OK. Tyres at 45/50 lbs. Should be 50/45. Pressure fluctuates. Brakes OK. Drove for two hours. Change and exhaust pipes fell off! Took over rear engine car. Back end collapsed. Time Front 3.12.5 [fastest lap], Rear 3.16. Motel, sun and…"

The day after the race Katie phoned to say she wanted to see Stirling in Miami but later cancelled the arrangement. It was not a good day as later he was caught for speeding and, this time, did not get away with it. "Norm, Chris, Joan, Bev and I off at 12.15 to Miami. $25 ticket. 65 in 45 zone! Unfair, I was

Skating with Stirling

"In those days," recalls Dauvergne Morgan, "the smart thing to do was to go ice skating at Queens Ice Skating rink on Monday. It was always a Monday – the only day anybody went. It was a great place to meet young of one sort or another. I was a hopeless skater but he was good, as you would imagine. He always said to me that if we saw a gorgeous creature coming towards us, it was up to me to fall down, which wasn't difficult for me to do!

"I think the same applied if I saw someone I wanted to say hello to, Stirling would do his best to accost him. But I think the only time that happened some chap asked him about a car and didn't show the slightest interest in me. He was just longing to chat to Stirling. As you can imagine, he was a great hero.

"It was great fun for me and I used to laugh myself silly. He was a terribly dashing young man.

"He was a very good skater because he had such good balance and co-ordination. But he always attracted so much attention. People would say, 'Ooh look, there's Stirling Moss'."

Brother and sister, right, and two of the best-known names in the driving business. Never before have they raced together. But on March 24th, at Sebring, Florida, *Stirling Moss*, thirty-one, and his sister, *Pat Moss*, twenty-six, are both driving Spinzel Sprites in the Four Hour Grand Touring Race. Though both are members of John Sprinzel's team they will be in fierce competition with each other. For Pat, European ladies' rally-driving champion, it will be her first big race. She will continue driving in rallies—has planned to drive in Italy, Holland, France and Belgium this year—but intends to devote more time to show jumping, where she first made a name for herself. Comments *Stirling*: "She should stick to driving."

The Queen 15.3.61

Stirling Moss ...

WAS MONEY THE MOTIVATION?

PP: "You were still racing a whole variety cars from Austin Healey Sprites right up to Formula 1, so presumably it was still very enjoyable to you, or did you do it for financial reasons?"

SM: "No, no. I mean, I wouldn't on principle race for nothing. It's just a principle; it wasn't a case of whether I needed the money or not. Also, I wouldn't accept less money than somebody else. They paid if they wanted me.

"However, I really did enjoy racing.

"The reason I raced the Sprite, which is the last thing in the world one would want really, was because I liked Donald Healey. We got along well and I thought. 'Well, we will have a bit of fun. I mean, it's not going to win against the Abarths and so on, but I can, at least, do the best I can. With all the cars that I drove, I drove them because either I enjoyed the race particularly or I liked that car particularly, or a combination of the two."

PP: "Or the people?"

SM: "Or the people, exactly. You have got to realise, and of course it seems completely foreign now, but when you are in a position where you are doing something you love and you are being paid for it, you then begin to select the people you like, because it is nice to be with them. Then you translate that to the cars you enjoy, because one car is nicer than another. Then you take on little crusades, like with this Sprite, trying to beat the Abarths. It became a challenge really."

12-Hour Sebring Race
A TEST OF MEN AND CARS

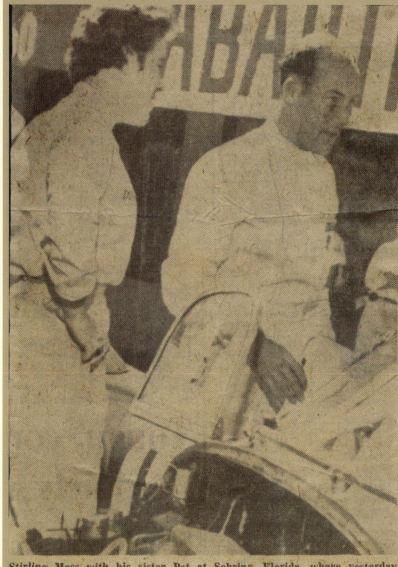

Stirling Moss with his sister Pat at Sebring, Florida, where yesterday they competed against one another in an endurance race, driving the same type of Austin-Healey. Moss was placed 4th and his sister 7th.

The Scotsman 25.3.61

The Sebring Four Hours

The Sebring 4-Hours was for GT cars under 1,000cc and was basically a battle between the Austin-Healey Sprites and Fiat Abarths. The twin overhead cam Abarths were driven by Dan Gurney, Harry Washburn and Bob Leiss and they dominated though Stirling was just about able to keep up with them. With the Abarths having a 10mph straight-line advantage, SM had to make up all the time he could in the corners.

Leiss and the three Sprites thrilled the crowd with a good bout of dicing. Pat Moss drove well but dropped back after a while and handed over to Paul Hawkins, the pair eventually finishing seventh. Gurney ran out of brakes and retired, leaving the race to Washburn. Suffering from clutch slip, Stirling's challenge faded and Hansgen led the Sprite charge, taking Leiss on the very last bend to beat him by a second.

PIT STOPS

Stirling Moss will compete in his first Canadian race on June 24 in a Lotus 19. The race is the Players 200 and takes place at Mosport, a new racing circuit 60 miles east of Toronto.

Stirling and Pat in big 'fight'

Stirling Moss ...

JOAN MORRIS

"Joan Morris worked on United Airlines; an extraordinarily spoilt girl!"

STIRLING AND PAT IN OPPOSITION

Stirling and Pat Moss in opposition

BRITAIN'S Stirling Moss was fourth and his sister, Pat, seventh in the four-hour endurance race for under-1,000 c.c. cars at Sebring, Florida, yesterday, reports Reuter.

It was the first time Stirling (31) and Pat (26) had competed against each other. Both drove Austin-Healey Sprites.

Moss, in a Maserati, is favourite for to-day's 12-hour Sebring Grand Prix, first event in this year's World Sports Car Championship.

Harry Washburn (Louisiana) won the four-hour race, covering 59 laps (305.8 miles) in an Abarth.

Yorkshire Eve Post 25.3.61

March — Stirling Moss Scrapbook

1961

doing about 50! Caught plane at 3.00 to N.Y. Town and met Shelley. Food and bed at 2.30am."

Next morning Stirling met Paul and Arledge regarding a TV film commentary on Le Mans. "Off at 3.00 to Chicago. Cold and windy and wet. Met by George Reed and to his fabulous house." A 6.20am start and SM headed off to Meadowdale Raceway where was going to instruct Chicago Region SCCA members in race-driving. "Taught 14 chaps from 9 – 4.30 solid. Sore throat. Met SCCA execs and food. Talked to 600 SCCA members from 8.30 till 11.10pm! Home and bed at 2am."

He looked round the shops next morning before flying American Airlines back to New York. After a drink with Anita, he flew BOAC overnight to London where Val met him and drove him to the office. He worked till 7.30 that evening before he "met Caroline, Dave and Karen and saw Lena Horne EX. Home and bed at 3.30am."

The month ended with work, a BRP (British Racing Partnership) drinks reception and going to see the Peter Sellers film *Mr. Topaz* which he did not enjoy. "Lousy."

The Birdcage Maser was a brilliant machine when running well but notoriously unreliable and this one sadly failed Stirling and co-driver Graham Hill at Sebring

Sebring circuit plan

Camoradi Racing Team

Camoradi was the name smooth-talking wheeler dealer Lloyd Perry 'Lucky' Casner gave to the team he formed in 1959. This curious name is made up of the first two letters of the following words: Casner Motor Racing Division. The team ran Birdcage Masers throughout 1960 and into 1961. On their letterhead, the team modestly described themselves as the world's major independent racing team!

"Lovely man, unbelievable shambles! I drove a Maserati at Sebring and, before the start, I said to one of the guys, 'Is the battery properly charged?

"'Yes,' he said.

"I ran across the road and the battery was flat. That really was unforgivable."

FERRARI SUCCESS AT SEBRING
Index Award Goes to Porsche

FILLING seven of the first 10 places, Ferrari completely dominated the 12-hour International Sports Car Race at Sebring, Florida, last Saturday, the winners being Phil Hill and Oliver Gendebien; they drove a 3-litre, V-8 TRI 61, 1,092 miles (210 laps), at an average speed of 91.30 m.p.h. The pair, in the course of their run, set a new sports car lap record in 3 min. 14.4 sec.

At the start, Stirling Moss with one of the Camoradi Maseratis was delayed with battery trouble, after which he moved up to second place and hotly challenged the 2.5-litre rear-engined Ferrari which was then in the lead. The Ferrari ultimately went out with suspension trouble and the Maserati with a fractured exhaust pipe. Moss then took over the second Camoradi entry and this, too, broke down.

For a long period, the Rodriguez brothers in a Testa Rossa were well in the lead; then, three hours from the end their car had dynamo trouble and Hill and Gendebien moved to the front and stayed there.

Not altogether unexpectedly, the Index of Performance went to Porsche, the car in question—a Type RS61—being driven by two Americans, Bob Holbert and Roger Penske, while a woman driver, Miss Denise McCluggage, shared with Allan Eager the wheel of the Ferrari Berlinetta that came out top in the Grand Touring class.

=== Provisional Results ===
1. Hill/Gendebien (Ferrari TRI 61), 210 laps, 1,092 miles, 91.30 m.p.h.
2. Ginther/Von Trips (Ferrari TRI 61).
3. P. Rodriguez/R. Rodriguez (Ferrari Testa Rossa).
4. Sharp/Hissen (Ferrari Testa Rossa).
5. Holbert/Penske (Porsche RS61).
Fastest Lap: Hill/Gendebien (Ferrari), 3: 14.4 (new record).
Index of Performance: Holbert/Penske (Porsche).
Grand Touring Class: Miss McCluggage/Eager (Ferrari).

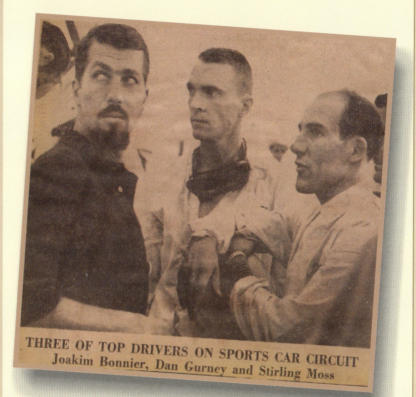

THREE OF TOP DRIVERS ON SPORTS CAR CIRCUIT
Joakim Bonnier, Dan Gurney and Stirling Moss

John Sprinzel's Sebring Sprites were driven by Stirling and Pat Moss in the four-hour race at Sebring for G.T. cars up to 1,000 c.c. Weighing only 11 cwt. all-up, this model has a maximum of over 110 m.p.h.

The Motor 29.3.61

Ten Ferraris for Sebring 12-hour race

TODAY'S 12-hour sports car race at Sebring is the first important International race of the season and it has attracted a big entry, mostly of foreign cars.

Ferrari is represented by ten cars, of which three are entered by Enzo Ferrari with Phil Hill, Olivier Gendebien, Wolfgang von Trips, Willy Mairesse, Ritchie Ginther as drivers, plus A.N. Other.

Camoradi have Stirling Moss, Graham Hill and American Masten Gregory.

Also among the big stuff are five Chevrolet Corvettes.

Then there are a number of Porsches with the works entries driven by Hans Herrmann and Dan Gurney and Edgar Barth and Jo Bonnier.

Among the G.T. cars are four Sunbeam Alpines, two entered by the works, one by Jack Brabham and the other a private nomination by Fillipo Theodoli, a New York advertising executive

OPPOSITION

Chief opposition to the Prancing Horse stable will be five Maseratis, three of which are nominated by Briggs Cunningham, and the other two by Camoradi.

The Briggs Cunningham cars will be driven by Walter Hansgen and Bruce McLaren, Briggs Cunningham and Bill Kimberly and John Finch and Dick Thompson.

and a former official of the Sebring circuit.

The other Sunbeam drivers are Paddy Hopkirk and Peter Jopp and Americans Vince Tamburo and Ed Wilson with the works cars and the Brabham entry handled by Peter Harper and Peter Proctor.

Two M.G.'s and some Lolas and Lotuses are also engaged.

In the Four-Hour race for G.T. cars up to 1,000 c.c. which precedes the big event, John Sprinzel has entered two Austin-Healey Sprites, which will be driven by Stirling Moss and his sister Pat.

Sporting Life 25.3.61

Cars

SEBRING SPRITE

The Sebring Sprite was developed by BMC in conjunction with John Sprinzel. It was produced in four states of tune – Road, Sports, Competition and Race. The race version had a light alloy body (£100) and more aerodynamic fibreglass bonnet and aluminium hardtop. The Formula Junior engine produced 62bhp as opposed to the 45bhp of the standard original Sprite. The Sebring Sprite could claim three class wins at the venue of that name.

Pat Moss Carlsson

"Stirling's clutch went in practice. So there was one duff car and, being a nice sister, I let him have my car. Obviously he would be quicker than me so I said, 'Take my good car,' and I had his with the duff clutch.

"Another thing I remember is that it was a Le Mans start and I beat him into the car. I was very proud of that. But then I had to start it on the key because of having no clutch."

PP: "Was he very competitive, even with you?"

PMC: "Oh yes, we have always been competitive. If we play cards together, we're competitive fiends! If we play Scrabble, I can spell and he can't. Dad couldn't spell and neither could Stirling, but Mum and I could. Yes, we were always competitive and very committed."

PP: "Had Stirling's attitude to motor racing changed in any way by 1961?"

PMC: "Not from Day One. From the very first hillclimb he did, he was always in there to win. No, he hadn't changed. He was always very dedicated. He was in motor racing, as I was in rallying. You're not there to mess about; you're there to win.

"I never went motor racing. When he first started, they used to drag me along but I did not like motor racing, either to do it or watch it. Obviously, I wished Stirling well but I didn't want to go and see it. To me motor racing is boring! You just see the cars flash by and, to drive it, it is the same every lap. It didn't appeal to me at all. I only did a few races."

Circuits

Moss on: SEBRING

"Sebring was a difficult circuit, because in those days it was never laid out properly as a circuit, you know. It was very difficult to drive on because you couldn't see where the track went with no natural features. There was not much character and therefore not really a very good circuit."

1961

Stirling Moss Scrapbook

They Won It In The Past

DEC. 31, 1950
6 Hours — 401.7 miles (tie). Speed 66.95 m.p.h.
Cadillac-Allard — Fred Wacker and Frank Burrell
Cadillac-Allard — Jay Davidson and George Weaver

MARCH 15, 1952
12 Hours — 754 miles. Speed 62.83 m.p.h.
Frazier-Nash — Harry Grey and Larry Kulok

MARCH 8, 1953
12 Hours — 899.6 miles. Speed 74.96 m.p.h.
Cunningham C4R — John Fitch and Phil Walters

MARCH 7, 1954
12 Hours — 883.6 miles. Speed 73.63 m.p.h.
OSCA — Stirling Moss and Bill Loyd

MARCH 13, 1955
12 Hours — 946.4 miles. Speed 78.86 m.p.h.
D Jaguar — Mike Hawthorn and Phil Walters

MARCH 24, 1956
12 Hours — 1,0008.8 miles. Speed 84.07 m.p.h.
Ferrari — Juan Manuel Fangio and Eugenio Castilotti

MARCH 23, 1957
12 Hours — 1,024.4 miles. Speed 85.36 m.p.h.
Maserati — Juan Manuel Fangio and Jean Behra

MARCH 22, 1958
12 Hours — 1,040 miles. Speed 86.6 m.p.h.
Ferrari — Peter Collins and Phil Hill

MARCH 21, 1959
12 Hours — 977.6 miles. Speed 81.466 m.p.h.
Ferrari — Phil Hill, Olivier Gendebien, Dan Gurney, Chuck Daigh

MARCH 26, 1960
12 Hours — 1,019.2 miles. Speed 84.933 m.p.h.
Porsche — Olivier Gendebien and Hans Hermann

Maserati T61

The Tipo 61 became known as the 'birdcage' Maserati due to its construction consisting of a multitude of small diameter tubes. Suspension was by double wishbones and coil springs at the front and de Dion at the rear. The power unit was a 2,890cc 4-cylinder, traditionally front-mounted and inclined at an angle of 45°. Transmission was by a rear-mounted five-speed 'box. The T61 was generally quick but fragile. In 1960 it held together to win the Nürburgring 1,000km race.

The Sebring Twelve Hours

Ferrari versus Maserati was how it was billed but Enzo's machines took the honours as the Maser challenge gradually fell apart. Stirling's race proved the point. He began in the front-engined Tipo 61 which had a flat battery and this was particularly galling to the Le Mans-start specialist. He was sharing the car with fellow Brit Graham Hill and after SM had worked hard to recover the lap and a half lost and get back on terms with the leaders, actually getting up to second position, Hill had the exhaust manifold break which spelt retirement, but not before Graham burnt his feet and was nearly asphyxiated.

Not to be beaten, Stirling took over the new Masten Gregory/'Lucky' Casner rear-engined Maserati T63 but he was soon in the pits complaining of a loose wheel. He continued but 15 minutes later was out for good with rear suspension failure. His only consolation was a new lap record in the older car.

The race saw the Ferrari of Phil Hill and Olivier Gendebien take the honours but the heroes were a couple of very young brothers from Mexico, Pedro and Ricardo Rodriguez, in a 1960 Ferrari.

Jinx hits Moss —in two cars

BAD LUCK HITS STIRLING AGAIN

STIRLING MOSS DID THE FASTEST LAP

Race officials have corrected two results and the lap record for last Saturday's 12-hour sports car race in Sebring, Florida.

Britain's Stirling Moss (Maserati), who retired early in the race, was credited with the official lap record of 97.4 m.p.h. This was previously given to Phil Hill's Ferrari, winner of the race with 96.3 m.p.h.

Ferraris were given the first five places in the official correction, the Hall-Constantine Ferrari replacing the Holbert-Penske Porsche in the fifth position, the Porsche was placed sixth.

The lap total for the winning Hill-Gendebien Ferrari was reduced from 210 to 208, at an average speed of 90.13 m.p.h., not 90.0 m.p.h. as previously announced.

Mosses 4th and 7th

MOSS DOGGED BY BAD LUCK

Out of Endurance Race After Lying Second

A works-entered Testa Rosa Ferrari, driven by Phil Hill (United States) and Olivier Gendebien (Belgium), on Saturday won the Sebring 12-hour endurance race for sports cars at a record average speed of 91 m.p.h.

They covered 210 laps of the 5.2-mile course to bring off a double; they won the race in 1959, also in a Ferrari.

Stirling Moss was plagued with bad luck. He entered a front-engined Maserati after deciding at the last moment not to drive the much-heralded "Birdcage" rear-engined Maserati because he was not satisfied with its handling.

At the start, the battery was flat and he lost a lap while it was being changed.

Mexican Brothers

The front-engined car overheated early in the race, and Moss switched to the rear-engined model. Just before the four-hour point, the car developed suspension trouble, and Moss was out of the race for good. At one point, he had been lying second.

Chief feature of the race was a duel between the Hill-Gendebien car and another Ferrari driven by the Mexican brothers Ricardo and Pedro Rodriguez.

Birmingham Post 27.3.61

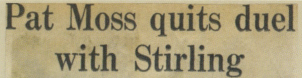

Cars

Maserati Tipo 63

The rear-engined sports racer was of similar construction as the front-engined 'birdcage' cars with multiple small-bore tubing and, said 'Motor Racing' magazine, "seemingly as complicated"! The four-cylinder engine was inclined to the right at an angle of 33° and the five-speed transmission was in unit with the differential. Front and rear independent suspension used tubular wishbones and coil springs.

Pat Moss quits duel with Stirling

PAT MOSS and her brother Stirling roared off on their first big race together yesterday.

But Pat was forced to quit halfway through the race at Sebring, Florida.

Relief driver Paul Hawkins took her car and finished seventh — three places behind Stirling.

Said Pat afterwards: "Stirling lost me on the first lap. I was forced to go into the turn in the wrong gear."

She was the only woman among the 24 entries and drove a Sprite, like her brother.

★ ★ ★

Stirling finished fourth — beaten by Bruce McLaren of New Zealand who came second in a Sprite, and by two Americans driving Italian Abarths.

But Moss gave a brilliant performance against the faster Italian cars. Many times the 15,000 spectators gasped as he overtook his opponents on the inside of the track's hairpin bends — only to lose what he had gained on the straight.

He said later: "There weren't enough turns."

Daily Express 25.3.61

March

Stirling Moss Scrapbook

1961

APRIL

Calendar

- **3** Easter Monday Goodwood, Sussex, UK – Lavant Cup (InterContinental race) – 1st in 2.5 Cooper-Climax T53P; Glover Trophy – 4th in 1.5 Lotus-Climax 18; Sussex Trophy – 1st in Lotus-Climax 19; Fordwater Trophy – 3rd in Aston Martin DB4 GTZ
- **9** Brussels GP, Heysel, Belgium – unclassified in heat 1, 8th in heat 2, 2nd in final heat, unclassified overall but unofficially 7th in 1.5 Lotus-Climax 18
- **16** Vienna Preis, Aspern, Austria – 1st 1.5 Lotus-Climax 18
- **22** Aintree 200, Liverpool, UK – ret'd in 1.5 Cooper-Climax; Sports Car Race – 1st in UDT/Laystall Lotus-Climax 19
- **25** Syracuse GP – ret'd in 1.5 Lotus-Climax 18
- **30** Targa Florio, Tribune do Cerda, Madonie, Sicily – ret'd in Porsche RS60 1.9 (sharing with Graham Hill)

Easter fell on the first weekend in April and Goodwood had a packed programme for their traditional race meeting. Of the six races, Stirling took part in all but two. His mounts consisted of the new Rob Walker 2½ litre Cooper-Climax for the Inter-Continental race, though he practised with Walker's Lotus as well, a Lotus 18 for the Formula 1 race, a Lotus 19 for the sports car race and an Aston Martin DB4GT Zagato for the grand touring contest.

Saturday went as follows: "Up and off to Goodwood. Practice. Sports OK. F1 Lotus good. Get 7,300. 4th too high. FIc Cooper better but not enough miles and gearbox mounting broke away at back. Two laps only on FIc Lotus. Holds back at 6,000. Aston pretty awful. On to John's. Collected Judy from Brighton. Food and bed at 2am."

F1: SM 1.27.8, Surtees 1.28.8, Roy 1.28.8, Hill 1.28.8, Innes 1.29.2

F.Ic: Bruce 1.24.2, Hill 1.24.6, C. SM 1.24.8, L. SM

Cars

Cooper-Climax T53P

Stirling had given the Cooper marque its first GP win in 1958 and Jack Brabham had gone on to win the World Championship in the works Cooper in 1959. For 1960 Cooper's response to Chapman's rear-engined Lotus 18 was a new 'lowline' Cooper. It had coil spring suspension all-round and reduced frontal area. For 1961 these were put into small-scale production and run with either 1½-litre Climax engines for the new F1 regulations or larger engines for the Tasman and Inter-Continental series. Walker's example was fitted with a 2½-litre Climax power unit.

The temperamental, but brilliant, Alf Francis

Left: Classic shot of Stirling winning the Lavant Cup at Goodwood in the 2.5 Cooper-Climax. Above: Stirling also won the Sussex Trophy race in a Lotus 19. Below: L to R - Henry Taylor, SM & Cliff Allison

 Cars

Aston Martin DB4 GTZ

In 1959, Aston Martin supplemented the DB4 coupe with the shortened, higher performance DB4GT with a twin plug head and Weber carburettors. Then, at the 1960 London Motor Show, they introduced the even higher performance Zagato version built by the Italian coachbuilder of that name. The GTZ was built on the shortened chassis of the DB4GT but was lighter and handmade by Zagato. Top speed was 153mph and the 3,670cc engine now produced 285bhp @ 6,000rpm. Specification included manual 5-speed gearbox, independent front suspension and beam axle/trailing arm, coil sprung rear. This model could reach 60mph from standstill in 6.1 secs. Just 19 were produced between 1959 and 1963.

April

Stirling Moss Scrapbook

1.25.2, Brooks 1.25.2
  GT: SM 1.37.2, Parkes 1.37.4, Innes 1.38.2.
  Sports: SM 1.28.0, Henry [Taylor] 1.30.8, Cliff [Allison] 1.33.4

Sunday was spent relaxing. He ate with UDT/Laystall team mate Henry Taylor and went to the "flicks".

On Monday: "Up at 10am. Judy off to town. B'fast. Later circuit. Wet. FIc Bad start due to gearbox mounting breaking. Lost 10 secs. To 1st and brake locked, 2nd, then 1st and won. Bruce close 2nd. F1 Good start, Surtees flew past, held 2nd then into 4th [gear] but selected 2nd [gear] 8300! Finished 4th. Won Sports. Easy race. GT 3rd. Car lousy. Axle tramp. John's and food + Caroline, Val, Herb, Ilia and Ma and Pa. Town and chat and bed at 2.30am."

"Up at 11am. Mary H! Cooked b'fast. Work. Lunch with Mr. Winstone & Co. More work. Haircut and work till 10pm! Little bit of food with CN 36 and KM phoned re divorce at 12.00pm. Bed at 2am."

On the Wednesday Stirling opened garages for BP at Dagenham and Welwyn. He then took CN to the premiere of *Greengage Summer* (VG) and dined at the Columbia Club, together with Val and Charles Walters. "Bed at 3am."

Next morning he called on his lawyer regarding Katie and the divorce before wandering into Harrods and other shops in the area. By 6.30 he was at London Airport and flew by Sabena Caravelle to Brussels, checking in to the Atlanta Hotel at 8.45pm. He was due to race in the non-Championship Brussels GP at Heysel but it was not to be a happy weekend.

Friday: "Up late and circuit. Had terrible troubles with the car and finished up dead slowest in practice! It seems to be dirt in the carbs. Wet all day. Later collected Dave from Airport. Cocktail do. Food + Mike Cooper-Evans. Bed at 2am." It was no better next day and the best he could do was sixth fastest. At least he had the consolation of meeting some local crumpet. "Later met Paula Pascale and sister Yvette."

Race day was hardly better. "Up late & circuit. 1st heat. Car awful. Last. Changed mag. 2nd heat one from last, changed fuel pump and removed body panel (thought mag overheating), lowered fuel level. Better. 6,800. Behind Jack 7,300! 11 mph extra. 2nd. Good dice with JB. Had 50yd lead on last str. Lost it all. 2.04.4. Food, prizes and bed at 2am."

In its editorial *Autosport* felt moved to comment that, though Moss was far behind Brabham on points scored in the two previous heats, he continued "to give of his best". That was the 'racer' in him.

April 10 saw Stirling in Paris, buying shoes and going to *Mr. Perouse* with Jo Bonnier. (VG). He then

Easter Monday International Goodwood

In the Inter-Continental race Stirling and Bruce McLaren had what Autosport called "a stupendous duel" for the Lavant Cup with Stirling shaving it by 0.6 secs. He was less lucky in the F1 race as John Surtees and his Yeoman Credit Cooper-Climax were on unstoppable form. Stirling trailed him for much of the race until his engine went off song with a suspected bent valve caused, presumably, by his selection of second instead of fourth, a most uncharacteristic error from the maestro.

In the Sussex Trophy race Stirling led from start to finish in the Lotus Monte Carlo with Taylor finishing 2.2 secs adrift. The Zagato-bodied Aston gave Stirling a challenging time in the GT race and although he was initially second, he could not push Mike Parkes in the lead and also had to give best to Innes Ireland's 'standard' DB4GT before the flag.

Tony Robinson (centre) and other mechanics chat with Taylor, SM and Allison

Circuits

Moss on: GOODWOOD

SM: *"Goodwood is a lot more difficult than people realise, actually. When you go into the bend after the pits you have got a double corner there, which you can take as one and that makes a big difference to how fast you go through Fordwater, which again is a difficult corner, as is the rest of the track round the back. It's only short, but I think that Goodwood is a lot more interesting than people give it credit for."*
PP: *"You are working on most of the lap, apart from the Lavant Straight?"*
SM: *"Yes, you are."*

Start of the International !00 race for F1 cars at the Goodwood Easter meeting with a front row, from left to right, of SM, Surtees, Salvadori and Hill

Drivers

Moss on: BRUCE McLAREN

SM: "Bruce was a really, really nice guy, a very pleasant Kiwi. He came over here with quite a lot of talent but not knowing that much. I remember one year that he couldn't qualify for Monaco and I said, 'Well follow me around,' and he could do it very well. So he did have a lot of talent."

PP: "Could you be too nice to be a competitive Grand Prix driver?"

SM: "Yes. I think that Bruce is one of the ones who falls near that."

PP: "You need a certain ruthlessness to compete?"

SM: "Yes. I can't believe that Bruce would ever be ruthless, Walt Hansgen I am sure could be, and probably Dan [Gurney], but I can't see Bruce being ruthless."

1st big win... John Surtees hugs the bowl.

WOW! I have beaten Stirling Moss

McLaren (leading below and standing above right) and Stirling had a rare d dice for the Lavant Trophy. However, the photo above is a bit of a ser. Though in Stirling's scrapbook as Goodwood, we are convinced it not! Any suggestions?

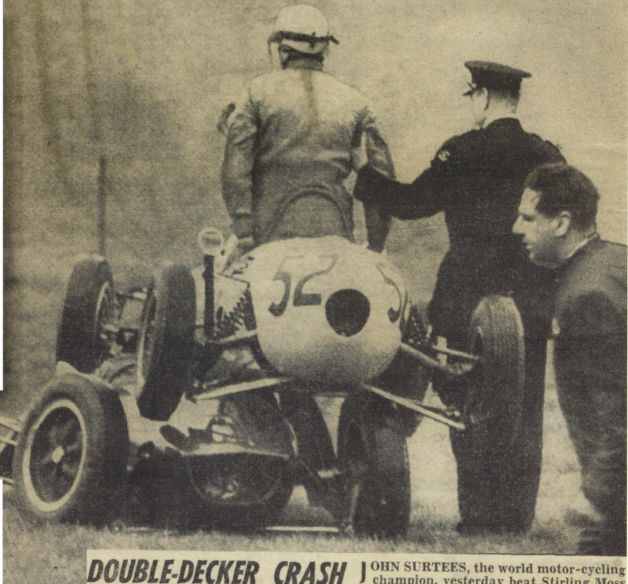

DOUBLE-DECKER CRASH
Helping hand for driver Parkes as he climbs out of his Gemini-Ford after a double-decker crash with A. B. Rees's Lotus-Ford at Goodwood yesterday. No one was hurt. *Sketchpic by Geoffrey White.*

JOHN SURTEES, the world motor-cycling champion, yesterday beat Stirling Moss in the thrilling International 100 at Goodwood

Surtees, in a Formula I Cooper Climax entered by the Yeoman Credit team, led all the way to win by more than half a minute.

1961

flew to Gatwick where Val met him and drove him to the office. After cocktails next day with BP, he took CN to see "*Alamo* (EX) 3½ hours. Food at Candlelight and bed at 2am". He felt awful and listless when he arose next morning but worked all day. In the evening he met Herb and went to "see Judy at Phoenix VG. On to see Lena Horne. Fab. Chat. I drove at 1.30am! Bed at 4am. Judy said ciao."

He was off to the airport next day with David Haynes and Val, plus Basil Cardew of the *Daily Express* and Denis Holmes of the *Daily Mail*. They flew to Vienna. "Food and Club Eve. Danced and watched fantastic stripper. 6 ft plus. Nadja Nadlova. Met girl called Katia. Bed at 4am."

Having done a TV interview the day before, it was radio's turn on Friday. He then met Ruth Maxouvitch and went to a press reception. "Shop. Shoes … and then Martin Pjundes' for cocktails and food. On to Maxims and Eve with Shane [Summers]. Bed at 2.30."

This was to be a rather better, though not very challenging, weekend. "Up at 10.15 and met Inge at 11.05. On to track. Practice delayed by no bales. Lunch and practice. I get 115 mph max. Car oversteers but feels nice. To hotel. SM 1.13.7, Shane 1.15.3." Sunday: "Up at 10.00. Circuit. 50,000 people. Race. No fast competition. Held back and used only 3rd and 4th. Changed at 6,800! Gears good. Car oversteers, engine fair. Ftd at 1.12.2 (1 lap), other 1.15 plus. Later hotel, food and prize giving. Packed and bed at 2.15."

Tuesday April 18 saw Stirling back in the UK and travelling down to Goodwood with Caroline Nuttall. He tested the Inter-Continental Cooper and the revolutionary Ferguson. "Latter has clutch slip and 1.5 engine. There is a flick on presentation to the corner, and understeer in the corner. Brakes are fantastic. Uses 15 x 500 @ 35lbs. Later saw *Saturday Night and Sunday Morning* (F). Snack, chat and bed at the Fleece 1.30."

Having stayed overnight, he was back at the circuit next morning and was testing the Ferguson again. "Car is still much like yesterday. Town, work and later snack and work till 1am. Bed at 2am. Ken and Nym had a baby boy today, 6 ½ lbs. Depressed re J.C."

Clearly, Judy Carne had finished their relationship, an unusual situation for Stirling, and he was sad about this.

On Thursday Stirling had lunch at the Savoy with Bob Gibson Jarvie and used his scooter to get there which must have caused the odd raised eyebrow if he parked in the famous short road to the hotel entrance, the only thoroughfare in the UK where one

Daily Mail 4.4.61

Daily Sketch 4.4.61

Stirling Moss …

DIVORCE FROM KATIE

SM: "It was one of those things that happened. Unfortunately the marriage wasn't a success. I get along with her very well now. It was just the wrong time for the wrong people really and it was the wrong life for us."
PP: "The racing life?"
SM: "Yes. The strain was obviously quite big at one time."
PP: "Did splitting up affect you?"
SM: "Yea, I was pretty upset for a while. What it made me do, really, was put more time into racing and working, rather than sitting around."
PP: "But you weren't short of female company."
SM: "No, no, luckily…"

Grand Prix of Brussels

The Brussels event, run to the new F1 rules, was split into three 100-kilometre heats. In the first Stirling pitted and a spark plug was discovered to be loose. In the second heat, he was short of a cylinder which is quite significant when you have only four at best. Finally, for the third heat, the motor was on song and he came through the depleted field of 10 to chase Brabham who led. They had a fine ding-dong which entertained the crowd but clearly Stirling's engine was still not comparable with Black Jack's and he was beaten by a whisker.

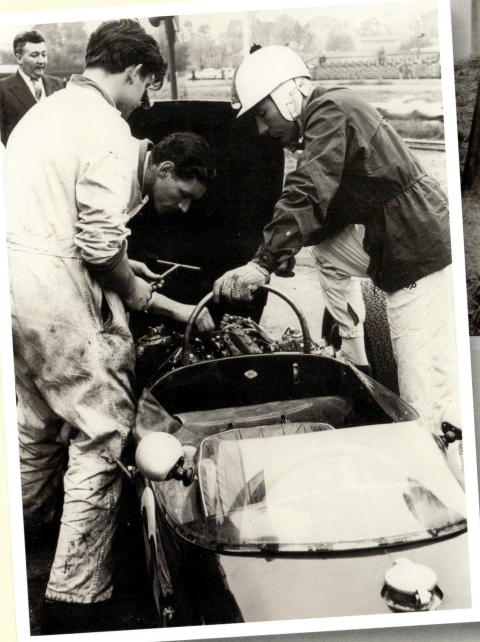

Stirling chases Salvadori during Brussels GP

Stirling Moss ...

INGE

"I had quite a long-lasting affair with Inge Kirmse. She worked for one of the airlines and was a German girl with one brown eye and one blue eye."

1961

drives on the right. After working until eight, he ate with Ken and they visited Gregory's wife in hospital. "Depressed." He was obviously missing Judy.

Bearing in mind that work is a great healer, "Up early and work. Off at 9.30 + Shane to L'pool via Manchester. Rootes lent a car. Hotel and track. Cooper F1 duff as usual. Ran big ends in 7 laps! Sports Lotus had mag trouble. Did one lap in Henry's car 2.01.2! One in Ashmore Lotus 2.02.0 Geared to 6,400! Hotel. Food + Shane and Jenny. Later met Caroline…"

Saturday, April 22: "Up at 8.45. Circuit. Sports. 6th row. 2nd at lap two and then 1st. Stayed and did ftd. 2.00.2. Henry 2nd. Engine fair. F1 9th row. Good start and to 5th/6th and big-ends. Rain all later day. Caught plane from Manchester + Herb, Shane and Jenny. Out to Astor + Stephanie. Bed at 4.15am."

On Sunday David Haynes drove his best friend to London Airport where Stirling met up with Graham Hill. They flew to Rome, met Shirlee Adams and travelled on to Catonia. There they hired a Fiat and headed for Polite where they met up with French photo-journalist Bernard Cahier.

On Monday the drivers practised for the Syracuse GP with Stirling in the Rob Walker Lotus 18 but the engine was far from healthy. He commented that it was "holding back as in Brussels. Gurney 1.56.9, Ferrari 1.57.0 (Baghetti), Surtees 1.57.8, Hill 1.58.1, Brabham 1.58.3, Bonnier 1.58.5, SM 1.59.2, Roy 1.59.9, etc." The race took place on the Tuesday and things were no better for Stirling. "Car bad. Gears sticking, engine missing and SM not driving well either! Was 7th could have been 6th but the mag. drive sheared two laps to go."

There was clearly a fundamental problem with the Climax engine or its ancillaries. Next day, he set off for Sicily and the uniquely challenging Targa Florio in which he was to share a Porsche RS60 with that great character Graham Hill. He arrived at Cefalu in three hours 45 minutes and did two laps in the 1100 Fiat hire car. The first was clocked at one hour, three minutes and 24 seconds. He then checked in at the Santa Lucia.

Thursday April 27 was Judy's birthday. Meanwhile, Stirling and Graham were at work. SM "did three laps with Graham in the 2 litre Carrera. Ex (51 mins) lunch and then a lap + Huschke, then two with Shirlee (50 mins). I now know the course pretty well. Bath, food and bed at 11pm."

Friday: "Up at 7.15 out to circuit and scrutineering. Practice. I did 43.08 in the 1700 with new tyres. G. Hill did 43.16. I then took the 2 litre Mule out and did 40.28. Car felt good. Got 228 kph in 1700 and 223 in 2 lit. Later hotel and bought goggles,

ON THE DAY THE LORDS DEBATED THE NEW TRAFFIC BILL…

Moss gets the freedom of the road again!

In the back seat as Stirling Moss becomes legal

Jubilation… moment of freedom which made Moss say: "It feels like coming out of prison"

AND HE KEEPS THE NEEDLE STEADY AT 40

by BASIL CARDEW

BRITAIN'S most famous accelerator foot pressed down gently, the automatic transmission took the Ford Zephyr away from the kerb in a smooth murmur. … Stirling Moss took a firmer grip of the wheel, grinned, and said: "It feels like coming out of prison."

Diligence… hand signal from a racing ace

Daily Express 14.4.61

Stirling Moss wins Austrian race
Lotus cars fill first three places

VIENNA, Sunday

STIRLING MOSS won the Prize of Vienna in an international motor race for Formula I cars on the Aspern Airfield course near here today. Moss, who drove a Lotus, set a track record with a time of 1 minute 12.2 seconds at an average speed of 75.12 m.p.h.

Moss covered the 55 laps, totalling 83.20 miles, in 1 hour 10 minutes 16 seconds at an average speed of 76.42 m.p.h.

Lotus cars were also second and third with Seidl (Germany) second in 1 hour 10 minutes 53.0 seconds and Trinoth (Italy) third, one lap behind. —Reuter.

Yorkshire Post 17.4.61

Moss Back Behind Wheel on Highway

LONDON (UPI)—British auto racing star Stirling Moss—free to drive on British roads for the first time in 12 months—motored to London airport in a new grey sedan yesterday to catch a plane for Vienna.

Moss said it felt "wonderful" to be back behind the wheel for the first time since a British court suspended his driving license after he was convicted of a traffic offense last year.

"I've been such a nuisance to my friends, having to be carted about," he said.

Moss will compete on Sunday in the Vienna Grand Prix.

U.S. Cutting 15.4.61

Vienna Grand Prix

A Frenchman by the name of Prineth, who was driving a Lotus, led away at the start, followed by Tim Parnell, also Lotus-mounted. Stirling was third and Shane Summers fourth as they approached the hairpin for the first time. Leading was too much for Prineth and he succumbed to the pressure and spun, causing Parnell to take to the grass and allow Stirling and Summers through.

On lap 13, appropriately, Summers retired with a broken drop-arm bolt, caused by the rough nature of the track. Stirling's engine then appeared to onlookers to go off-song allowing Parnell to make some inroads into his lead, to the entertainment of the crowd. Then Parnell dropped out with a broken drive shaft. Moss, whose engine came back on tune, "really started to motor now" and won very easily, having set a new lap record in the process.

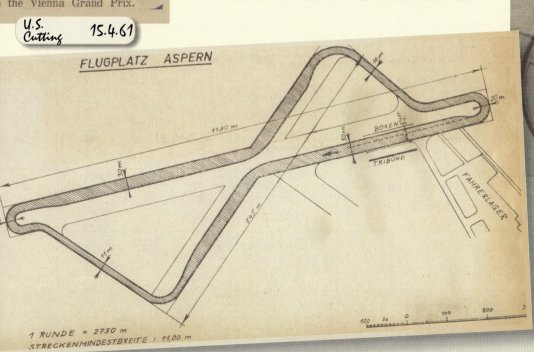

Stirling Moss gewann überlegen
11.000 Autos beim Flugplatzrennen

1961

etc. Bath and food and bed at 12.30pm."

On Saturday Stirling went to Palermo, had a haircut and returned to Cefalu. He did one practice lap and was in bed at 8.30pm, rising at 5am on the morrow. "Start. I led for four laps by 1½ mins from Joe and two odd from Ferrari. Graham did two [laps] and I took over –76 secs from Ferrari. Got back to lead + 60 secs by one lap to go. Was on sub 40 min lap and then 8 kms from finish the axle broke!" It was cruel luck after a brilliant performance.

Saturday Night and Sunday Morning

This 1960 film, an influential example of Free Cinema, starred newcomer Albert Finney and launched his career. It was kitchen sink drama, adapted from his fifties novel by Alan Sillitoe. Set at the end of that decade, it portrays a dreary existence where young working class men have only work, booze and death in their lives. Finney's smouldering anti-hero, Arthur Seaton, tries to break out of this straight-jacket and fight the system. "Don't let the bastards grind you down," is his famous message. Rachel Roberts won a Bafta for her performance as the sexually liberated Brenda, as did the film. It was directed by Czech-born Karel Reisz who, in 1981, would make 'The French Lieutenant's Woman'. The jazz soundtrack was by Johnny Dankworth and the success of the film allowed producer, Harry Saltzman, to buy the rights of Ian Fleming's James Bond novels.

I reckon that Stirling's push-button home will cost £30,000

STIRLING MOSS, who once described himself as a prosperous man with expensive tastes, is certainly proving the point with the new house he is building himself in Mayfair. Though it's only three doors from the Shepherd Market home he is living in at the moment, the new house is a whole world apart in luxury fittings.

After visiting it yesterday I estimate that when 44-46 Shepherd-street is finished he won't get much change out of £30,000.

Stirling is designing it with the aid of an architect —and is incorporating some remarkable features.

It will have a three-car garage with radio-controlled doors. Drive up to the garage, press a button in the car, and the garage doors open automatically.

The bathrooms will be even more of a lazy man's dream.

"They will all be push-button remote control," his secretary tells me. "By pressing a button build an electronic dream house.

But culture gets a look in too. He started painting about a year ago, soon after his separation from his wife Katie.

He has had lessons from Elizabeth Walker, wife of his friend Rob Walker. So there is to be a roof-top studio with patio which, incidentally, overlooks the London Hilton Hotel, now being built.

Reluctant

Stirling has already sold his home in Shepherd-street to business man Mr. Peter Werth, a wealthy hearing-aid specialist.

"I just bumped into Stirling walking down the street. He was a bit reluctant to sell his old house as the new one won't be ready for some time," said Mr. Werth.

"But I told him I didn't mind buying now and moving later, so the deal was done."

Moss, who is in Sicily at the moment, says : "Everything will be very nice when it is finished, but I don't expect to move in before next September."

In the bedroom you can run a bath to the exact depth and temperature required."

On a more utilitarian plane there will be a fully-equipped and up-to-date ground-floor office to handle Stirling's 10,000 letters a year—from fan mail to business.

Stirling, who built a house for himself in Nassau, has picked up many American ideas. It was always his ambition to

Stirling going pop..pop..pop

● Yes, it IS Stirling Moss, ace British motor-racing driver. No, he is NOT turning over to the two-wheeled game— just saving time around the paddock. Hundreds of fans saw him pop-popping about yesterday at Goodwood (Sussex) where he was practising for today's big motor meeting.

Stirling Moss, Shepherd Street, London W1, Engeland

Fleece Inn

"The Fleece Inn was near Goodwood and was run by John Brierley who had helped me with the 500s. I once took a girl there and they put cayenne pepper in my pyjamas! It was a terrific place and great fun."

The Fleece Inn, which alas no longer exists, was in Chichester and dated back to 1602. It was originally owned by William Cawley who was one of the signatories to Charles I's death warrant. Brierley owned the pub from 1950/51 until 1966. He was a race mechanic and worked on Coopers before taking on the Fleece Inn. "Stirling always used to stay with us and we would be virtually taken over by the Moss family, plus Ken Gregory and Alf Francis. We did have some fun and games. It was such a jolly place."

WIN FOR STIRLING MOSS

Vienna, April 16. Stirling Moss, driving a Lotus, won the International Vienna Airport car race today, setting a new lap record. He covered the 93 miles (55 laps) of the race in 1hr. 10min. 1.6sec., at an average speed of 82.021 m.p.h. Second was Wolfgang Seidel (Germany) in a Lotus, 52 seconds behind, and third, Ernesto Prinoth, of Italy, also in a Lotus. British cars filled the first eight places.—British United Press.

The Guardian 17.4.61

As Stirling has a photo of the E-type, which was launched the previous month, in his scrapbook, he was clearly impressed

BP PROGRESS
No. 28 APRIL 1961

AIRBORNE AGAIN

Stirling Moss flies to visit two BP stations near London

A COUPLE of days after Easter, Stirling Moss once again climbed aboard a BP-chartered BEA helicopter at Battersea Heliport, London, to drop in on two more BP Dealers. This time he visited Dagenham, Essex, and Welwyn Garden City, Herts, and at both places he received a tremendous welcome both from the crowds and from the local Press.

At Dagenham, the home of Ford cars, he called in at the site of H. J. Reader and Sons Ltd and met the four Reader brothers, Leonard, Eric, Victor and Horace, who run the station. This is on the edge of the vast Ford factory estate which reaches down to the River Thames.

Old/New

Len Reader told BP PROGRESS that the family business had been situated on that same spot in Rainham Road South since 1899, when they traded as blacksmiths and wheelwrights. 'Fords was only a field when we came here,' he said. By 1926 a garage had been opened and it had one of the first petrol pumps in Dagenham. 'It was hand-operated as here was no electricity in these parts then,' Len told us.

opens next year, the station is expected to do a bigger trade than ever, as it is on the direct route to this new link between Essex and Kent.

In the afternoon, Moss's helicopter chopped its way north-west to Welwyn Garden City, one of the first of the 'built-to-plan' communities now known as 'new towns'. One of the latest of them, Stevenage New Town is next door. And at Welwyn's smart Stadium Service Station, beside the very impressive sports arena, Stirling was welcomed by BP Dealer Mr Denis Barley, who told us of his site's success.

Phenomenal

'We've only been open three weeks,' he said. 'In the first week we did 5,720 gallons, and now we're

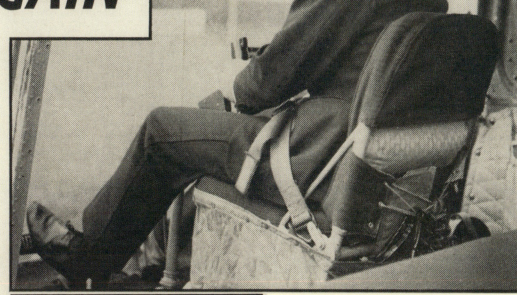

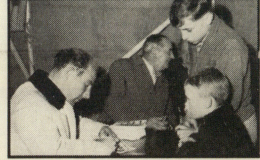

Top: Moss takes over the controls of the BP-chartered helicopter—but only for the photographer's benefit. Above: one of the 700 autographs Moss signed during the day. Right: Stirling meets the Reader brothers at Dagenham, Len, Eric, Vic

"THE GREENGAGE SUMMER"
Premiere at Odeon, Leicester Square

1961

AINTREE
INTERNATIONAL '200' MEETING

Aintree

In practice for the main Aintree 200 race, both Stirling and Jack Brabham had their sessions curtailed when the bearings went in their respective Climax-engined Coopers. Most unusually, Stirling found himself on the sixth row of the grid with some 22 drivers ahead of him but it was all pretty academic because in the race his bearings went again within just two laps.

The sports car race was a different matter. Due to his magneto trouble in practice he was again in an unaccustomed lowly grid position. Stirling was up to second by the end of the first lap, enjoyed a dice with team mate Henry Taylor for several laps before taking the lead and opening up a seven second gap. As well as the chequered flag, he took the lap record.

Shirlee Adams with SM at Syracuse

ENTE AUTONOMO CIRCUITO DI SIRACUSA

XI GRAN PREMIO SIRACUSA
25 Aprile 1961

Indianapolis

An American sponsor called Al Dean contacted Stirling around at this time to try and entice him to the Brickyard. He offered him a choice of two cars which he claimed were potential winners. When SM politely thanked him but said he would only be interested if he could drive a British car, Dean responded that he respected Moss's views and therefore would like to offer him a British mount.

Stirling Moss Scrapbook

ITALY FINDS SECOND NUVOLARI

'NEW BOY' BEATS WORLD ACES

From TOM WISDOM

SYRACUSE, Sicily, Tuesday.

A "NEW BOY" soundly beat all the world stars in the curtain-raiser of the world championship grand prix season today.

British and German drivers were shown the way a race should be won by Italy's 26-year-old Giancarlo Baghetti.

This is a man to succeed the heroes of old, Nuvolari and Ascari. He led all the way.

He was driving the "old" rear-type Ferrari in the new ½-litre grand prix formula. Germany and Britain had their new cars here.

STIRLING MOSS
Retired seventh.

Moss out

The best we could do was world champion Jack Brabham in fourth place, a lap behind.

Stirling Moss retired two laps from the end while lying seventh, but was counted as a finisher.

John Surtees, Tony Brooks and Innes Ireland retired—Ireland escaping when his pedal stuck and he hit a tree.

The Porsches driven by Dan Gurney and Jo Bonnier were second and third.

Grand ... explained—Page 3

Daily Herald 26.4.61

The MEN — Most drivers make their name first in local club races, then in national meetings

Stirling Moss 31, regarded as world's best driver, has not yet won world championship.

Jack Brabham: 34, Australian, non-smoker, non-drinker, world champion for last two years. Ex-speedway rider.

John Surtees: 26, four times world champion motor-cyclist. Drove in first car race last year.

Innes Ireland: 30, newcomer, ex-apprentice engineer, jumped to fame last year by beating Moss twice in one day.

Tony Brooks: 28, former dentist, now garage-owner, started racing for fun. Runner-up for world title 1959.

Roy Salvadori: 39, has been racing since 1946. Once a motor dealer, he now has a big garage business.

Syracuse GP

Roy Salvadori, in his book 'Roy Salvadori, Racing Driver,' comments, "Siracusa was not a circuit I liked because the roads were narrow, the cambers were bad and the surface was appalling."

The non-championship Syracuse GP gave a foretaste of the season ahead and it was not a very palatable one for the British teams. Young rookie, Giancarlo Baghetti drove the prototype rear-engined Ferrari to the marque's first GP win with the engine behind the driver. It did not help that the British teams missed the first practice as the cars had to be flown out by Bristol Freighter from Gatwick, due to participation in that weekend's Aintree 200.

However, the clearly superior straight-line speed of the V6 allowed even Formula 1 debutant Baghetti to take a fine win over the Porsches of Gurney and Bonnier. The British cars were humiliated and fourth-placed Brabham, the reigning World Champion, was lapped. Stirling had a miserable race with a misfiring engine. Finally, the magneto drive broke and he had to push the car over the line to be classified eighth.

Above: Stirling in the pits at Syracuse.

Left: Chatting with Roy Salvadori who was alongside Stirling on the third row of the grid.

45ᴬ TARGA FLORIO

1961

Stirling Moss Scrapbook

The Targa Florio

The 45th Targa Florio was run over 10 laps, totalling 450 miles with over 7,000 bends and a variation in height from sea-level to 2,000 feet. There were works teams from Ferrari, Porsche and Osca and some 60 entrants in total. Phil Hill/Olivier Gendebien and Wolfgang von Trips/Ritchie Ginther had 2.4-litre rear-engined Ferraris, while Ricardo Rodriguez/Willy Mairesse had a front-engined 12-cylinder 3-litre. Stirling, sharing with Graham Hill, had a new experimental 2-litre engine in his Porsche RS60, as opposed to the usual 1,700cc unit. In practice Stirling was said to be sensational and smashed his own lap record by some 26 seconds, the fastest of the Ferraris being almost three minutes slower.

At the end of the first lap Stirling was three seconds ahead of team mate Bonnier in a similar 2-litre Porsche, with von Trips some 42 seconds adrift. Bernard Cahier, writing in Motor Racing magazine, noted that Stirling was "Driving like a true master… He seemed to be enjoying himself immensely and, although he was travelling at record speed, he was nevertheless always finding time to wave at his friend standing on the side of the road." Was this Cahier himself?

At the end of the fourth lap, Stirling handed over to Graham Hill with a lead of one minute 45 seconds over second-placed Bonnier and one minute 55 seconds over von Trips. With Phil Hill having crashed out on the first lap, Ferrari team manager Tavoni shrewdly substituted sports car specialist Gendebien for Ginther and the Belgian drove brilliantly to move the von Trips car up to second spot and then take the lead.

When Stirling took over again, delayed by a longish pit stop, he was over a minute behind the flying Ferrari but had a pit stop in hand. By the eighth lap the maestro was back in the lead and by the end of the penultimate lap was a minute ahead again. Then, with four miles or so to go, cruel luck. The extra torque of the 2-litre engine was too much for the transmission, which seized, and it was all over with the flag virtually in sight.

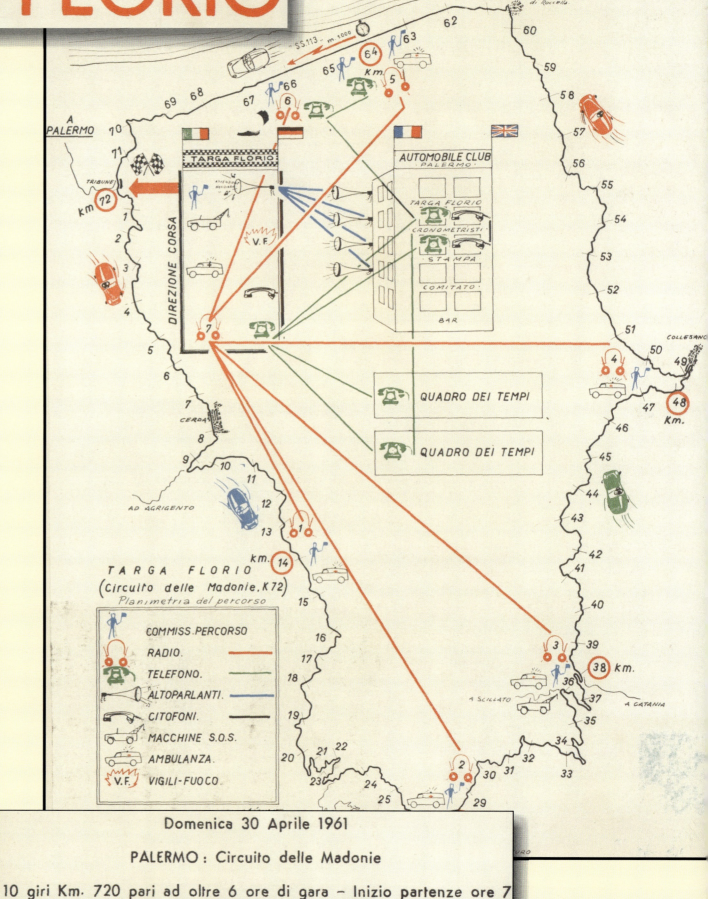

Cars

Porsche RS60

The origins of the RS60 are rooted in the 356-based RS (Rennsport) Spyder of 1956, with spaceframe chassis and five speed gearbox, evolving into the RSK of 1959. A change in sports car racing regulations in 1960, which required a full-width windscreen not less than 25cm (10in) high, resulted in Porsche completely redesigning the bodywork. The wheelbase was accordingly 4in longer than the RSK's, the wheels were smaller and there was the choice of 1.5, 1.6, 1.7 and 2 litre four cylinder engines. Four works cars were built and a further 12 made available to private owners, making a total of 16 constructed.

The uniquely challenging Targa Florio was a perfect showcase for the prodigious Moss talents and, in a lesser-powered machine, he crushed the opposition until cruelly robbed of victory with the chequered flag virtually in sight

Circuits

Moss on: TARGA FLORIO

"Terrific. Very challenging but one could learn it. I could learn the whole circuit and that to me was great because then I would feel now I can really have a go. A lot of corners I didn't know that well, but they didn't matter. What one had to know was the ones that did matter and there weren't that many of those. You see the speed was not that high. The average was 60/65mph so you hadn't got that many high speeds corners.

"I was not that keen on being in Sicily but it was a terrific event."

1961

Stirling Moss Scrapbook

From left, Maurice Trintignant, SM, Nino Vaccarella, Ricardo Rodriguez and Hans Herrmann

GENDEBIEN - VON TRIPS - FERRARI WONNEN DE TARGA FLORIO

...en de grootste pechvogel heette weer Stirling Moss...

Zes jaar heeft het geduurd, eer het Targa Florio-gemiddelde van 96,29 km per uur, waarmee Stirling Moss en Peter Collins met Mercedes in 1955 de oudste wegrace ter wereld wonnen, verbeterd is. Gendebien-von Trips brachten in deze 45ste Targa Florio hun Ferrari „2400" met een totaalgemiddelde van 103,433 km per uur over de eindstreep. Een paar kilometer voor die streep stond Stirling Moss met een stuk-gedraaid differentieel van de Camoradi-Porsche, waarmee hij op het 720 km lange parcours van begin tot eind ongenaakbaar aan de kop had gelegen...

Gedurende het verbeten gevecht tussen Moss en Gendebien verbeterde de Belgische coureur ook Stirlings ronderecord van 102,147 km per uur (Aston Martin, 1958) met ruim 5 km per uur. Het staat nu op 107,847 km per uur. De voorsprong van Gendebien-von Trips op de Porsche van Bonnier-Gurney bedroeg 4½ min. en ruim 17 minuten was het verschil tussen de Ferrari en de Porsche van Hermann en Barth. Voor de rest luidde de uitslag: 4. Vaccarella-Trintignant (Maserati); 5. Maglioli-Scarlatti (Maserati); 6. Pucci-von Hanstein (Porsche GT); 7. Strähle-Luige (Porsche GT).

Van feestvieren kwam voor Olivier Gendebien helaas weinig terecht, omdat hij na de race, samen met von Trips in een kleine Fiat een aanrijding kreeg, die hem op een gebroken linkerpols en een shock kwam te staan. Waar hij, zoals hij later verklaarde, achteraf heel blij mee was, omdat er van de wagen niets meer was overgebleven...

Stirling Moss ...

TARGA FLORIO 1961

"Oh my God, 8 kms, I think it was. That was awful. That was the most frustrating race, because I really wanted to win it and we were ahead of everybody. It was secure. I mean we certainly could have won it and the bolts in the back axle actually just stretched a bit and let the oil out and the axle seized, so we couldn't push it or anything. That was so frustrating after 1,000 kms and the car was so good. It really had gone terribly well: nice to drive, a very rewarding car and a very rewarding circuit."

Drivers

Moss on: GRAHAM HILL

SM: *"Graham Hill was a good, fast, steady driver. I mean, he has an enormous amount of credits to his name: five Monaco wins, an Indianapolis and God knows what others. I just think that shows his versatility. I think he was fast, but nowhere near the fastest. He was fast enough to be a good competitor with the sort of cars that he chose. I think that he would make the best of the car that he had got."*

PP: *"And brave? Perhaps more bravery than pure natural skill?"*

SM: *"I don't know that he was particularly brave. He certainly wasn't stupid and bravery and stupidity are very closely related you know! I think, just a good, fast, steady driver."*

PP: *"He once said that if you don't have any imagination you will kill yourself."*

SM: *"I think he certainly had adequate imagination."*

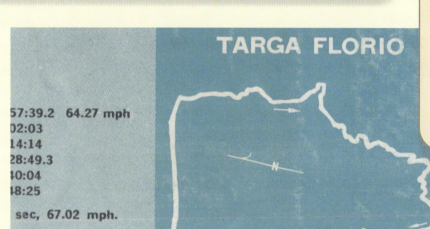

Relaxing with Jo Bonnier

Targa Facts

The winning von Trips/Gendebien Ferrari set up a new record average speed (though Stirling's average would have been, of course, even higher had he and Hill finished) of 64.272mph. The previous race record was held by a certain S. Moss driving the Mercedes-Benz 300 SLR with P. Collins back in 1955.

The fastest lap of 40 mins 03 secs was recorded by von Trips in the Ferrari, being an average of 67.015mph for the 44.74 mile circuit. The previous lap record was held by one S. Moss, set in 1958 in the Aston Martin DBR 300, averaging 63.480mph.

MAY

1961 Calendar

- **6** BRDC International Trophy, Silverstone, UK – (InterContinental race) 1st in 2.5 Cooper-Climax T53P; sports car race – 1st in Lotus-Climax 19
- **14** Monaco GP, Monte-Carlo – 1st in 1.5 Lotus-Climax 18
- **22** Dutch GP, Zandvoort, The Netherlands - 4th in 1.5 Lotus-Climax 18
- **28** 1,000 Kms, Nürburgring, Germany – ret'd in Porsche RS61 1.7 (sharing with Graham Hill), took over Porsche Carrera, 8th overall & 1st in 2-litre class

After 3¾ hours sleep, Stirling was up at 5.45am and departed from Sicily on a plane to Rome at eight. He looked around the city and was in London by 4pm. "Worked with VP till 1.30am.." Next day he addressed a Faculty of Architects and Surveyors luncheon, did some work and went down to Goodwood. He was due to test the Ferguson but it did not happen as Jack Fairman had "had a slight shunt". Shirlee Adams was clearly in town as Stirling saw her that evening.

He saw Judy Carne the following evening and on Thursday, after yet more press interviews, headed off for Silverstone where a major race meeting was taking place that weekend. The main race was for Inter-Continental cars and Stirling had a choice of Walker's Cooper or Lotus. He was also due to compete in the sports cars race in a UDT-Laystall Lotus 19.

"Practice. Cooper. Got 160mph in 2½. Dampish in places. Sports. OK. Lotus FIc not good."

GP	SM	1.35.2
	Bruce	1.35.2
Sports	SM	1.40+
	Cliff	1.43+

On Friday, he noted, "Cooper is flapping its front wheels badly and lifting a wheel a lot. Tried REALLY hard for 1.34.8. Lotus Sports fab. Cooper geared a lot

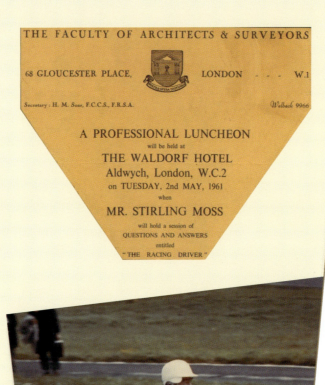

Circuits

Bruce McLaren on Sebring

Writing in his May column in Motor Racing, Bruce McLaren made a few interesting comments about the Sebring 12 Hours in March. He had been invited to drive a Maser for Briggs Cunningham who then offered him a drive in a Sprite for the 4 Hour race.

"I managed to get away first from the Le Mans start – what was Stirling hanging about for? – and got to the first corner in company with the Moss family, both Stirling and sister Pat. I suppose I was too much of a gentleman to cut Pat up on the inside, and so lay third for a time.

"For a lot of the race, Stirling, Hansgen and I had a merry old dice. I had a higher third than Stirling, and was quicker for the first half of the straights, but the better streamlining of his coupé compared with my soft-top gave him an edge on top speed.

"One of my pleasantest memories about the race was the way we could carry on conversations – partly mouthed and partly by hand waving – along the straights."

As to the Cunningham team, he commented, "Driving for Cunningham is like staying in a first class hotel. He has a mammoth caravan… There you can have orange juice, hot chocolate, coffee and tasty meals at any time of the day and night. There is a hot shower in the van, and constant supplies of hot towels. What a change! The delightful Kiwi was amazed to find in practice that the front-engined T61 Maserati was much quicker "than the newer rear-engined job. We weren't the only ones to discover this. Stirling Moss and Graham Hill, after trying both the Camoradi Maseratis, elected to drive the front-engined car."

LOCATION UNKNOWN

It was hardly cricket. **Stirling Moss**, in world championship form, won the go-kart challenge race between the British Racing Drivers' Club and the Lord's Taverners at Brand's Hatch yesterday.

But at the finish there was no trophy for him.

Innes Ireland, top racing driver and last year's winner, failed to deliver the gold-plated cup he has held for 12 months.

Why? An embarrassed Mr. Ireland explained to officials: "The cup is in the boot of my car—but I don't know exactly where the car is.

"I did so badly at Silverstone yesterday that when I got back to London I went on the town with **Graham Hill**.

"Then I forgot where I had parked...

Daily Mail 8.5.61

The BRDC International at Silverstone was run to the InterContinental formula for 2½ litre cars. Stirling much preferred the larger-engined single-seaters because the premium was more on skill with judicious use of the throttle a big factor, especially in the wet

Stirling Moss ...

ROB WALKER

PP: *"Why did you stick with Rob Walker? Why did you not join a works team? Presumably you could have gone anywhere you chose?"*

SM: *"Probably, yea, I probably could have done. I raced for one reason. I raced because I enjoy racing. I was lucky enough to be good enough to make some money, so therefore, it was not [financially] necessary for me to go anywhere else. Rob was a lovely man. The whole crew were a great team and, at that time, we were as good as any other team, I reckon. Therefore, from my point of view, it was a really good alternative to going into an ordinary team. And, of course, the freedom I got with Rob was important. If I wanted to go anywhere in the world, if he half agreed, he would send the car. Also, I could race any other cars I wanted to race whenever I wanted to race them. So there were very few restrictions put on me. We would test and do all the things we normally did. I just found it more enjoyable."*

PP: *"As a true competitor, was it perhaps necessary to handicap yourself a little bit to make it more challenging?"*

SM: *"Well, it did work that way, because people wouldn't sell us the latest car. I mean, Chapman refused. With John Cooper, we had to get our own gearbox. That was a problem because we had a fantastic gearbox called a Colotti, but it was really not up to it and was really not as good as we had hoped. I think the materials were not so good and so on, but we were forced into that. As far as the Lotus was concerned, Rob did everything he could to make it as good as possible. For example, he had the drive shafts changed for every race, unbeknown to me actually."*

Alfred Neubauer

In October 1955, when Mercedes-Benz shocked everyone by announcing their retirement from motor racing, putting Stirling out of work, he and legendary Team Manager, Alfred Neubauer made a pact (as recounted in the Stirling Moss Scrapbook 1955) to meet in 1961. As far as Stirling can recall, it never happened but in May 1961 Neubauer, who had just celebrated his 70th birthday, was made Manager of the Racing Department at the new Mercedes museum at Stuttgart.

B.R.D.C. 13th INTERNATIONAL TROPHY MEETING
PRIVILEGE
SILVERSTONE 6th MAY 1961

1961

too low (3.8+). Work on book and to John's. Herb and Brandy to food + Ken, Celia and Bunty."

GP	Bruce	1.34.2
	SM	1.34.8
Sports	SM	1.38.0
	Cliff	1.42.

Saturday was to prove a very successful day. "Up early and circuit. Sports race. Easy win from Roy [Salvadori] + ftd. F1c Fair start in pouring rain. Car still shakes at front. Drove and won by over 1 lap and 1 min from Jack and ftd! To John's Guide Dog Barbecue and then G. Hill's party and SA [Shirlee Adams] and VP [Val Pirie] and Shane. Home and bed at 3am."

There was no relaxing on Sunday. "Up earlyish and work. Off to Brands for BRDC v LT [Lord's Taverners] Kart race. I won my heats and the final. Town and food and Jenny, Shane and DH [David Haynes] and Shirlee. On to see *Green Helmet* F. Bed at 3am."

On Monday he had lunch with "Desmond Fitzgerald and Don McClure. Sold Des a scooter. Work and then off to Paris + SA. Miami [presumably a Paris restaurant or club], food and Crazy Horse. Bad." Next day he drove from Paris to Monte Carlo in 13 hours 45 minutes. He called "at Ali Baba and explained". Stirling has no idea to what this cryptic phrase refers!

First practice for that weekend's Monaco Grand Prix was on Thursday. "Lotus holds back due to fuel blockage. Ratio too high." He ate with his parents that night. "Up at 6.30 and practice. Car broke fuel pump on lap 1! OK later. Ratio pretty good. Time no better. Did 3hrs with Walter Cronkyte for US TV."

On Saturday he was working on a TV film in the morning. "Later practice. Car overgeared. Ftd. Poor Innes had a shunt at the tunnel when he got 2nd by mistake for 4th. Later saw Syd Van de V. Then hospital and garage." Syd van der Vyver was a South African engine specialist who had been very successful in Africa and, according to the SA press, Stirling wanted him to build an engine for him to use in F1.

SM	1.39.1
Ginther	1.39.3
Clark	1.39.6
Hill, G	1.39.6
Hill, P	1.39.8

Sunday: "Up early and snack. Race. I had a fair start. 3rd. Clark (2nd) fell back and I took Ginther for 1st at lap 14. Led to finish with gap of from 3 – 10 secs. Drove flat out ALL race. Ftd with Ritchie @ 1.36.3. Organisers didn't give lap prize because I didn't

Stirling Moss ...

LOTUS'S REFUSAL TO SELL 1961 CAR

For 1961, there was a conflict of interests within the Lotus camps which resulted in the refusal of Chapman to sell Rob Walker a Lotus 21.

PP: "Of course, you were with BP and Chapman and Lotus were with Esso weren't they?"

SM: "That made it a lot more difficult. Conversely, it made it a lot easier for Chapman not to help us, if you like."

PP: "So the BP/Esso situation was an excuse then?"

SM: "I think probably..."

PP: "That is extraordinary."

SM: "Esso wouldn't have been very keen on Rob's team, because I was the one person that might be able to beat them and, therefore, I think that they were able to stop him selling us a 21. I can understand it. I think it was the right thing for them to do really. I mean, I was their biggest competitor [within the camp] and so they took away from me the most up-to-date machinery. The biggest problem I had, of course, was when Jimmy Clark came along. He was a very, very proficient driver. I said to Rob, 'It is not going to be easy to run an old car against a guy as good as this, you know. I really need the same machinery.' On certain circuits I was alright. But additionally, I sensed a lack of cooperation from Chapman."

That it was wet for the InterContinental race at Silverstone can easily be seen. The Lotus 19 had earlier provided an easier win in dry conditions

Circuits

Moss on: SILVERSTONE

"Silverstone, as it was, had one of the most difficult corners; that was Abbey. It was just on to take it flat. That was very difficult and there were a few other quite fast corners there. Considering that it was just an aerodrome originally, it worked out quite well."

an ENICAR watch goes with STIRLING'S success

Says Stirling Moss: "To a racing driver Time, of course is all-important. It's reassuring to know you're wearing a watch you can really depend on in all circumstances — like my ENICAR Sherpa".

ENICAR prices range from £9 . 10 . 0 upwards.
From fine jewellers everywhere

The Hatton Jewellery and Watch Co. Ltd., Minerva House, 26/27 Hatton Garden, E.C.1

Stirling Moss at Maidstone car show

BRDC International Trophy, Silverstone

Run for Inter-Continental cars to the old 2½ litre formula, the 233-mile BRDC Trophy race took place on a rain- and oil-soaked Silverstone circuit. McLaren was on pole with SM just 0.6 secs adrift. Jack Brabham and Graham Hill completed the front row. Brabham led initially with McLaren next and then Moss, as cars spun in all directions. One to succumb was McLaren who lost his Cooper in a big way. Hill had spins on laps two and five. It seems Moss had been biding his time but then he showed his class, as Autosport reported.

"Moss's drive was a shattering demonstration of his unrivalled genius as a wet-weather driver. He took the lead on lap 23 and proceeded to drive with such uncanny skill that 30 tours later he had lapped the entire field at least once."

On lap 54 Stirling lapped the World Champion. "A truly incredible performance," said Autosport. "Ireland made a two-minute stop to have his suspension looked at, but looking never helps much and he went out again and promptly spun at Abbey."

It seems just about everyone spun. "Meanwhile, Stirling Moss was still hammering around at a seemingly impossible pace, his passage through Woodcote being something to behold. He was almost on the grass every time as he passed the pits, the tail coming out a bit each time, but with judicious use of the throttle Stirling applied just the right amount of extra power at the right moment and went on at unabated speed. This was indeed a dazzling display of supreme artistry."

Stirling Moss ...

TARDY REACTION FROM COVENTRY CLIMAX

PP: "Why were Climax so slow to react and build a V8, giving Ferrari such an advantage?"

SM: "I think that they were happy doing what they knew. When you think about it, the whole Climax thing started with a fire pump engine and then they just got better and better. They changed things, but you are still talking of people with a relatively narrow horizon. I think to take the step and go to a V8 was a bit more than they wanted to do if they could help it. I may be wrong but personally I rather feel that making an entirely new engine, as of course, the V8 had to be, was probably pushed upon them, rather than their choice."

PP: "There were financial considerations. The Brits spent a lot of time lobbying hard to try and retain the previous formula. That meant that, when they failed, they were slow getting off the mark as a result."

SM: "Yes. The other thing is that we had nowhere near the experience that Ferrari had. Ferrari had made so many different sizes of engine in every configuration - 4 cylinders, 6 cylinders, 8 cylinder and, of course, mostly twelve cylinders. Whereas over here, we weren't like that. I mean Jaguar brought out one engine [the XK] and they had modified that all the way through from the late forties to the mid-seventies."

1961

Stirling Moss Scrapbook

break old record. !X! 500NF Called on Innes and then party at Hotel de Paris. Bed at 4am."

Monday was pretty leisurely, by Moss standards. After some more filming, he spent the day relaxing and in the evening took Herb and SA to the Chevre d'Or and the casino. Tuesday consisted of more of the same, though according to his diary he had a haircut on both Monday and Tuesday – obviously such a big job it had to be split in two! He called on Innes again at the hospital and drove to Italy, having dinner in Turin and staying the night in Como.

Next morning he was shopping in Como before driving on to Zurich and then to Solitude where he did three laps of the circuit before heading, via Düsseldorf, to Zandvoort. He had dinner with a crowd of chums including SA.

Friday was spent shopping in Amsterdam and on Saturday he was practising for the Dutch Grand Prix. "Used Cooper with old engine. (129mph). Lunch and practice with both cars. Lotus – better brakes and gearbox, same speed but engine, the new one, wrongly timed (valves). Get 7,100 only. Cooper feels good, bad gearbox. Correct gears!. Home and drivers' meeting... Bed at 1.30am."

SM	Lotus	1.36.2
Gurney	Porsche	1.36.5
Brab		1.36.6
Trips		1.36.6
Ginther		1.36.7
G. Hill	BRM	1.36.7
Surtees		1.36.8
Brooks	BRM	1.36.9
Clark		1.37.0

Sunday, May 21: "Up early and stooged around. Practice. I did 1.37.6 with Lotus with old engine. Cooper and new engine NBG (?manifold). Windy."

P Hill	1.35.7
Trips	1.35.7
Ginther	1.35.9
G. Hill	1.36.3
Gurney	1.36.4 etc.

The Grand Prix took place on the Monday. "Up and stooged around. Circuit. Over 70,000 people! Race. Had a fair start and then came thru to 5th behind Trips, P. Hill, Clark and Ginther. Had a dice with Ritchie and in the end took him on the hairpin inside on last lap! Entered at 40 yds up, had about 1ft on the line! He messed me about on braking but increased my max to 7,900. My car ran at 95 - 100° all the race due to blanking! Hotel took 2¾ hours due to traffic. Food and bed at 2am."

 Bunty Scott-Moncrieff

Bunty Scott-Moncrieff was very much a gentleman of the old school and an extraordinary character. Prior to WW1 it was not done for a 'gentleman' to go into trade but the Kaiser war changed all this. "By the time I got into the motor trade in the late nineteen twenties," he once wrote, "it was considered almost as respectable as being a wine merchant or stockbroker." Learning from the rogues, he was not above a few roguish tricks of his own. One speciality was to spend the summer in Monte Carlo. When "some rich young silly" had gambled away everything, Bunty would appear and offer him a modest amount for his Bentley, Rolls or Bugatti, drive it back to England and make a tidy killing. He traded for many years under the unforgettable title of "Purveyors of Horseless Carriages to the Nobility and Gentry since 1927".

Jubilee extensions at Haynes Bros.

FAMOUS racing driver, Stirling Moss, came to Maidstone, on Monday, when before more than 400 people he officially opened the Haynes Brothers new body, paint and commercial works at Ashford Road, Maidstone, together with their "Golden Jubilee Show Week."

Haynes Brothers, Ltd., were celebrating 50 years' association with the Ford Motor Company. To mark this, they were presented with a commemoration plaque and a showroom clock by Mr. Brian Harnby, Ford's Car Sales Manager.

Looking extremely tanned and wearing a light grey suit, Mr. Stirling Moss congratulated Haynes Brothers on their show.

Mr. Moss, who is a great friend of Mr. David Haynes, sales director of the firm, arrived in a Ford automatic Zodiac, which was supplied to him earlier in the year by Haynes Brothers, Ltd. He quipped: "Now they have built this place for me—to service it in!"

PROGRESS

The Mayor of Maidstone, Councillor A. H. Clark, said the occasion was yet another important landmark and development of Haynes Brothers—"this friendly family business which has been going on since the first William Haynes came to Maidstone 129 years ago."

Continuing, the Mayor added: "It is only right and proper that Maidstone, the County Town, should set an example to the rest of the county, and this you certainly did when you became the first Ford distrubutors in Kent just 50 years ago

"Tribute," he said, was paid to the foresight and business acumen of the late Bernard Haynes when he ordered the first five Ford T. cars, but I doubt whether he visualised that 50 years later you would be selling 750 a year."

The tradition of "service" was evident in the story of the Haynes family. The first William Haynes was twice Mayor of Maidstone. His son, another William, held the same office on three different occasions.

He felt the same spirit had animated the present directors, Mr. Ronald and Mr. Phillip—both in peace and war.

Before the opening, Mr. Moss was shown around the modernised passenger workshops and service bays, the new commercial vehicle works, the new body and paint shop and the new extension of the stores division.

MODERN

In all, over 12,000 square feet of additional workshop floor space has been added and the new shops are equipped with the most modern Ford precision tools and are staffed by Dagenham-trained specialists.

During Haynes' "Golden Jubilee Show Week," special exhibitions and displays can be seen. The "old and the new" theme runs through the show. For example, on display

S.E. Gazette 9.5.61

This lady looks rather taller than Stirling, until you realise it's the hair!

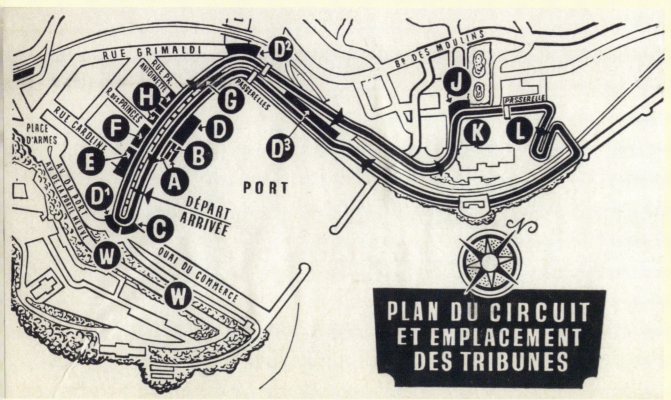

Stirling Moss ...

ADAPTING TO REAR-ENGINED CARS

PP: "This was the period of the changeover from front to rear-engined cars. Did some drivers take to rear-engined cars better than others?"

SM: "I suppose, probably that is true. It didn't worry me, but I am very lucky because I like to feel that I can adapt to just about any car. I mean, the Ferguson was probably the best example of having to change my style and I didn't find that too difficult, whereas others did. Therefore, I didn't notice the transition from front to rear engine as being that difficult."

PP: "You had a very open mind and were always looking for something that was better to give you the advantage over your competitors?"

SM: "Yes! Absolutely."

Stirling Moss ...

THE WORLD CHAMPIONSHIP

PP: "How important was winning the World Championship by this stage in your career?"

SM: "By this stage, it didn't matter so much but it certainly did originally. I was very upset because I felt I was the best driver and I just missed out again and again. And then I began to think, 'Well, the thing I do have is the respect of my fellow competitors'. People could compare the times and see what I was capable of and achieving. Therefore the fact that I wasn't the World Champion didn't really matter. The people that worry you most are, first of all, your team mates because they are using the same equipment, therefore the times are directly comparable and show when you were not being as quick as you'd like. The other factor was the other drivers and I think I had their respect. The title didn't worry me too much. The world title is a fantastic thing, but when you reckon Fangio had five of them, winning six would not have made me a better driver than Fangio. There were drivers who won the title whom I could consistently beat. Having not won the World Championship gave me a certain exclusivity, you know!"

PP: "There is no question that you inherited Fangio's mantle as the best in the world."

SM: "Well, I think when he retired I was expected to be the World Champion, yea, and that, of course, was worth a lot to me, psychologically. That helped, that and the fact that everything I did Rob was pretty thrilled with and we had Alf and so on. So we were a fairly complete outfit. Our biggest problem was that we just could not get the things that we wanted. Today reliability isn't a major issue, but then it was."

Daily Star Beirut 13.5.61

May — Stirling Moss Scrapbook

On Tuesday Stirling said good-bye to Shirlee and flew back to London where VP met him and drove him back to the office. Next day he saw his architects to discuss the new house in Shepherd Street and that evening took Caroline to the Candlelight Room.

After working until 3pm, he was in the air again next day and flying to Amsterdam. There he collected his Facel Vega and was in Lochműhle by 11.15pm. It was the Nűrburgring 1,000 Kms that weekend and he was to share a Porsche RS61 1.7 sports racer with Graham Hill.

Friday was not a very happy day. "Up at 9 after a bad night. Circuit. Wet. I did 10.31 in our 2 lit and 10.27 in Joe's [Jo Bonnier] car. Ours feels better on the road, but has a vibration. Ferraris 10.34. I can't see in the wet. Ratios req'd. 2nd 120kph, 3rd 160, 4th 185, 5th 210."

Saturday was barely better. "Up early and practice. 1700 with correct ratios. Damp and used SP tyres and did 9.43 and on D9 9.37.1. Could do 9.25 if dry on D9. To hotel and the damn car burst an oil pipe from the gearbox and lost all the oil. Left it." Presumably this was the Facel.

Race day was Sunday. "Up at 6.30 and to circuit with Graham, whose car was broken into and had the passports stolen! Took 1 hr. Start and I was 2nd to Jimmy Clark. Took lead behind pits and lead for one lap and then Phil [Hill] pissed by! Dropped to 3rd and then GH. He did 5 laps and then rain; I continued and came to 2nd and bang. Took over 2 lit disc Carrera and won 2 lit sports class. Went in ditch twice. I got 207 down the Foxhole and flat up back hill! in sports 1700. Hotel for prizes. Given gold cup for triple win. Lochműhle and bed at 2am."

On Monday he flew back to London where Ken Gregory picked him up. He worked and went out for dinner, retiring at 4am. After a full day's work on the Tuesday, he gave a talk at Eton in the evening and did an interview for Life International. The last day of May consisted of work and heading "off in Rob's Facel to Silverstone. Tested [Ferguson] 99 1.42.6 and Lotus 1.38.0. Get 7,900 with 4.55 axle. Home via B.R.P. Took Audrey Hale for food."

Circuits

Moss on: MONACO

"Monaco is interesting because it was difficult to pass there, but there are quite a few places where you can make a bit of time. When you come over the brow into the Casino Square, you want to be in the right place when you take off, so that you can land in the right place. It's quite a precise circuit. Going into the tunnel, it's critical to turn in at the right time. If you turn in a bit too early, it's not that good. I would say that Monaco requires quite a lot of precision, not high speed precision, low speed precision. It really was quite a slow speed circuit. The hairpins were really quite difficult because you would just scratch around - you can't really make up that much on a hairpin. St Devote was a very important corner. It was one of the few high speed corners. Important to get it right so you got sufficient speed up the hill. So, I would say it was one of my favourite short circuits, actually."

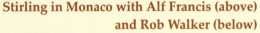

Stirling in Monaco with Alf Francis (above) and Rob Walker (below)

Formula 1 Prospects

Before the first Grand Prix of the year, Autosport previewed the season ahead under the title of 'Formula One Prospects'. "If figures are to be believed, the ultra-low Ferraris will be extremely difficult to beat on any circuit, but even an Italian estimate of 190bhp for the 120 degrees V6 seems to be more than optimistic, and must represent the highest output ever claimed for a water-cooled, multi-cylinder i.c. [internal combustion] engine on a bhp per litre basis, without the aid of a supercharger.

"The F1 cars will be of two types, both rear-engined. In one case the 1,476cc power unit will be a 120 deg. V-6, and in the other a V-6 of 60 deg., of 190bhp and 180bhp respectively."

Right: Spectating in Monaco was sister Pat (right).

Below: Stirling entertains a bevy of beauties in the famous and stylish principality of Monaco. They were to witness one of the greatest Grand Prix victories of all time

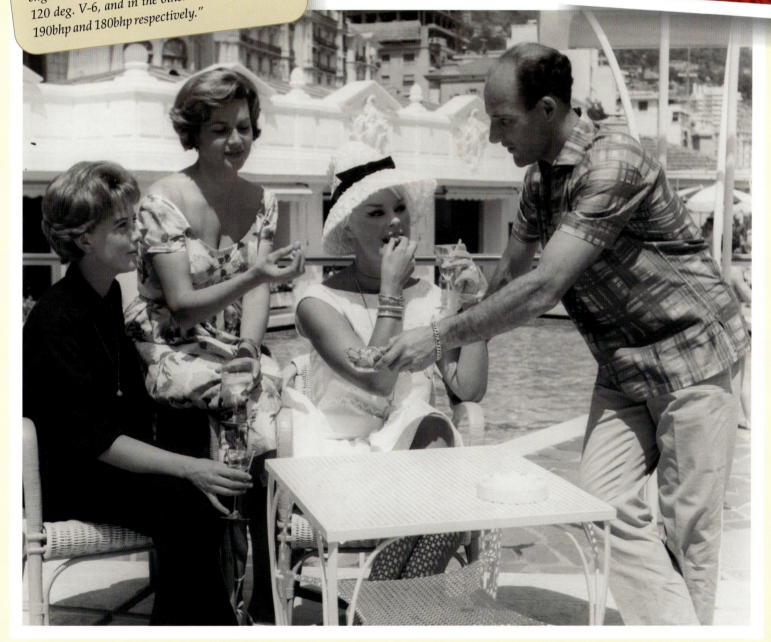

'I DO NOT BELIEVE I HAVE ANY CHANCE AT ALL OF WINNING THE CHAMPIONSHIP THIS YEAR...'

MONTE CARLO, Thursday.

Cars

Lotus 18

Multi-tubular chassis frame, independent double wishbone suspension front and rear, telescopic dampers, helical springs, 16" wheels, Colotti gearbox, dry single plate clutch, Coventry Climax FPF 1,496 cc in-line four cylinder engine producing 155hp, twin overhead cams, alloy block, Weber carbs.

May

Stirling Moss Scrapbook

1961

Stirling Moss Scrapbook

MOSS GOES BY SCOOTER

NOTHING like a change .. so Stirling Moss goes to the Monaco Grand Prix race track by mini-scooter.

Stirling was making practice runs at the track yesterday for Sunday's big race.

It's a world championship event—and Stirling is in good form. Last week he won at Silverstone, beating world champion driver Jack Brabham.

Daily Herald 13.5.61

Practice Incident at Monaco

Stirling's mate Ireland had a very nasty shunt in practice when he selected the wrong gear in the ill-lit tunnel and the rear wheels locked up. In his wonderful book 'All Arms and Elbows', he writes, "For me, it was the most extraordinary experience because, being in almost pitch darkness, I had no idea which way the car was pointing. I think the car was, in fact, going backwards when it hit the wall and I was thrown out of it. By an absolute miracle, I was projected straight out of the tunnel at the far end, instead of being dashed up against the wall. I was thrown, I suppose, some 50 or 80 yards and to this day I can recall the impression I had of flying through the air.

"Anyway, I hadn't been there long before Stirling Moss came round and stopped. He was very good, I remember. He took charge, obtained a cigarette for me from one of the crowd and tried to make me comfortable."

The Green Helmet

Moderately entertaining British film made in 1961 and starring Bill Travers, Ed Begley and Sid James. Storyline based on fading racing driver and antagonistic relationship with his younger brother who wants to supplant him. Racing footage from Sebring, Goodwood and several European tracks. Cameo performances from real racers Jack Brabham, Roy Salvadori, Mike Salmon, John Coundley and 'Lucky' Casner. Billed as 'The men who love speed and the girls who love them' and 'He lives at the pace that kills'.

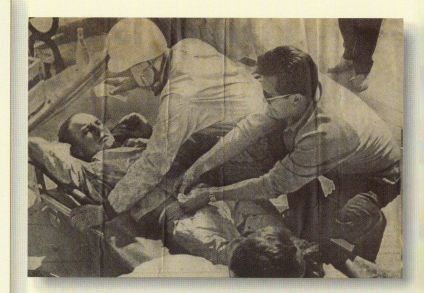

PALS...

THEY are the keenest of rivals when they race . . . but, in moments like this, the comradeship of track aces is uppermost.

Innes Ireland has crashed on the Monte Carlo Grand Prix course and fractured his knee. Stirling Moss, one of the first to reach him, kneels anxiously at his side. As Ireland lies on a stretcher, he is given an injection in the leg . .

Daily Sketch 15.5.61

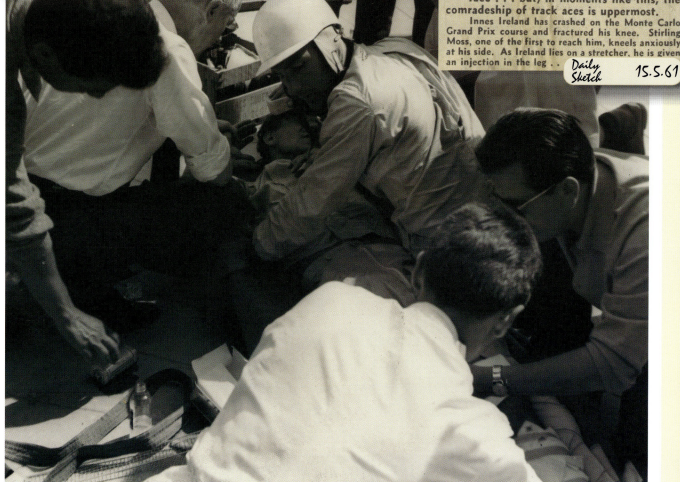

AS THEY LINE UP ON THE GRID FOR THE FIRST GRAND PRIX OF THE YEAR -----
Stirling Moss predicts *defeat*

May

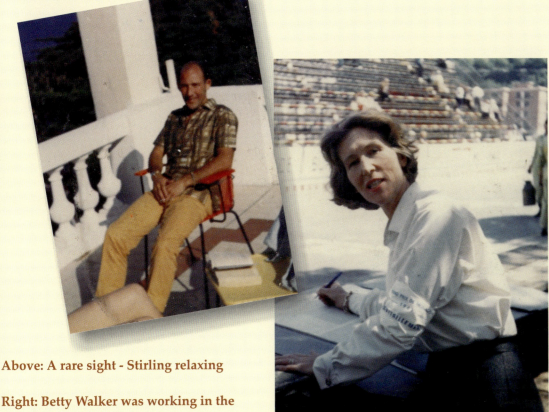

Above: A rare sight - Stirling relaxing

Right: Betty Walker was working in the pits, as ever, at Monaco

Far right: On the grid, shortly before the off, Stirling takes on personal fuel

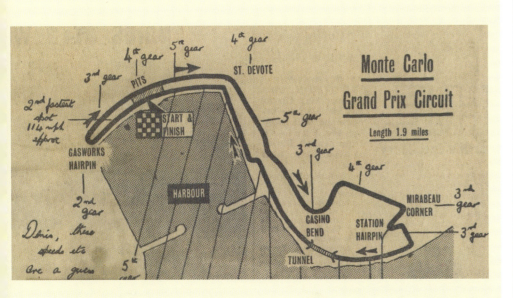

Stirling Moss Scrapbook

1961

Monaco Grand Prix

The 1961 Monaco GP was quite simply one of the finest races of Stirling's remarkable career. It was real 'David and Goliath' stuff!

He arrived at Monaco thinking he had not a hope in Hell. The Climax engine, even the new FPF Mark II which SM had for this race, was well down on power in comparison with the new Ferraris and his Lotus was last year's model. Furthermore, the Walker equipe had been suffering from misfiring problems. Eventually, during practice, Alf Francis traced the problem to the Weber carburettors which lacked a small drilling in one of the castings.

Stirling then managed to set fastest lap in practice and occupied the front row with Ritchie Ginther in the Ferrari 120° V6 that was reputed to have nearly 25% more power than the Climax engines and Jimmy Clark in the latest Chapman Lotus. Further back were Ginther's team mates, Phil Hill and Taffy von Trips, and the feared Porsches of Bonnier and Gurney.

Ginther used his power to make the best start and led from Clark and Stirling but Clark pitted almost immediately. Driving brilliantly, Stirling took the lead on lap 14 and Bonnier also supplanted Ginther. Moss led by two seconds and was already lapping the backmarkers after 15 of the 100 laps. After another 10 laps Ferrari instructed Ginther to let Phil Hill through to take up the challenge. Two laps later Hill took Bonnier.

At 30 laps SM led by a reducing 9.9 secs, followed by Hill, Bonnier, Ginther and von Trips in pretty close company. Eleven laps later Ginther took Bonnier and closed up on Hill. There were now two Ferraris remorselessly in pursuit of the old Lotus in the lead. All the while, the race average speed was increasing and the lap times were coming down. By 54 laps the lead was down to four seconds.

The gap fluctuated – 3.8 seconds at 60 laps, 4.9 at 70. Then Hill was signalled to let Ginther through to head the Ferrari challenge. They signalled, 'FASTER, FASTER", then "GINTHER GIVE ALL". Stirling's pole lap had been a 1.39.1. Now Ginther did 1.36.9, then 1.36.3 and was now within three seconds of the maestro who calmly equalled his time. Stirling later told Rob Walker that he took every single bend absolutely on the limit.

It was said the Ferrari personnel were "almost going berserk in their pits", but Stirling withstood the unbearable pressure and headed the three Ferraris home by just 3.7 seconds to win one of the greatest races of all time. Autosport called it "a miracle drive". Walker described it "as the greatest drive, by any driver, that I had seen in my entire life".

Monaco front row. Stirling (foreground) in last year's Lotus lines up alongside Ginther in the latest, far more powerful sharknose Ferrari and Jimmy Clark in the new Lotus 21

The master at work, with the side panels famously removed to aid cooling. With the Hotel de Paris in the background, he is going through Casino Square

Wonderful Michael Turner painting of the snarling Ferraris of Ritchie Ginther and Phil Hill mercilessly in pursuit through Casino Square of the masterful Moss. *Reproduced by kind permission of Michael Turner*

 *Stirling Moss ...*

MONACO GRAND PRIX

SM: *"At Monaco I got pole position. I think you will find that if I had done all 100 laps at my pole position time, the race would only have lasted 40 seconds longer than it did. I didn't take the lead until lap 14. To begin with I was just happy to be in the first group. Then the leading Ferrari started to pull away and I thought, well I am going to have to go and break away from the others and there were people like Jim Clark in the race. Then I took the lead and held it to the end."*

PP: *"And the Ferraris took turns to put pressure on you?"*

SM: *"Which, of course, I didn't know. I thought in the race, because it was one then the other, they were just messing around, waiting to pick me off at the end."*

PP: *"Of course, you famously took the side panels off the Lotus 18. Was that because of heat or weight?"*

SM: *"Heat. To get more air around. It could be pretty hot inside those things for 2¾ hours."*

PP: *"How do you personally rate Monaco '61 of all your races?"*

SM: *"I would say it was one of the hardest races I ever had. I can remember quite distinctly I would start a lap and say, 'Right I am going to try to do the perfect lap from here'. Then after five or six corners I wouldn't be quite perfect so I would say, 'Well then, I am going to try and do a perfect lap from here and I kept trying to force myself, to make the fastest lap, to see if I could gain a fraction of a second here and there. And then they would inch it back. I would think probably my toughest race in Formula One."*

PP: *"You were absolutely flat out?"*

SM: *"Yes, 86 laps, absolutely as fast as I could go."*

PP: *"Ten-tenths?"*

SM: *"Yes."*

PP: *"At ten-tenths, are you taking risks?"*

SM: *"No, I was driving myself as hard as I could. I was going through the tunnel flat, you know, all the time, not just once or twice. And then if a backmarker got in the way, I would not try and get passed immediately but would leave them [the Ferraris] with the problem of overtaking where it was less ideal. I really was absolutely hard on it."*

PP: *"Must go down as one of your very best, the Ferraris having so much more power and there being three of them ranged against you. You said at the time that it was your greatest drive and a very emotional moment afterwards, because you had been trying so hard. I presume you were emotionally drained?"*

SM: *"Very much so. It was very hard. It was a tremendous relief when I saw the flag and I had got it first. I couldn't believe it."*

1961

Stirling Moss Scrapbook

Today this car is in the amazing Donington Collection where it is claimed to be the most famous GP car of all time

Removing the side panels

Famously, Stirling ran without side panels at Monaco. It was a last minute decision by him but had Rob Walker worried that it would be against the regulations. He dashed off to see M. Taffe, the Clerk of the Course, who gave his approval, providing the race numbers were clearly visible. Someone rushed to the lorry and obtained another set of numbers and affixed them to the rear engine cover. "Eventually," recalled Walker, "we pushed the car on to the grid well after the five-minute signal had been given."

Stirling's diary entry for one of his very greatest races. Note that he says he was "flat out all race" with 'all' underlined twice. Such emphasis is unusual, if not unique, in his diaries and normally understated comments. One can also see his anger at not getting the cash prize for making fastest lap because he did not break the old lap record - a matter of 500NF (introduced in 1960, a new franc equalled 100 old francs). After calling on poor old Innes in hospital, he partied at the Hotel de Paris. Next evening he took Herb Jones and Shirlee Adams to two of the fashionable nightspots

Another superb Michael Turner painting of the Monaco action with the trio negotiating the Mirabeau corner. *Reproduced by kind permission of Michael Turner*

Drivers

Moss on: RITCHIE GINTHER

"I must say, Ritchie Ginther did a good job at Monaco, he really did. He kept the pressure on. I think he had quite a lot of knowledge of the car, having done a lot of testing. I would say Ritchie was really very similar to Phil [Hill] in ability."

1961

MOSS WINS BY 3 SECONDS

Ace Moss pips the Ferraris

Stirling Moss ...

ALF FRANCIS

PP: "You and Alf Francis had a very long relationship. He was with you in the early days and I suppose you parted for several years while you were driving for Mercedes and Maseratis and then you came back together again."

SM: "Alf was an incredible character. I had enormous respect for him. I mean, half an hour before the start of the Monaco Grand Prix he welded up a cracked chassis tube with a tank full of fuel inches from the tube. There are not many people who would do that but with Alf that is what he would do. He was very temperamental. He would get the tools and throw them in the air and say, 'I'm finished, this is not happening' and he would walk out, he would literally walk away. The best you could do was just shut up and keep out of it. There would be a big eruption, not because of me or Rob, but because he was really pissed off at something or other, and then everything would be alright and he would go back and collect the tools and get back to work. He was very, very temperamental."

PP: "But at the end of the day he did the work and did it very well?"

SM: "Brilliant mechanic. He had only one failing. Quite often you have a girl that is a fantastic secretary and then thinks she can run the business, but it isn't the same. Being an incredible mechanic, doesn't mean you can design a car. He did try, with reasonable success, but not what you would expect from a guy who was probably the best racing mechanic of the era, you know. His skill was taking things and making them do and fettling and all that sort of thing, which couldn't happen now, of course. It was totally different in those days. I had an enormous respect for him because he would find ways round problems that ordinary people couldn't."

THE MONTE CARLO GRAND PRIX

A foretaste of things to come this season? Richie Ginther's Ferrari leads the field into the Gasworks hairpin at the start of the Monaco Grand Prix, the first of the grandes épreuves counting towards this season's championship. Following close behind the Ferrari are J. Clark's Lotus (No. 28) and Stirling Moss in a privately-entered Lotus. After one of the most brilliant drives of his career, Stirling Moss won the race through the Monte Carlo streets, although hotly pursued for most of the race by the Ferrari team. He finished only 3.6 seconds ahead of Richie Ginther, with Phil Hill and W. von Trips, also in Ferraris, third and fourth. Monaco was the first of the Grand Prix run under the new Formula One: it appeared from the Ferraris' impressive showing that they may well upset the British domination in motor racing of recent years

The spoils of gladiatorial victory most magnificent. Note Colin Chapman clapping on right. Looks like Alfred Moss behind him

MOSS TRIUMPHS AT MONACO
Ferraris are defeated

ACE'S MOTHER 'ARRESTED

As Moss gets surprise win

AS Stirling Moss flashed across the finishing line to win the Monaco Grand Prix yesterday his mother dashed out from the crowd to congratulate him—and was promptly "arrested."

For the rest of the cars were still completing the circuit at more than 100 miles an hour.

Police grabbed Mrs. Moss before she could reach him.

She said last night: "A race official explained who I was. They escorted me off and let me go.

"They were perfectly charming."

She had seen Moss win a race he expected to lose—and take the lead in the 1961 world championship.

Last minute

He switched from a Cooper to a Lotus at the last minute. But he still feared the Porsches—with powerful new engines—and the strong Ferrari team.

In the 14th lap he overtook American Richie Ginther, driving one of the bright red Ferraris.

Victor's smile from Stirling Moss as he receives the trophy.

Daily Sketch 16.5.61

Where are Prince Rainier and Princess Grace? Ironically, they appear to have missed what was probably the greatest Monaco GP of all time!

1961

Stirling Moss Scrapbook

Stirling being interviewed by football commentator Kenneth "They think it's all over" Wolstenholme for the first ever use of the new Eurovision link for a TV commercial

Stirling Moss, immediately after winning the Monaco Grand Prix 1961, is interviewed by Kenneth Wolstenholme for the Dunlop TV commercial, the first ever to use the Eurovision link.

DUNLOP USE EUROVISION LINK

Last Sunday the Eurovision Link was used for the first time for a TV commercial.

Publicising Dunlop tyres, it showed an on-the-spot interview between Stirling Moss, winner of the 1961 Monaco Grand Prix, and Kenneth Wolstenholme.

This outstanding commercial TV "first" was achieved by Dunlop in association with their advertising agents, Charles F. Higham Ltd., and the TV and advertising films division of Associated-British Pathé.

Moss crossed the line in his Lotus-Climax at 5.35 pm. Minutes later the interview had been transmitted directly over the Eurovision Link to Teddington Studios of ABC TV.

The interview was then inserted into a 75-second commercial, which was screened over the entire commercial TV network at 10.07 pm.

Advertisers Weekly 19.5.61

Stirling's dream fades

BLUE CLOUD, the house Stirling Moss built in Nassau three years ago, is up for sale. The price—£25,000.

The buyer will get a luxurious house with two bedrooms, dressing rooms, modern kitchen, two reception rooms, and a balcony 50ft. above sea level with a view over the Caribbean.

Blue Cloud was the dream house for Stirling and his wife Katie. They designed and helped build it. They did the decorations.

Now they are living apart. And another dream has taken the place of Blue Cloud — the £30,000 gadget-packed home that Stirling is having built in Shepherd-street, Mayfair.

Daily Express 18.5.61

Dutch Grand Prix

Practice was a frustrating affair for Stirling. Initially he was fastest but the three 120° V6-engined Ferraris had the wrong axle ratio. With these changed, the trio filled the front row of the grid. Meanwhile, SM had asked Alf Francis to swop the engine, as Stirling notes in his diary, into the Walker Cooper. However, the combination were 1.4 seconds slower, so he reverted to the Lotus for the race and started on the second row, best of the rest, and alongside Graham Hill.

The German Count von Trips led in his Tipo 156 Ferrari from American Phil Hill. Soon Clark was up to third and dicing with Hill, P. Over many laps they swopped places several times and, being only just adrift of von Trips in the lead, Clark had the Italian team concerned. Hill, G held fourth and then came another race-long battle between Ginther and Moss. When they took Graham Hill, they were battling for fourth. One cannot help but reflect where Stirling might have been placed had he the benefit of the current Lotus like Clark.

During the last laps Ginther had the advantage over Stirling but then the Englishman 'did him' on the penultimate lap and then somehow held off the more powerful Ferrari to win their duel by no more than a tenth of a second. However, the Ferraris, which finished first and second, were now on a roll and would be very difficult to stop from hereon. This race, though, was remarkable for being one in which there were no retirements or accidents.

"Hiya, Stirling Moss!"

Circuits

Moss on: ZANDVOORT

"I enjoyed Zanvoort, because I like the Dutch people and it was near Amsterdam, which was a lovely city. A lot of sand, of course, which used to blow around in the old days particularly. A couple of quite demanding corners, one was a long corner, right hander into a straight, so it was quite important, because it would effect your speed down the straight, but quite a nice circuit."

1961 — Stirling Moss Scrapbook

Ferrari domination (above) very evident at Zandvoort

Drivers

Moss on: TONY BROOKS

SM: *"Tony Brooks I have always thought was the best driver who was never as famous as he should have been. He did make it, but was never very well known. However, he had tremendous capabilities in Formula 1 and sports cars, and not many drivers could mix both that well."*

PP: *"Why was this?"*

SM: *"I don't know why that is. Maglioli was a good example, Taruffi is another example. There were really quite a lot who were quite stunning in sports cars, but never really made it in Formula 1. But Tony was not like that, Tony in my mind made it in both."*

May

Stirling Moss Scrapbook

1961

Read text in number order

①

Technical Report: MOSS MARK III

by Brock Yates and Gordon Bruce

What did Britain's sacrosanct Ministry of Speed Sports do when faced with a dearth of drivers? They created one — of course!

► The project started during the bleak years following World War II. While dozens of Englishmen labored at their drawing boards planning cars the equal of 158 Alfas and San Remo Maseratis, a tiny, confidential group was embarking on a scheme that would shake the sport to its core.

This organization was convinced the first step in making Great Britain a racing power was not the creation of a potent G.P. car, but the development of a driver superior to the contemporary greats like Farina, Ascari and Villoresi. Seaman was long since dead and Mays and Howe were retired, leaving only Reg Parnell and George Abecassis to shoulder the British burden. They reasoned if a talented young Englishman could star on a continental team, the resultant national enthusiasm would bring dozens of new green cars to the grid.

The original plan was to locate a brilliant youth and train him intensively for several years. However such a prospect was not to be found and they were forced into their fantastic alternative: the *construction of the ultimate racing driver*.

After rejecting a proposal for an out-and-out robot sloshed over with a heavy coat of B.R.G., the group decided their new device should look and act as a mortal . . . but would drive with flair, precision, and courage that no human could duplicate.

DOMINANCE BY MK I

The enterprise began with a grant of 500,000 pounds from the hush-hush Ministry of Speed Sports. A basic layout of the machine was set down by Dr. Reginald Wollstonecraft-Shelley, whose paternal grandmother, Mary Godwin-Shelley, had been a pioneer in the field.

Dr. Shelley and a team of 17 top engineers and cybernetics experts took 11 months constructing the MK 1 prototype. The first field test was a secret run up Prescott on April 24, 1947. Driving an ancient 1.5-liter Delage, it easily shattered the hill's record by 7.3 seconds.

The machine was named "Stirling Moss" for several reasons. "Stirling," despite the modified spelling, symbolized the integrity of the English pound and the Empire. "Moss" simply stood for "Ministry of Speed Sports."

Stirling Moss, MK 1, began racing on tiny 500 cc Coopers and Kiefts. From the start he dominated the class, turning the tricky Brands Hatch course into his personal playground.

POWERPLANT ALTERATION

Between races, technical improvements continued. The power supply was altered from electrical to a highly efficient, perfectly muffled two-stroke, air-cooled engine. The original system had run directly from the car's magneto, but complications like the long cord necessary for Le Mans starts forced the change to internal combustion.

By the early 1950s Stirling was giving an excellent account of himself on such varied automobiles as the B.R.M., Jaguar, and H.W.M. And in 1954 his big chance arrived with the fabled Mercedes-Benz Grand Prix team.

Work on the MK II began in 1955 after one unpleasant fact became apparent: the MK I could be beaten. Granted, only one man was capable of the feat, but as long as Juan Fangio remained active, Moss could not reach the pinnacle of racing.

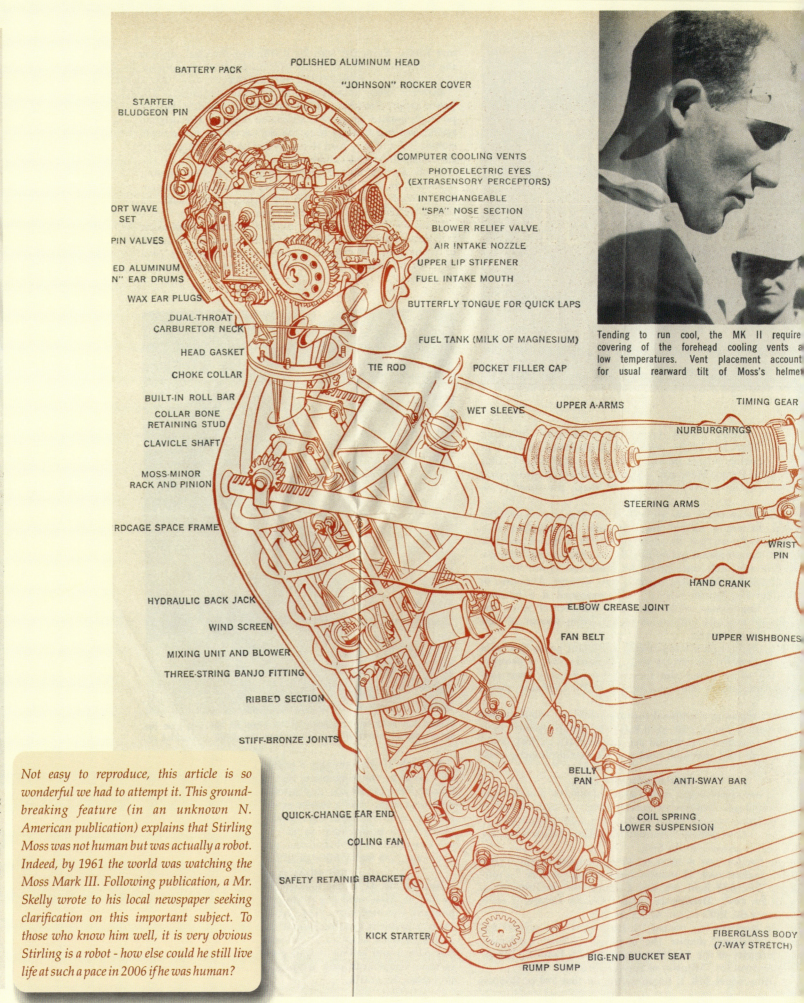

Not easy to reproduce, this article is so wonderful we had to attempt it. This groundbreaking feature (in an unknown N. American publication) explains that Stirling Moss was not human but was actually a robot. Indeed, by 1961 the world was watching the Moss Mark III. Following publication, a Mr. Skelly wrote to his local newspaper seeking clarification on this important subject. To those who know him well, it is very obvious Stirling is a robot - how else could he still live life at such a pace in 2006 if he was human?

Stirling Moss Scrapbook

Having no equipment to adjust speed according to the healthiness of his conveyance, Stirling Moss MK II would continue on at full bore until he won or the ailing part shattered to pieces.

Moss's personal mechanic, Alf Francis (who everyone assumed worked on his cars) labored to inject a sense of restraint into the works. But on and on Moss went, leaving a trail of fastest laps and ruptured gearboxes across Europe. The whole thing came to a horrible climax at Spa in 1960 when a wheel parted from his Lotus at 140 mph. The driver was bent beyond repair.

While the public was informed the great man had suffered a pair of broken legs, the organization rushed into building the MK III. Construction went ahead of schedule and the motoring world was pleasantly shocked when Moss's fractures knitted in a brief five weeks.

SPEED VARIATION EFFECTED

The MK III is the last word. Outwardly the same as its predecessor, it is equipped with a new variable-speed computer that adjusts itself to any driving situation. Moss now only drives at the peak when necessary, thereby ending his frantic, inexorable rushes for the lead. A perfect performance came at the U.S. Grand Prize at Riverside, where he dawdled along, letting the others scrap up ahead. Then full power came on at the proper moment and he slipped by his bewildered rivals to win effortlessly.

The plot was almost ruined a few years back when the R.A.C. discovered what was going on and reacted with expected huffiness. Moss had his driver's license yanked on the pretext of a traffic violation but the Club's director's were persuaded to keep silent for the good of the sport and the Commonwealth. Nonetheless the story was made public recently when a young Nassau go-karter spotted Francis replacing an oil line in Stirling's chest and blabbed to the press.

There is little reason to fear that Stirling's career will suffer now that the secret is out. Most racing authorities have accepted the revelation graciously, being more shocked that such a machine works than that such a ruse was attempted. They are in general agreement that, barring mechanical difficulties, Stirling Moss MK III will be a force to be reckoned with for many years to come.

—BY & GB

A curious group — among them Bob Holbert — looks on as a mechanic adjusts spring tension in Moss's right foot.

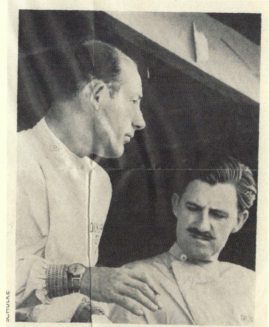

Graham Hill looks on incredulously as he hears for the first time the smooth purr of pumps and gears issuing from the midriff of Moss Mk III.

The MK II was seemingly a perfect machine. Lighter by 16.5 pounds, the magnesium and plastic-compound body housed the most sensitive and intelligent computing devices known to man. After a season of development, "he" began to come into "its" own. Lap records were accumulated for nearly every major circuit in the world and after 1957 it was universally accepted that what appeared to be this pleasant young man was the finest of all racing drivers.

ONE FATAL FLAW

But the MK II had one failing: it lacked prudence. Once in the car, Moss would flog it around in a blinding series of perfectly executed shifts, slides, brakings and gear changes. Every movement would be carried out flawlessly and his car would circulate lap-a-lap at the maximum. Unfortunately this pace would continue despite drops in oil pressure, rises in water temperature, badly wearing tires or ominous crunchings from the gearbox.

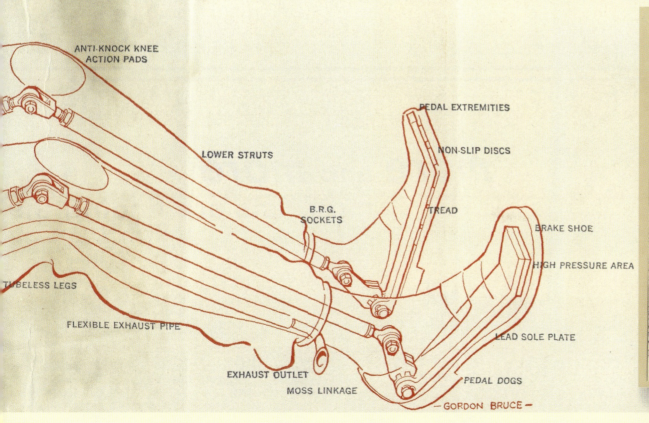

Race Pilot Just Robot?

NO HOAX, MOSS REALLY HUMAN BEING

Dear Mr. Lauring:

I was shocked to read in a recent issue of a legitimate "car" magazine that Britain's Stirling Moss, who recently won the "Monte Carlo Grand Prix," was a robot.

The article told of how the robot operates and of some of the problems his inventors encountered. It said the robot that is now racing is actually the third of its kind; the other two were damaged in previous races.

The article went on to say that when the second robot was damaged beyond repair, the public was informed that Moss was in the hospital with both of his legs fractured. In the meantime, while he was supposedly in the hospital recovering, his makers were busy constructing a new robot.

If the article were a hoax and Stirling Moss really isn't a robot, it would be impossible to believe that a man could go into the hospital with two badly fractured legs and in a relatively short time (8½ months) return to racing as healthy as ever.

I would appreciate it very much if you would answer personally or in your column and let me know if you have any information on or know anything else about Stirling Moss. My friends and I are trying to determine if this is a hoax or if Stirling Moss really is a robot. I also wonder why nothing has been said of this in the newspapers.

Sincerely yours,
TONY SKELLY.

Los Angeles Examiner 26.5.61

1961

Stirling Moss Scrapbook

Nürburgring 1,000 Kms

The seventh 1,000 kms sports car race at the ultra-challenging Nürburgring circuit in the Eifel mountains gave Stirling an opportunity for a spot more 'Goliath-bashing' when he and Graham Hill shared a 1.7-litre Porsche with about 100bhp less than the fastest Ferraris. Nevertheless, the British duo were second quickest in practice in the rain. Porsche gambled, after two days of rain, and fitted the new rain tyres for the race even though race day dawned bright and dry. As a result, though Moss led the first lap, he was soon consumed by the larger-engined beasts, first the Ferrari of Phil Hill which was consistently lowering the lap record and then the similar car of Ginther.

At 11.30am, after some two-and-a-half hours racing and the first round of pit-stops, with Graham now in fourth place, it began snowing! The slippery conditions suited the rain-tyred Porsche and Hill began closing in on those ahead. Then he handed over to Stirling who went faster and faster as the leaders slowed. As the mist closed in, Stirling moved up to a brilliant second place and then it was all over as matters mechanical intervened.

Stirling and Graham took over a disc-braked Porsche Carrera Coupé and proceeded to overhaul the 2-litre class-leading Lotus to at least take modest honours. At the dinner that night, Stirling was awarded a gold cup for his previous three consecutive wins in the Internationales ADAC-1,000km Rennen.

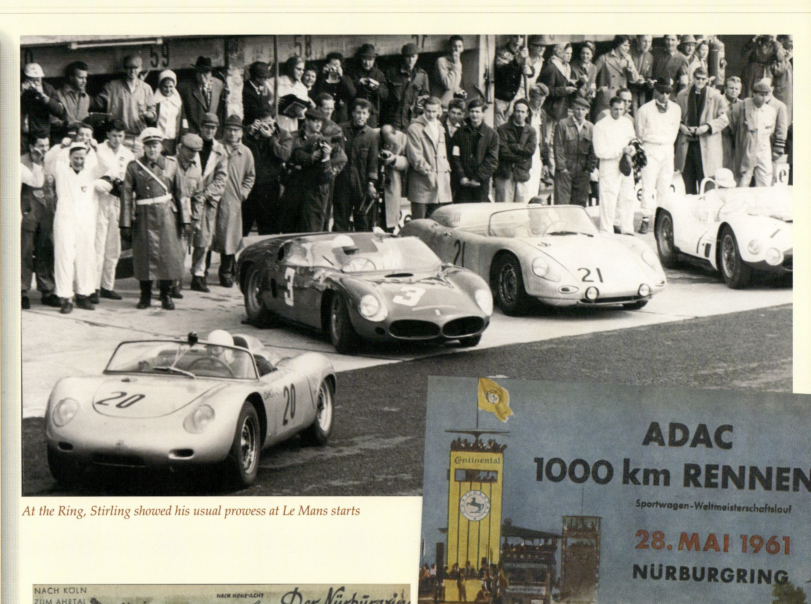

At the Ring, Stirling showed his usual prowess at Le Mans starts

Stirling Moss ...

FACEL VEGA

SM: *"A terrific car in its time for what it was. It had a large Chrysler engine and air conditioning and a radio and was automatic. Not a sporty car, but very comfortable. You would sit in luxury. It was very fast and great as a tourer. That is what it was a grand tourer really, rather like the later Jensen which was a similar thing. The Facel was a luxury car but very reliable because of the Chrysler engine and excellent gearbox. And it had electric windows! It was a super car, actually, for what I used it for, and that was just to cruise from one race to another. In those days you could fly to Brussels for a fiver and I could leave the car in Brussels, £5 each way. I would leave it in the car park, come over to England, and go back and forth. Very convenient."*

Stirling and team mate Graham Hill even encountered snow in their superb drive in the Porsche at the Ring but sadly their efforts ended in retirement

Below left: This is a card in Stirling's scrapbook. It was reproduced from a painting by John Paddy Carstairs. This extraordinary man directed over 50 films (he discovered Norman Wisdom), wrote 30 books and held exhibitions of his paintings at the Royal Academy and in Paris. Coincidentally, he was the first private owner of 9600 HP, the oldest Jaguar E-type in existence and the example that Jaguar used as the development car, launch car, road-test car and Press car. In its Press role, it would be lent to Stirling to open Britain's first 'Five Minute Car Wash' in June. The next owner was Jack Fairman, Stirling's co-driver at Jaguar and Aston Martin. To complete the set of coincidences, 9600 HP has been owned by Philip Porter since 1977

Stirling has a word with Tony Robinson who assisted Alf Francis throughout their long association

May

Stirling Moss Scrapbook

JUNE

Calendar

3	Silver City Trophy, Brands Hatch, UK – 1st in UDT/Laystall 1.5 Lotus-Climax 18/21
10/11	Le Mans, France – ret'd in Ferrari 250GT (sharing with Graham Hill)
18	Belgian GP, Spa-Francorchamps – 8th in Lotus-Climax 18/21
24	Player's 200, Mosport, Canada – 1st in heat 1, 1st in heat 2, 1st on aggregate in Lotus-Climax 19

The first weekend in June did not start well with the death of a friend in practice but Stirling managed to close it out of his mind and concentrate on getting pole position

Silver City Trophy, Brands Hatch

For the main race at Brands on June 3, Stirling drove a pale green Lotus 18/21 for the UDT/Laystall team run by his father Alfred which had not been having a very productive run with their Formula One cars. All that was destined to change and the magazine Motor Racing headed their report "Moss Mastery at Brands".

Moss, and Surtees in a Yeoman Credit Cooper, qualified fastest with identical times and Clark was just a fifth of a second slower in the works Lotus 21. Surtees led Clark with SM biding his time in third. With just over a third of the race gone, Surtees selected bottom gear by mistake and spun off. Stirling now began a relentless pursuit of Clark in the newer works car. Both were driving brilliantly but then the Scot buzzed his engine which knocked the edge off his performance and Stirling took him. The battle continued but SM retained the advantage and lowered the lap record in the process, leaving it at 1.4 seconds under the old 2½-litre record.

June began sadly. Thursday practice for that weekend's Silver City Trophy event at Brands Hatch took place in the wet and Shane Summers, with whom Stirling had become quite friendly, had a fatal accident. "Poor Shane was killed at Paddock Bend," wrote Stirling in his diary. He also noted, "Discussed new manager" but nothing seems to have come of that.

As to practice times, Stirling, whose aging Lotus 18 now had the benefit of some of the latest parts developed for the factory Lotus 21s, could not quite match Clark in the works car. He recorded a 1.54.8 to Clark's 1.54.1 with Surtees on 1.54.4. That evening he went to Keith and Betty Ballisat's to eat.

Things were a bit brighter next day, in various senses, but not all was well. "Practice. Car feels good. Brakes bad, gearbox bad and oversteer. Home and work. Met Dave at 8.30. Food and saw *3 Ring Circus*. Bad. Bed at 2am." At least, he was now equal quickest and the margin over the Coopers was substantial.

SM	1.42.8
Surtees	1.42.8
Clark	1.43.0
Brooks	1.43.2
Salv	1.43.8
Hill	1.43.2
Bruce	1.44.2
Jack	1.44.6

Saturday was race day. Though the result was a good one for Stirling, he sounded far from happy in his diary. "Race. Won. Covered in fuel for 30 laps.

The UDT/Laystall Lotus 18 had now been updated to semi 21 spec and the bodywork certainly looks more 21 than the boxy 18. It would prove effective at Brands, clocking up yet another win for the maestro

June

Stirling Moss Scrapbook

1961

Brakes and gearbox bad. Car slower than Clark's. Home, bath and we met Caroline and food at Lotus. Home and bed 2.15." The reference to food at Lotus should not be taken as the Lotus works canteen. This was a local London restaurant (in Edgware Road) that was a particular favourite called the Lotus House! David Haynes recalls it was "open very late". "You could always get a meal there," says Val Pirie.

Sunday was spent at his parents' place at Tring and next day he had the TV cameras filming him in his office before a meeting with his architects to discuss the ambitious house project. "Later called on Kiki then took Jennifer W. for food. Bed at 1.30am. Tried to call Shirlee." Transatlantic calls were not quite as easy or 'normal' as they are today. On Tuesday Stirling and Graham Hill flew to Paris and on to Le Mans where they were to share a 250GT Berlinetta Ferrari for the endurance classic that was probably Stirling's least favourite race.

Wednesday, June 7: "Up late and stooged around. Scrutineering. Car weighed 1,017 kgs. Practised. Tried 650 x 15 and 550 x 15 @ 50lbs but car understeered. 600 and 650 seemed better except for wander. Get 7,700! Set lights and then food and bed at 1.30am."

Next day, they practised in the wet after lunch. "Seat is better. Fitted softer dampers. Car slides a lot in wet on D10s. Dunlops promised D12s and D9s. Food and bed at 1.30am." Friday was pretty leisurely. Stirling spent time at the garage where the car was being kept and prepared before being involved in a TV film and retiring at the comparatively early hour of midnight in deference to the 24-hour race starting on the morrow.

This car was built to order for Messrs Dick Wilkins and Rob Walker with righthand drive, a light alloy body, laterally sliding Plexiglass side windows, painted "Dark Blue with White band on front, as we have done on car n° 2119/GT", trimmed Blue Connolly VM 3087 hide, blue carpets, light grey headlining and fuel tank "to 1961 Le Mans regulations". It was to be ready in time for Le Mans at the latest.

On June 6, "One new Ferrari 250 GT Berlinetta" was invoiced to Pippbrook Garage (Walker's company) for 5,500,000 Lire.

The bill for preparation of the car for Le Mans, including an additional battery system, light system for the race numbers and fire extinguisher (including labour), came to 85,368 Lire.

At the end of July, Ken Gregory wrote on behalf of The R.R.C. Walker Racing Team of Duke's Head Yard, Highgate High Street, London to Col. Hoare regarding two invoices. The first was fine but the

Pictured above is 16-year-old Gordon McIsaac, of 14 Parawai Crescent, Grey Lynn, Auckland, holding his painting of British racing star Stirling Moss at the wheel of a red Maserati in which Moss won the 1956 Grand Prix of Monaco.

Melbourne Sun 3.6.61

Tops in traffic

Not as fast as the powerful racing cars he normally drives, but British ace Stirling Moss finds this miniature motor scooter more useful in London's busy traffic.

Wet Weather Tyres

At the Aintree 200 in April, Dunlop had introduced a new rain tyre for the first time. Stirling had not been able to benefit as he was forced to retire within two laps with engine troubles. However, Jack Brabham, who won, reckoned they were worth "at least three or four seconds a lap.

"This was the first time I had tried them, and the thing I found most difficult to get used to was how far they would go before breaking away. It took me several laps to get used to the idea that I could get round the corner on the wet surface far quicker than with normal tyres."

Dunlop had been experimenting for some while with high hysteresis rubber but warned that the wet weather tyres wore out 20% faster in the dry than normal racing tyres. They were denoted by a green spot on the tyre wall and hence became known as 'Green Spot' tyres.

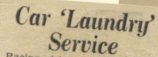

Car 'Laundry' Service

Racing driver Stirling Moss is to open Britain's first automatic car "laundry" in London next week. American equipment will enable the "laundry" to handle up to 250 cars an hour, producing a vehicle clean inside and out every 15 seconds.

The owners say that a genuine five minutes service will be offered to motorists, who will be served free coffee while they wait.

Coventry Eve. Tel. 9.6.61

Wontners

Jennifer W. was Jennifer Wontner and she was a member of a very well-known and distinguished family. Arthur Wontner was a famous actor manager who made his name in the 1930s playing Sherlock Holmes. He had a successful career in theatre, film, radio and later television. His son Hugh (later Sir Hugh and later still Lord) Wontner ran the Savoy Hotel for many years and is credited with much of the success that that great hotel enjoyed. For many years he fought off the advances of the Forte family who were pursuing the Savoy Group. He was also a highly regarded Lord Mayor of London in 1973.

A Fair Question

In its June 9 issue, Autosport published a letter from a Mr. Millensted from Oundle School (was he a pupil or a master?). He began by stating that Stirling currently led the World Championship jointly with von Trips but that even SM's brilliant driving would be no match for the much faster Ferraris and that Stirling "will very soon move right down the chart driving the 1960 model of the Lotus. Please could you tell me why Rob Walker has not yet got hold of the new, and very much improved, 1961 Lotus, which has been out for a little time already?"

Moss 104 m.p.h. at Le Mans

Stirling Moss and Graham Hill averaged 104.3 m.p.h. in a Ferrari in the first practice for the Le Mans 24-hour race on Saturday.

Another Ferrari, driven by Ritchie Ginther (U.S.) and Wolfgang von Trips (Germany), had the fastest time of the 55 cars, averaging 123.9 m.p.h.

MOSS WAITS IN THE WINGS...
...then steals the show in last act

STIRLING MOSS is driving better now than he has ever done. In the 200-mile Silver City Trophy race at Brands Hatch on Saturday he elected to wait in the wings, letting others have the early limelight, before stealing the show in the last act.

Cars

Ferrari 250GT SWB

Ferrari produced both road and competition versions of the short-wheelbase 250GT Berlinetta. Two competition cars were built in 1959, 45 competition versions and 15 road cars in 1960, 25 competition versions and 41 road cars in 1961 and two competition versions and 33 road cars in 1962. Chassis construction was tubular frame with two main oval section steel tubes. 2,953cc V12 engine, producing (competition) 260-280bhp at 7,000rpm, 3 x 46 DCL3 Webers, 4-speed gearbox integral with engine, front suspension by independent top and bottom wishbones and coil springs, rear suspension by semi-elliptic springs with solid axle. Dunlop disc brakes. Max speed around 155mph (250km/h). 1961 version had bigger valves and was lighter at 1,017kg.

THE HOUSE OF MOSS

Johanna Norton Griffiths

THE first thing I noticed about him was his hands. Medium sized, beautifully kept; long, thin fingers. Strong and masculine, yet soft and firm at the same time.

The hands of an artist—but not the kind who wields a brush and palette.

Stirling Moss is an artist behind the wheel. A mechanical magician whose skill and dexterity on the racing circuits of the world have made him an international idol.

Yet the world's greatest racing driver carries his crown modestly.

He is the son of a dental surgeon who is also a farmer living in Tring, Hertfordshire. His sister Pat is the famous show jumper and rally driver.

Moss, 32, first showed interest in motor racing at the ripe old age of ten. Ten years later he became a professional. In 1957, at the peak of his career, he married a pretty Canadian girl, Katie Molson. They went to live, when they had time, in Nassau. But the marriage did not work out and they are now separated.

Now he is trying to sell his old home in the Bahamas and is building another to his own specifications in a small village in the heart of London's Mayfair.

What is he really like, this man whose public image is that of a garlanded hero regarded as sometimes difficult, temperamental and full of his own importance? I think he is the most misunderstood personality I have ever met.

Here is a famous man, not just known in one of two countries but all over the world. Boys model themselves on him. Some young men go further and think they are him!

What impression did he make on me? Amusing, gay fun, completely at ease, frank, sincere, but often seeming lonely in his fame. Perhaps the most endearing quality of all is that he is sympathetic.

We talked of houses and the building and designing of them. I've just bought one and he's just building one. We were lucky to find something in common so quickly. Even so, I don't think anyone could feel ill at ease with him.

Wherever he goes to race, he collects gadgets and odds and ends to improve his new house. He is like a child with a new toy, only perhaps more willing to share his enthusiasm with others.

"It's going to have every modern implement and idea I can find," he told me proudly. He takes great interest in the smallest details.

It seemed all out of place to me — a dare-devil dicing with death one minute, the next a houseproud young man longing for his own home.

What are his plans? Does this mean he intends to retire? I don't think even he knows.

He told me: "When I retire I shall go into designing —and I don't mean birdcages. It simply infuriates me that you can't buy a wall fittings which doesn't have screws showing!" I'd never thought of it!

I should like to see the house when it is finished. With his impeccable taste, it should be the best equipped in London. Perhaps its owner will even stay at home more to benefit by it.

London American 8.6.61

second one, referred to above, "relates to the preparation of the Berlinetta for Le Mans, and as Rob's car was borrowed by the Entrant who was in fact Luigi Chinetti of the North American Racing Team, these charges should most certainly be passed on to him – especially as the car was lent free of charge. You will no doubt appreciate that Chinetti is the Ferrari concessionaire for North America, so I am sure there will be no difficulty in arranging for him to pay the account direct to Ferrari."

"Up late and circuit," began his diary entry for the Saturday. "I began race and averaged 191 kph for 1½ hrs. (21 laps. 25/26 possible on 127 lit) [fuel] Lap 4.08.0. Then Graham for 1½ hrs and then SM two spells till 11.00pm approx. Then 3rd GH again, then SM. 1 lap and we had had it. A fan blade flew off and cut the water hose and the head gasket went! Stooged around + Gerda. TV. Met Mylene D. No bed."

Next day, Stirling had a snack with his father, did another TV interview, and then he, Graham and Val flew from Orly back to London where Val treated him at the Lotus House. Later Herb Jones came to stay for a week. After a solid day of work at the office on the Monday, SM, Herb, Val and Diane Aubrey went to the Wellington. Next day he and Rob Walker drove to Silverstone in a Mini. "1 hr. 20. Tested Lotus with new suspension and body. Only get 7,600 with high 5th (=7,700 low) and 7,800 in 4th after Stowe. 6,600 in 5th round Woodcote. 1.38.7. Home at 9.30 and took Sally D. to Candlelight Room. Bed at 2.15." Sally D. was Sally Ducker.

Wednesday was an intriguing day. His services were employed to promote London's first 'Five Minute Car Wash' and Pathé News were there to film. The Jaguar E-type had just been sensationally announced at Geneva in March. The impact was such that examples would be mobbed in the street but they were still incredibly scarce as Jaguar had only produced a relative handful and virtually all those were for export. Jaguar's Press Car was borrowed and this was the same car as had been involved in the 150mph road tests and the unveiling at Geneva. Distinctively registered 9600 HP, according to the Pathé News commentator, it was Stirling's own car. This was not actually so but, coincidentally, it has been owned by Philip Porter since 1977. Stirling described the day as follows:

"Up and work. Opened 5 min car wash. More work. Re-opened car wash. Met Carol Cole. Work. Called at 'The Village' (Alex Sterling) and then to Ronnie and Leo's for food. Work and bed at 2.15."

Stirling did not sleep well that night but, after just four hours slumber, worked until 9pm. "Then took Jean Lockwood to 55. Bed at 2.30." There is some

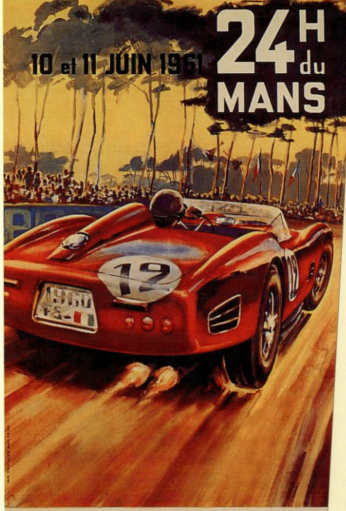

Stirling having a little fun with French photographer and journalist, Bernard Cahier who took a number of the photographs in SM's scrapbooks

Background to Le Mans

Back in February, Rob Walker had written to Col. Ronnie Hoare of Maranello Concessionaires (the UK Ferrari importers), through whom the new Ferrari 250/GT was being supplied. He stated that, "it now seems unlikely we will enter the Ferrari for Le Mans because they refused to give us starting money and Stirling, quite rightly I think, refuses to start without having starting money as he doesn't wish to create a precedent". Walker went on mention there was a G.T. race at Rouen on June 4th and if the car could be ready in time he would very much like to enter. He suggesting the factory was not told, "as this might slow them up a bit".

In April, Maranello Concessionaires wrote to Ferrari saying that at Sebring Mr. Moss had tried a 250 GT Berlinetta fitted with six twin-choke carburettors. He understood this set-up was being homologated and, if so, he would like 'his' car to be so equipped.

Ferrari replied saying they were surprised at this information as they had no car at Sebring equipped in this way. "…no Granturismo Berlinetta is expected, at this time, to be fitted with six carburettors… We would like to confirm that the car intended for Mr. Stirling Moss is going to receive our best care, and in the hope that it will completely satisfy its competent owner, we send you our best regards."

Hoare them wrote to Walker to say he had been in Modena the previous week and had raised the question of the six carburettor engine with Mr. Ferrari. "It is quite correct that a Berlinetta has been fitted with an experimental six carburettor engine, almost identical to the Testa Rossa, and that this car was the one Stirling tried recently at Sebring." He continued that Enzo maintained the unit was still undergoing development and there would be considerable difficulties homologating it. "There have, however, been certain important modifications carried out to the head of the engine and also to the carburettor size and exhaust system and I hope your car will be producing at least 15bhp more than your old one with a slight reduction in overall weight."

Then Enzo Ferrari himself wrote to Stirling. He firstly confirmed the car would be ready for Rouen. He then stated that, "The 12 carburettors have been homologated, looking forward to a future installation, next year..." He said the homologation would be completed on 1st July, 1961. "I would advise you, however, that we have adopted an advantageous solution, having homologated, starting from 1st March 1961, the installation of three new double-bodied DC carburettors that Weber has manufactured for us, marked 46 DCF3.

"With this arrangement, we actually lose 8 or 9 h.p. at 7500 revs, but, as compensation, we obtain a better regularity and a better pick-up at low and average ranges.

"I can assure you, in any case, that the engine of the Berlinetta 61, as it was established during the tests at Le Mans, develops 300 h.p. at a maximum of 7500/7700 revs.

"You can surely rely on my best interest, and with this opportunity, please accept my best regards. Yours sincerely, Enzo Ferrari."

With an eye to 1962, Ferrari was courting Stirling as we shall see later in the year.

Stirling with Graham Hill in the pits at Le Mans. They made a good pairing

Note the NART sticker on the rear but the car was actually owned by Wilkins and Walker

Moss on: LE MANS

PP: *"I know you never enjoyed Le Mans as an event, but what about the circuit?"*

SM: *"The circuit. Le Mans circuit was quite good actually. The straight is rather boring, but getting the right spot to brake, correct gear ratios and all that sort of stuff was quite interesting. The track was so smooth, very good condition. But it is a long time 24 hours – too long."*

1961

mystery as to what 55 refers. Other numbers refer to houses that SM owned in Shepherd Street but this does not. It seems it was most probably a club.

On Friday Stirling flew by BEA to Brussels. "On by car to Spa. Practice. Did tests. Get 146mph! Food and bed at 1am." More of the same followed next day. "Car seems OK but slow. Poor Cliff [Allison] had a shunt on 1st lap. Two legs and car gone. Food with Wisdom and Henry [Taylor] and Li and Denis (D. Mail) [Holmes] Bed at 1am."

Hill	3.59.3
Trips	4.00.1
Gende	4.03.0
Surtees	4.06.0
Ginther	4.06.1
G Hill	4.07.6
Brooks	4.07.9
Moss	4.08.2
Bonnier	4.08.3
Gurney	4.08.4
Jack	4.08.6

The 1961 Belgian Grand Prix was one of the least satisfying races Stirling Moss ever took part in. The Rob Walker Lotus 18 had now been updated with 21 rear suspension and more streamlined bodywork which was important for the high speed Spa-Francorchamps circuit. Nevertheless, the car was just well off the pace. The previous year Stirling had had an enormous accident in one of the infamously fragile Lotuses and perhaps memories of that still plagued him. According to pre-eminent motor racing historian, Doug Nye, this was the only event in his entire career when SM did not give it his absolute best shot. His diary entry was suitably terse.

"Up and race. Bad start and lay about 14th. Up to 11th and then 8th. Car fair. I'm fair. Caught Webbair home. Press interview at 12.30pm. Bed at 2.15am."

After a day of work, he consoled himself next day by taking Carolann Cole to the Candlelight Room and was, again, in bed at 2.15am. The following day saw him up early and packing for his next trip which was to Canada, to Mosport where he was to race in the Players 200. His mount was to be the sports racing Lotus 19.

At London Airport he, "Changed from TW to BOAC because of delay. NY met Shirlee and Ian and off in charter plane to Bridgehampton. Talked, etc. Bed at 1am. Up at 6am after NO sleep. Over-tired. Filmed for Dave Garroway show with Healeys. Did all sorts of shots and talk. Drove a little way towards NY. Bed at 12.30am."

Next day, which was Thursday June 22, he drove on to New York "by Healey. Caught AA plane with Shirlee and Ian. Met by Alan Miller. Hotel. Food, two

I'M DRIVING IN A RACE I HATE..

STIRLING MOSS, one of the stars at Le Mans today, has a heart-to-heart talk with his old friend TOM WISDOM

A LONELY, rather subdued young man is driving today in a motor-race he hates.

He hates it because, though he has won 50 races and crashed eight times in 11 years of big-time speed-bids, he thinks this particular event is unnecessarily dangerous.

The man is my friend Stirling Moss. The race: the famous Le Mans 24 Hours.

I talked with 31-year-old Stirling after his victory at Brands Hatch last week-end—his third success in five races this season.

His light blue overalls were stained with petrol that had leaked from an overfilled tank. His legs and back were burned raw by the fuel.

"What about the flame-proof overalls you've been designing?" I asked him.

For many the 250 GT swb Berlinetta is the most beautiful Ferrari of all. It looks good from any angle

Le Mans Race

For the 1961 Le Mans 24-hour race Stirling teamed up with BRM GP driver Graham Hill and they drove a Ferrari 250GT swb entered by the North American Racing Team (NART), though this brand new 1961 car actually belonged to Dick Wilkins and Rob Walker. Moss and Hill were in the GT class and could not, on paper, be expected to live with the pure racing jobs, the sports racing prototypes, as they were known.

The honour of being first away from the Le Mans start, which almost always fell to SM, was taken on this occasion by Jimmy Clark who was even more fleet of foot and lead under the famous Dunlop Bridge. However, Stirling, taking first stint, initially held an amazing fourth place. "Moss, Salvadori and Clark [in works DBR1 sports racers] were having a proper dust-up, and no one has ever seen a GT car being driven as fast as Stirling's was going," stated Autosport. "Moss caused great amusement by passing both DBR1 Aston Martins in front of the pits, only to be overtaken again in the Esses. His GT car was actually quicker than the Feltham sports-racers on the straights."

After two hours and a change of drivers, Graham Hill was going great guns in eighth place and after another two hours was up to sixth. Meanwhile, the conditions were deteriorating with steady rain. At midnight, with a third of the race run, Stirling had made the most of the slippery conditions and the duo were up to an extraordinary fourth place, just two laps behind the leading Ferrari, a lap behind the second-placed one and on the same lap as the example in third place. They were no less than four laps ahead of the Ferrari GT that was second in their class.

Then it all turned pear-shaped. As Stirling says in the book he wrote with Doug Nye, 'Stirling Moss, my cars, my career', "Unbelievably, NART had not removed its standard road-going fan, and since we had been holding high revs for so long one of the fan blades had flown off and slashed clean through a radiator hose. This stupid retirement was enormously frustrating, because it was so unnecessary and unprofessional."

To add to the frustration, Moss and Hill had been leading the Mairesse/Parkes prototype Ferrari which went on to finish second overall.

Moss, seen here on the right with his wheels astride the white line, was up to an amazing fourth on the first lap

June

Stirling Moss Scrapbook

TV shows and bed at 1am.

"Up at 9.00 and to Bowmanville and Flying Dutchman hotel. On to circuit and practice. Car was wrongly geared. Get about 137 mph 39/38 35/42 33/44 (needs lower 3rd 31/46) Sadler is much faster accelerating !X! Rain. SM 1.39.2."

After the frustration of the European season, this Canadian interlude proved a good fillip. Saturday dawned. "Up at 9.00. Police escort to circuit. Parade lap. 1st heat and I won by 1 lap and from Joe. Ftd in 1.40.0 (reckon 1.38 possible) Car did 16.8 mpg 'cos I was so easy not to break the axle! 2nd heat and I won from Joe. 40,000 spectators. Saw Jimmy and Lucy Morton and Jill. Hotel, 'do' and bed at 1.45am."

Next morning, he drove to Toronto and once again took to the skies with American Airlines. Later he saw Shirlee off to LA and checked in at Belmont. As he had not been shopping lately and must have been suffering withdrawal symptoms, he repaired that omission during Monday before meeting Shirlee at the International Hotel and flying, by Alitalia, back to London. "No bed – no sleep."

In spite of that, he did a day in the office and "At 7.30 met Carolann and we had food at 55. Bed at 1.15am." '55' is sounding more and more like a restaurant or club.

No time for relaxing as the relentless schedule continued with the French Grand Prix in the heart of Champagne country that coming weekend. "Up early and work. Off to LAP [London Airport] at 10.45 and BEA [British European Airways] to Bourget. Facel to Reims. Crystal Hotel and practice. Geared to 161 @ 8,000. Get 7,500 – 7,600 alone. 7,900 behind the Ferrari! Car handles badly due to rear suspension. Hotel and food with the Taylors and chatted. Bed at 2am." At that time, as recounted elsewhere, Stirling kept his Facel Vega abroad. His comment about achieving 7,900 behind the Ferrari refers to the higher revs he could reach when slip-streaming the more powerful Italian machines. Apparently he irritated von Trips considerably by getting a 'tow' from him which pulled Stirling up to fourth fastest and well clear of the non-Ferrari rest. It is interesting to note how much the 'tow' was worth.

P Hill	2.24.9
Trips	2.26.4
Ginther	2.26.8
SM	2.27.6
Clark	2.29.0
G. Hill	2.29.1
Surtees	2.29.1
McLaren	2.29.4
Gurney	2.29.6
Clark	2.30.3

Graham Hill

Val Pirie: "Stirling was quite close to Graham because in the old days Graham didn't have a penny and we used to give him a lift to the airports, etc. I remember coming back from Le Mans I was sitting in the middle and I kept operating the piddlers [windscreen washers] and Stirling said, 'If you do that again, I'm going to chuck you out of the car,' and Graham believed him. So, every time we went round a corner, Graham would hold me because he really believed Stirling would turf me out."

Thanks to some demon driving from both Stirling and Graham Hill, aided by slippery conditions, their GT Ferrari was up amongst the sports racers which must have been incredible to watch

Who WANTS to go to HEAVEN?

Perhaps **Stirling Moss** gave the frankest reply of all. "I would like to survive after death, as long as I could be sure of meeting past friends or of starting up new and interesting acquaintances," he said.

"The only thing that worries me is that it would be all too perfect. Maybe I wouldn't fit into this new life."

Today 17.6.61

LISTE OFFICIELLE DES ENGAGÉS

Concurrents		Conducteurs	Voitures
SEFAC FERRARI	2	W. von TRIPS	FERRARI
SEFAC FERRARI	4	P. HILL	FERRARI
EQUIPE NATIONALE BELGE	8	O. GENDEBIEN	FERRARI
EQUIPE NATIONALE BELGE	10	W. MAIRESSE	EMERYSON
EQUIPE NATIONALE BELGE	12	L. BIANCHI	EMERYSON
R.R.C. WALKER RACING TEAM	14	S. MOSS	COOPER ou LOTUS
PORSCHE SYSTEM ENGINEERING	18	I. BONNIER	PORSCHE
PORSCHE SYSTEM ENGINEERING	20	D. GUERNEY	PORSCHE
YEOMAN CREDIT RACING TEAM	24	J. SURTEES	COOPER
SCUDERIA SERENISSIMA	26	M. TRINTIGNANT	COOPER
COOPER CAR CY	28	J. BRABHAM	COOPER
COOPER CAR CY	30	B. MAC LAREN	COOPER
TEAM LOTUS	32	I. IRELAND	LOTUS
TEAM LOTUS	34	J. CLARK	LOTUS
OWEN RACING ORGANISATION	36	G. HILL	B.R.M.
OWEN RACING ORGANISATION	38	T. BROOKS	B.R.M.
Concurrents devant se qualifier :			
SEFAC FERRARI	6	GINTHER	FERRARI
H et L MOTORS	40	J. LEWIS	COOPER
UNITED DOMINIONS TRUST	16	H. TAYLOR	LOTUS
TONY MARSH	42	T. MARSH	LOTUS
CAMORADI INTERNATIONAL R.I.	44	M. GREGORY	COOPER
SCUDERIA CENTRO SUD	46	L. BANDINI	COOPER
SCUDERIA COLONA	48	W. SEIDEL	COOPER ou LOTUS
C. GODIN de BEAUFORT	22	C. GODIN de BEAUFORT	PORSCHE

Stirling Moss …

MYLENE D

"Mylene Demongeot was an actress I met. She was working in a thing called La Plume de ma Tante and a very cute little girl. I saw the show and then I thought, 'Gosh!' The trouble was that if I called up anywhere and left a message with my name on it that was very difficult. I sent a note, saying how much I enjoyed the show and signed off in French and said that I hope we will meet sometime, or something like that. Then when I was going to the Tour de France, I got a cable sent to me saying, 'Good luck in your event'. And then we met up after. So that was quite a long-term effort to try and meet up."

A French actress born in Nice, she was, according to the Daily Express, being sought to appear in 'The Stirling Moss Story'.

THIS IS WHERE STIRLING CAME IN

THIS is where he came in. A year ago on the Francorchamps track—Europe's fastest circuit—Stirling Moss spun off the course at 140 m.p.h. He broke his legs and three ribs, and crushed three discs of his spine. Yesterday, he returned...

In the first practice run for tomorrow's Belgian Grand Prix he took 12th place, driving a Lotus. But he also went back to the place where he crashed.

Still in his tracksuit, he looks right to the spot where he so nearly died. On this track, too, four other Britons have been killed. Those are the facts. His thoughts are his own. Tomorrow, he races again.

Picture by Daily Mail Cameraman John Knoote

Daily Mail 15.6.61

1961

Baghetti 2.30.5
Brab 2.31.0
Roy S 2.31.2

Thursday was spent relaxing with time by the pool and some practice. Even though he was racing that weekend, he was not in bed until 3am!

Friday was an almost identical day except that he was involved in the "presentation of Nockolds painting to Reims and then lunch with the Prince and Princess du Polignac. Pool and practice. Car seems OK. Later food with Rob and Betty [Walker] and DD. Chatted and bed at 3am."

Stirling Moss ...

CO-DRIVERS

PP: *"Were there some people who were particularly hard on their machinery?"*

SM: *"Yes. When you were going to take a co-driver you would have to look at what they offered and the most important thing to me is the fact that if I give it to you, when you bring it back, I want it much the same. I don't expect you to do any great heroics, but give me back a car I can do something with. That was my main first requirement."*

Stirling Moss ...

GERDA

"Gerda was a German girl. I can't remember much about her but she was a bit of a messer [someone who is unreliable and wastes one's time], I think."

Grand Prix de Belgique

Francorchamps

With Alf and the other mechanics on the grid at daunting Spa where even the robot had an off day, proving even robots can be human!

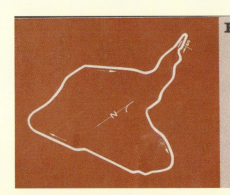

BELGIAN GRAND PRIX
STARTING GRID
(First 7 rows)

P. HILL (Ferrari) 3:59.3		VON TRIPS (Ferrari) 4:00.1		GENDEBIEN (Ferrari) 4:03.0
	SURTEES (Cooper) 4:06.0		GINTHER (Ferrari) 4:06.1	
G. HILL (BRM) 4:07.6		BROOKS (BRM) 4:07.9		MOSS (Lotus) 4:08.2
	BONNIER (Porsche) 4:08.3		GURNEY (Porsche) 4:08.4	
BRABHAM (Cooper) 4:08.6		GREGORY (Cooper) 4:10.2		LEWIS (Cooper) 4:11.1
	DE BEAUFORT (Porsche) 4:16.7		MC LAREN (Cooper) 4:17.4	
CLARK (Lotus) 4:17.5		BANDINI (Cooper-Maserati) 4:19.0		IRELAND (Lotus) 4:20.0

June

Circuits

Moss on: SPA FRANCORCHAMPS

SM: "Most people rate it as daunting, a daunting circuit. Spa, when you reckon that you are averaging 120mph plus with a hairpin thrown in, it gives you an idea of how fast you are going and because of the corners it was not at all easy. Not at all easy, actually. With a kink on the straight and so on, these had to be taken very, very fast and Spa is somewhere you find yourself being forced to keep your foot down and you have to brake rather late, because otherwise you don't get the time you want. Quite a difficult circuit to get a fast time on."

PP: "Were there some circuits you didn't enjoy?"

SM: "Spa has to go near that, because I never felt very secure. I always felt, 'God, you know you are going a hell of a lick. If anything goes wrong, you are in trouble.'"

PP: "Which it did of course in '60, in a big way."

SM: "A wheel came off and that was it… Into the bank. Spa seems the most daunting but a fantastic circuit."

Belgian Grand Prix

The whole event was just utterly soul-destroying for Stirling. First practice started as the 1960 race had left off. The previous year, two drivers had been killed and there were two major accidents, including SM's monumental one. This year, on his very first lap Cliff Allison crashed and broke both legs. There were four Ferraris entered with local man Olivier Gendebien joining the regulars and they filled the front row and took one of the two places on the second row.

As the quartet of Italian single-seaters headed off into the distance for their own race, leaving the rest at a rate of three seconds a lap, Stirling occupied a lowly 10th place. Due to retirements, that had improved a tad to eighth by the conclusion of proceedings but he only avoided the ignominy of being lapped by a slender margin. Not a happy day's work.

Stirling Moss …

ACCIDENTS & LOTUSES

PP: "You had had the very bad shunt at Spa in 1960. Did any accidents ever put you off. Did that one make you feel concerned about racing in general or about Lotus? Lotuses fell apart regularly didn't they?"

SM: "Yea, I mean, it was really quite strange to drive a Lotus, because they were not a very user friendly car like the Cooper. The Cooper was a much easier car, therefore, you could throw it around. You could get a Cooper and really do ridiculous things with it and it didn't hurt you. The Lotus you had to drive with great respect and feeling. At Spa in 1960 a wheel had come off. It worried me if the wheels could come off especially when we went to a place like Lisbon, or Porto, where there were a lot of trees right alongside the circuit. I would be going around a right hand corner fast and thinking, 'God, if a wheel comes off now, this is going to be awful' and that is why one needs great concentration. You have got to get your mind off it, you can't think about it and it is difficult to do so if you are concentrating on driving. So a Lotus never really gave me confidence, I must say, in all the time I drove them. I had great respect for the ability of Colin Chapman and what he had done. I mean, the cars were really terrific, but they were not easy and they were not strong."

PP: "Taking the point about Lotuses not being easy, was that because you needed to be more precise than with a Cooper, or because they would bite?"

SM: "No, it was just that the Lotus, for whatever reason, was a difficult car because it would oversteer and understeer. They weren't as constant as a Cooper…"

PP: "So you couldn't have the confidence. They were unpredictable?"

SM: "Yes, like an unpredictable woman really; you never know whether you are going to get hit, or she would be in a fit of passion. It was the same thing with the Lotus, whether she is passionate or annoyed. Because it was light, you could sometimes see an advantage over others. You could accelerate with another car with a similar engine and you got the edge a little bit. But not that much."

 Tommy Wisdom

Tom Wisdom was a great character. He was Motoring Correspondent for the Daily Herald and Sporting Life. He competed in all manner of events for many years and in rallies he would often team up with his wife Elsie (known as Bill). In January 1961 he was honoured by Prince Rainier of Monaco, having competed in every single Monte Carlo Rally since 1934. It was Wisdom who lent a young Stirling his semi-works XK 120 for the 1950 Tourist Trophy which Stirling describes as his first big break and which earned him a place in the Jaguar works team.

Coincidentally, he would borrow the E-type, 9600 HP, from Jaguar that coming Christmas to take it to Switzerland for a holiday.

I find a woman behind Britain's biggest car race eclipse in years

From TOM WISDOM: WATERLOO (BELGIUM), Monday

AN elderly grey-haired woman who does not drive a car took a leading part in Britain's greatest motor-racing defeat for a decade when Ferraris finished yesterday's Belgium Grand Prix in the first four places to head the world championship table.

Daily Herald 20.6.61

She is Signora Laura Ferrari, 60-year-old wife of the Napoleon of motor racing, engineer-designer Commendatore Enzo Ferrari.

The night before this critical race I, with the Grand Dame of Motor Racing and team manager Romolo Tavoni, was present at their nightly telephone conference with the great man himself.

The 62-year-old commendatore does not go to motor races any longer. His wife says: "His cars are his children, so he is sad when they fail, though delighted when they succeed.

"He prefers now to remain completely detached, but he is in touch all the time. By telephone he tells me what we should do and decides our tactics.

"My husband tells me—you are in the pits to be my eyes and ears. You are there to see —not to talk. So I sit in the pits while Tavoni gives the orders."

Secrets

While we talked together on the evening of the race, learning the secrets of the tactics to be adopted on the morrow, Stirling Moss approached, bowed and spoke with Signora Ferrari.

"My husband thinks you are a driver as great as the so magnificent Tazio Nuvolari," she said.

Tavoni backed this testimonial with an invitation for Moss to test the new Ferrari at Riverside, California, in October. Moss replied that he would be delighted to accept.

Signora Ferrari attends all races in which Ferraris compete. "I enjoy it—I am not nervous. That is part of the story of

From left: Olivier Gendebien, SM and Joakim Bonnier

 Spa Postscript

It may not have just been Stirling that was off form for the Belgian GP. According to the motor racing enthusiast's weekly 'bible', Autosport, in a subsequent article reviewing the race, "the engine was down on power as compared to Yeoman Credit and B.R.M. Stirling settled for a drive to finish, rather hoping that rain might fall and even things out a bit. When it did come, it was not heavy enough to make the roads slippery. Ironically enough, immediately after the race, the heavens opened. On the road to Liège airport at Bierset, Moss, accompanied by George Phillips [Autosport Chief Photographer], saw a Taunus crash right in front of the rented VW, some 20 kilometres from Spa. They pulled out the badly injured driver, and saw to it that he was taken to hospital."

Seems the whole weekend was jinxed for Stirling!

HIGH-SPEED CAR "LAUNDRY" OPEN

Daily Telegraph Reporter

The first of what its sponsors hope will become a national chain of high speed car "laundries" was opened in London yesterday by Stirling Moss, the racing driver. With this new automatic system, a car can be completely cleaned, inside and outside, in three to five minutes at a cost of from 9s to 12s 6d.

Mr. Hilton Lowndes, 37, from New Zealand, who has financed the £25,000 "Auto-Magic" washing installation in Brompton Road, hopes that in a few years the driver who washes his own car will be as rare in Britain as he is in the United States.

Daily Telegraph 15.6.61

 Five Minute Car Wash

The five minute car wash consisted of a car being hitched to a chain which dragged it through a series of water jets and brushes, after which about four men completed the operation by hand. For an investment of £25,000, it was claimed a car could be cleaned every 15 seconds!

Sally Ducker

"She was terribly grown-up," recalls her friend Dauvergne who was Rob Walker's daughter, "and she was absolutely gorgeous. She had very long eyelashes and she was very sophisticated. She was obviously very interested in young men and she was a friend of Stirling's for quite some time."

Val Pirie recalls she became a model and did the Fry's Turkish Delight adverts on television.

"Strike or no strike, we want the new car for our holiday. Stirling Moss here never looks at the instrument panel, anyway."

Daily Herald 23.6.61

Stirling Moss ...

ONE-OFF OFF DAY

PP: "Why do you think you had an off day. It was most unusual for you, to say the least."

SM: "Spa was one circuit I dreaded. I obviously wasn't particularly likely to win and I had these problems with Katie (impending divorce) and I just didn't get it together."

Ferrari invite Stirling Moss

Romolo Tavoni, manager of the all-conquering Italian motor-racing team, has invited Stirling Moss to try the new 162 m.p.h. 1½-litre V-6 Ferrari, writes TOM WISDOM.

If Moss likes the car, which is at least 15 m.p.h. faster than British Grand Prix models, he will be invited to join the Ferrari team for 1962.

Daily Herald 21.6.61

The Player's 200
FOR THE PLAYER'S TROPHY
SANCTION F.I.A.

Organized by Canadian Racing Drivers' Association

MOSPORT PARK June 24th, 1961 — Official Programme 50c.

— June — Stirling Moss Scrapbook —

1961

Dave Garroway Show

Dave Garroway was the first host of 'Today' which was considered a brash experiment when NBC-TV launched the morning television show in 1952. He fronted it until leaving shortly after his wife committed suicide in 1961. Described as the founding father of morning television, he also hosted the evening 'Dave Garroway Show' for NBC. He died by his own hand in 1982.

Player's 200 Mosport

This was the inaugural event at Canada's first major race track and was the first international race to be held in that country. Mosport is a contraction of 'motor sport' and the winding, undulating track of 2.459 miles was situated in the hills close to the north shore of Lake Ontario. The race distance was 80 laps (2 heats), equating to 196.72 miles (317kms), for which Stirling averaged 86.851mph (140km/h).

In the first heat, Stirling took the lead at the first bend and after just two laps was 16 seconds ahead of second-placed Jo Bonnier in a 1.6 Porsche who was followed by Olivier Gendebien in another Porsche. By the finish SM had lapped most of the field twice. After a slow start in the second heat, Stirling was only sixth at the end of the first lap, but was in the lead again within five laps. Bonnier and Gendebien were second and third overall, respectively.

Stirling had a happy and productive visit to Canada with a Lotus 19 for the inaugural meeting at Mosport

Stirling Moss Scrapbook

RUNAWAY DOUBLE BY MOSS IN CANADA

Ken Gregory Replies

In the June 23 issue of Autosport, Ken Gregory's letter of reply to Mr. Millenstead (different spelling!) was printed.

"Rob Walker has not purchased one of the latest-type 1961 Lotus Grand Prix cars, as used by the works team, only because Colin Chapman is unable to supply a car of this type, owing to contractual arrangements that he has made with his drivers. At the same time, I should like to point out that Colin Chapman has given every assistance, both to Rob Walker and Stirling, towards modifying the team's 1960 Lotuses in order to bring them up to as near the specification of the 1961 car as possible, and at the same time, maintaining faith with his own works drivers. These modifications include suspension and structural alterations, as well as undertaking the design of the new-type body, as used by Rob Walker and the UDT racing team."

One cannot help wondering if that was a tactful, or political, answer to avoid embarrassing the fuel companies.

STIRLING MOSS SAYS: I'M NOT AS FAST AS I USED TO BE

● LONDON, Tues.—World famous British racing driver, Stirling Moss, declared in a book being published today that he is "not as fast" as he used to be. The book, "a turn at the wheel," published by William Kimber is a personal diary of Moss's experience in Grand Prix driving between 1957 and 1960. "My whole outlook to motor racing," Moss writes, "has changed."

"I am not as dedicated as I used to be and I don't think I'm as fast as I used to be." Moss, who at 31 has won almost every major motor race in the world, says the closest he has ever come to being killed was in the Dutch Grand Prix last year when he missed a tree by four inches, after blowing a tyre at 120 miles an hour.

Singapore Free Press 21.6.61

ONE BAD INJURY, MANY CRASHES
Imitating Moss Is Deadly As Race Drivers Find Out

By JIM HUNT
Star Staff Writer

Mosport—The 20th century version of the dance of death — in polite circles they prefer to call it an automobile race — got its tribal ritual underway here yesterday with Stirling Moss in his accustomed role as chief witch-doctor.

Until the short, ordinary-looking Englishman checked into the race-200 race, there was about as much excitement here as is normal in the backwoods country where the Mosport track is situated. But once the 31-year old Moss bid the beautiful California airline stewardess, his lady friend, a fond adieu and slipped into his bright blue racing overalls, the electric current was in the air and the dance was on for real.

It isn't so much what breathtaking manner but the effect it seems to have on others far less experienced in the art. Yesterday, in a mere practice run, it produced one serious crash, a half dozen minor ones and numerous near misses.

Richard Austin, a 21-year-old from Toronto, was caught in the spirit of Moss as he took his car out for trial spin. He got to the second curve before manville hospital and then moved to Toronto General. His injuries today were reported as not serious but he will remain in hospital for observation.

Bill McDonald, also of Toronto, lost a wheel as he went into a corner but walked away without a scratch. Milt Wright of Orillia spun off the track and damaged his car but escaped personal injury.

took CBC radio man Bob McGregor for a spin to record an interview. Holding the mike in one hand and driving with the other, the English ace came close to the track record of 1.47 he was to shatter a couple of hours later.

Moss was the whole show yesterday and probably will be today. Fans flocked around him for autographs, gasped when

Toronto Daily Star 24.6.61

Webbair

Webbair was run by John Webb Air Services of Brompton Road, London. As an example of prices charged, flights to the Monaco GP, including hotel accommodation and "the best spectator tickets" could cost 29½ guineas (£30.97). "All inclusive: Champagne meals, complimentary drinks and cigarettes, served by special Webbair hostesses during flight." John Webb would later become a senior figure in British motor sport, running the Grovewood circuits including Brands Hatch.

JULY

Calendar

2	French GP, Reims – ret'd in 1.5 Lotus-Climax 18/21
8	British Empire Trophy, Silverstone, UK – (InterContinental race) 1st in 2.5 Cooper-Climax T53P; GT race – 1st in Ferrari 250GT SWB
15	British GP, Aintree – ret'd in Lotus-Climax 18/21, took over & disqualified in Jack Fairman 4WD Ferguson-Climax P99 (Fairman received push-start after pit stop)
23	Solitude GP, Stuttgart, Germany – ret'd in UDT/Laystall 1.5 Lotus-Climax 18/21

The first day of July was a Saturday and Stirling relaxed all day, which was a pretty unusual occurrence if not unique!

The French Grand Prix, which took place on the old road circuit outside Reims, was another frustrating one for Stirling, though it began well. "Had a fabulous start and followed the Ferraris. Gained quite a lot, then lost it due to others having Baghetti help them. Then rear (rt) brake pipe broke due to a stone. Lost 12 mins plus. On again. Followed [Phil] Hill, he spun and hit me! That was that. I got 7,900 with high 5th behind Clark (164 mph). P. Hill was waved to help Bag, he slowed and they all pissed past him! Ha Ha. Flew off + Lionel at 8pm. London, food with David H. Saw Herb and bed at 2.30."

In July, Stirling was quoted as saying that Canada's new circuit at Mosport Park "is the finest course of its length (2½ miles) in the world with the possible exception of Laguna Seca and Monaco. It is a case of concentration all the time, even the straight being a series of switch-backs guaranteed to catch out the unwary."

After a full day of work, he "met Maria Theresa (Terry) Shaw and saw *The Irregular Verb to Love* (EX). Food and bed at 2am."

Mid-week was spent working and on the Tuesday he saw Carolann and on the Wednesday he went out with Judy Carne again.

On Thursday, Stirling's mood was not improved

From left: Taffy von Trips, Jo Bonnier, John Surtees, SM, Jimmy Clark and Tony Brooks

Circuits

Moss on: REIMS

"A very unrewarding circuit. You would get in a slip stream and that could help tremendously. Of course, I cheated to get a fast time. I went up the escape road on the last bend and this enabled me to regain the circuit and approach the startline at a higher speed for a fast lap. But really not a drivers' circuit, so therefore, not what I would call very inspiring."

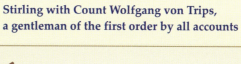

Stirling with Count Wolfgang von Trips,
a gentleman of the first order by all accounts

 ### French Grand Prix

The high speed nature of the Reims course leant itself to slip-streaming and in practice Stirling managed to follow von Trips for an entire lap which he reckoned gained him around three seconds over what he could have achieved without the tow. For this race, Ferrari had drafted in a fourth driver, a young Italian who had little experience but had already tasted success at the Syracuse and Naples non-Championship races. This was his first Grande Epreuve and he was given the slightly less powerful 60° engined shark-nose Ferrari.

Young Giancarlo Baghetti, in this fourth Ferrari, and Bruce McLaren had a rather nasty surprise during practice. As they shot down the Thillois straight, they came across a French farmer who had got on to the circuit and was motoring steadily towards them in his Peugeot 403. First McLaren and then Baghetti had to take evading action and neither could make the hairpin and had to continue towards the city!

As we shall see, several drivers were stoned in this race!

With the three regular Ferrari drivers on the front row, and SM and Clark on the second, it was being said quite openly, apparently, that it was von Trips's turn to take the seemingly inevitable Ferrari victory. The starter, the infamous 'Toto' Roche, was known for the shambles he normally created. Roche had stated he would drop the flag at any moment after the 30 second board had been shown. The Brits had concocted the idea of ignoring his flag but waiting until a co-conspirator dropped another flag moments later. It did not happen but all were kept on their toes as the 30 second board appeared five seconds after the minute board, and he dropped the flag and fled just 14 seconds after the minute board!

As the front row Ferraris surged away, Stirling briefly held third place on the first lap and again a few laps later. On his second he had posted a lap 2.1 seconds faster than Phil Hill and this would prove to be the fastest of the race. Initially there was a gap behind Stirling to a group of cars jockeying for position and including Baghetti. Ironically, the opportunity for slip-streaming which had so helped SM in practice, now worked against him because Baghetti, as Stirling noted in his diary, pulled the pursuing group up to him.

On lap 18 von Trips retired with overheating caused by a stone damaging his radiator. One down. A lap later Stirling stopped with, ironically, a stone having cut through a brake pipe. He lost five laps. Then he stopped again and lost more time but he now began slip-streaming Hill who was leading from Ginther. Then Clark who had been in the second group dropped back when a stone smashed his goggles. Phil Hill, trying to shake off Stirling, spun and they made contact, Hill losing time and dropping to 10th.

Amazing to relate but then the third invincible works Ferrari, Ginther's example, succumbed to lack of oil pressure. So now, for Ferrari, it all hinged on young Baghetti who did a superb job to hold off Gurney and Bonnier, winning it by yards and becoming the first driver ever to achieve victory in his very first Championship race. Alas Stirling had had to retire after Hill hit him.

Stirling's frustrating Formula One season continued at Reims for the French Grand Prix

1961

by having to get up rather early. "Up at 7.30 and to LAP to meet Norm. NOT THERE. The bastard. Work and to Silverstone. Practised the Cooper. Oversteered. Dropped the back wishbone. 35/38 tyres. Car still not too good. Alf put a high ratio in !X! 6,400 max."

Surtees	1.34.2
Moss	1.34.6
McLaren	1.34.6
Brooks	1.35.8
Hill G	1.36.4
Brabham	1.36.8 Vanwall

Stirling was practising for the forthcoming British Empire Trophy meeting at Silverstone at which he would be driving the InterContinental Cooper fitted with the 2½ litre engine and the Rob Walker/Dick Wilkins Ferrari 250GT SWB.

Friday: "Up at 9 and to circuit. Practised Cooper ICF. Get 6,600 on straight and 6,800 in 4th. Tried hard but slower than Surtees. (Bruce says he [Surtees] did 1.33.8 not 1.33.0!X!) Later Ferrari arrived. Wrong axle and tyres but did FTD. Oil pressure drops on braking. Stooged around and then to Castle Rd. Food with Celia and chatted. Bed at 12.30."

	FIc	G.T	
*Surtees	1.33.0	1.47.6	SM
SM	1.33.6	1.49.0	Sal – E-type
Bruce	1.33.8	1.49.6	Hill
Jack	1.33.8		
Innes	1.35.0		
*1.33.8			

Saturday was to turn out rather well with a productive day's work after an inauspicious beginning. "Race. My clutch broke on the line! I had a fair start and took the lead at Copse and led to finish. FTD at 1.36.4. Dampish. Car fair. GT race and same. Won by 22 secs from Bruce. Roy and Graham blew up. Won GP by 52 secs odd." Tring, where his parents lived and farmed, was conveniently between Silverstone and London. Staying there overnight, he worked on the design for his new London house on Sunday. That evening he went back up to London and saw JC.

On Monday he had a satisfactory check-up with his doctor, worked during the day and took Carolann, plus Betty and Keith Ballisat, out for a meal. Tuesday saw him taking part in the BBC television programme called 'The Asian Club', a pioneering discussion series which was broadcast from 1953 until 1961. On Wednesday, he took Freddy Ross to lunch. He then worked until 9.30pm when he popped into the 'Wheel' and met Jenny, Harriet and Terry.

On Thursday he attempted to fly up to Manchester as the British Grand Prix was taking

Left: Is Stirling looking with envy at the 1961 Ferrari? Being the under-dog with a chance for brilliance to overcome sheer power is one thing but having no chance whatsoever is another

Below: Superb Gunther Molter shot of the start at Reims, taken presumably from the Dunlop Bridge. Though the bridge has gone, the pits and stands are still intact to this day. This shot rather sums up the season

 The Irregular Verb to Love

'The Irregular Verb to Love' was written by Hugh and Margaret Williams and opened at the Leeds Grand Theatre and Opera house in April, 1961, transferring to London. It starred Joan Greenwood, John Standing, Diana Lambert and Derek Nimmo. "A typical light comedy of the period written by actors. Some pretensions to social comment and some laughs," says Ian McKellen who appeared as the hippie son of the household in a 1962 production.

Left: Is Stirling employing a little gamesmanship behind Phil Hill, who was leading Stirling by five laps after the Englishman's pit stop? Never one to give up, he was slip-streaming the race leader. Below: Whether it was pressure from Stirling or the slippery surface, is not clear but Hill threw the race away when he spun

A trio of Facel Vegas at their home GP

TURNING POINT. —The turning point of the race came when Phil Hill's Ferrari spun on Thillois and Moss rammed his front putting himself out and causing the Ferrari to stall and take several minutes to start. Here are the two cars seconds before impact.

July — Stirling Moss Scrapbook

1961

place at Aintree that weekend. He was at London Airport by 9am. "Flew up by Charter 'cos BEA cancelled due to cross-winds! 2nd Practice. Car overgeared. 123mph str [straight]. 126 past pits. Met Barbara Livingstone (Chidwell 5xxx). Bed at 2.30."

Trips	)	
Phil	)	1.58.8
Ritchie	)	
Joe	)	
SM	)	
Brooks	)	1.59.9

Friday: "Up late. 1st practice wet. Tried Fergy. FTD and in wet it was faster than others! 2nd and Lotus felt good. Met Barbara. Bed at 12.pm."

Saturday, July 15: "Had a fair start. Lay 4th to 3 Ferraris and then to 2nd and right behind Trips. Ginther then passed me. Engine felt a bit off. Later back brakes broke. Retired. Took over Fergy (already disqualified due to push). Lapped as fast as Ferrari. Later black-flagged due to Ferrari and Cooper !X! Caught 7.40 from Manchester + Ken and Jenny. Met by Norm and took Jenny to Basingstoke. 36 and chatted and bed at 2.30am."

Stirling worked Sunday morning, and then Val Pirie cooked lunch for a small bunch of chums with SM noting the food was excellent. He then went "to Graham's for Damon's Christening. Back, work till 8.30. Collected JC and to Beachcomber with Norm. 36 and bed at 2am." This was, of course, future World Champion, Damon Hill.

Monday was devoted to working, taking a Porsche Super 90 to Brands Hatch, working on a book for David Phipps and seeing "*Temptation Island* (F) with Norm. On to Enfant Terrible and collected JC and Janet. Food at 55 and to Winstons. Bed at 3.30am."

He was photographed for Vogue next day and in the evening he collected "Jenny W. and saw *Mort Sahl* (G). Food and bed at 2.15am." The following night, after a hard day at the office, he dined with Norm and VP at the Caprice, following which he packed for he was about to go on his travels again.

On Thursday, 20th he flew to Paris, picking up the Facel Vega. "Gearbox bad again. Slipping. On to Germany." Next day he began practising for the non-Championship Solitude Grand Prix in which he was driving the UDT/Laystall Lotus 18/21 hybrid.

"Up and off to Stuttgart. Checked in and practice. Car fair. 6mph down and gearbox bad. Food with Inge. Met Audrey's Dad and Norm up TV tower. Bed at 1am."

Moss fights shy of super car

By KEITH COLLING

STIRLING MOSS yesterday ruled himself out as a driver of the revolutionary Ferguson 2½-litre in tomorrow's 150-mile British Empire Trophy meeting at Silverstone.

He took the sleek, green car pioneered by the late tractor tycoon on a four-lap public debut at 108.1 m.p.h. on the Northants circuit.

Then he said: "I'm going to stick to a car I already know." He will be at the wheel of a Cooper.

Veteran 38-year-old driver Jack Fairman put the Ferguson through its paces over 15 laps in the first practice period for the big race.

Moss scored the fastest lap time with 111.3 m.p.h. The Ferguson, with Fairman, did 107.3.

Noel Newsome, Ferguson research director, was delighted. He promised that if the new car came up to expectations it may be entered for the British Grand Prix at Aintree next week.

Daily Mail 7.7.61

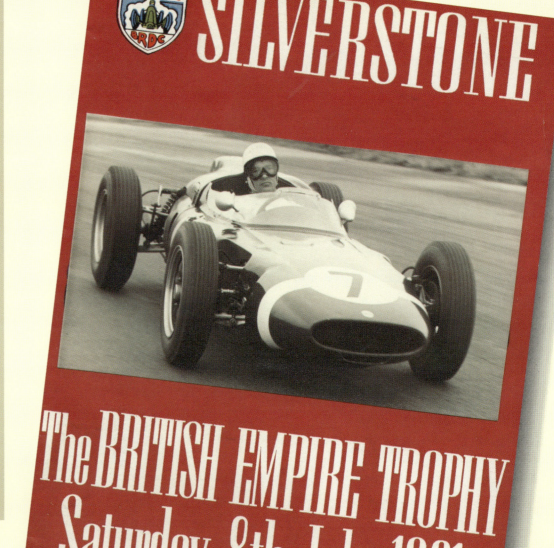

Silverstone Practice

The Ferrari 250GT arrived late on Friday afternoon, having left Modena on Thursday morning being driven by David Joliffe who then worked for Rob Walker. In 1989 Joliffe, writing in Supercar Classics, remembered the drive as one of the most memorable of his life. "Incidentally, that dash to Silverstone ended with a vivid reminder of just how good Moss was. The rest of the team had left, thinking I wasn't going to make it, but Moss decided to have a go at practising. We chucked my luggage out, pumped the tyres up a bit, and off he went… The opposition included drivers as good as Graham Hill, but Moss needed only three laps to get pole position. My mind's eye can still see him coming through Woodcote in a balanced drift, illustrating just how forgiving that car was if you had the balls to set it up a bit sideways."

According to Autosport, the car was fitted with rain tyres and this meant SM could only do three laps at a time before they overheated. "Also the car was understeering considerably and oversteering when Moss backed off for a corner."

WILL THIS BE THE PERFECT CAR?

By NORMAN AUBURY

Stirling Moss takes the new Ferguson, at speed, around Club Corner

Daily Sketch 7.7.61

ON the shimmering tarmac at Silverstone yesterday Harry Ferguson's ten-year-old dream came true.

In the 12 months since he died his "disciples" have turned their attention from the completed "people's" saloon car to the sleek, dark-blue racer which will make its debut in the 150-mile British Empire Trophy race on Saturday.

Driven by Stirling Moss and Jack Fairman, the new Ferguson astonished the experts yesterday by lapping at over 106 m.p.h on its first outing. The car was only five seconds slower than the lap record for this 2¾ mile circuit.

Afterwards Stirling said: "The car is extremely stable—almost too stable for a racing car.

"It demands an entirely new type of driving."

I do not believe that the 2½ litre Climax engined Fergusor can hope to win on Saturday.

But if the car finishes this fast and furious test, big firms throughout Britain and Europe will have to think again about taking up the Ferguson experimental transmission, designed to cut out skids.

In theory the remarkable four wheel drive should produce the perfect car—the herald, perhaps, of a great new era of super-safe motoring.

On Saturday we shall see.

Don't be fooled by the clear blue sky; Silverstone is often one of the coldest places on earth!

British Empire Trophy Race

Silverstone's main event at its July 8th race meeting was for single-seaters run to the InterContinental formula. Considerable interest was caused in practice by the revolutionary four-wheel-drive Ferguson which was to make its racing début. Fitted with a 2½ litre FPF Climax power unit, the Fergie was driven by both Jack Fairman, who had previously been doing much of the development driving, and Stirling in practice.

Stirling chose to stick with his Rob Walker Cooper but could not match John Surtees's time and started second fastest. He was then delayed leaving the line as he struggled to get into first gear as a result of the clutch breaking. However, he was soon heading the pack.

Shortly after the start, "Jack Fairman did some involuntary cross-country motoring when he drove on to the grass to avoid running into Salvadori," reported Autoport which is a delightful comment considering Ferguson were best known for making agricultural tractors!

The slippery conditions suited Stirling, who was pulling away at a rate of two seconds a lap and would have suited the Ferguson had it not stopped on the second lap with gear selection problems. "Stirling Moss, the supreme artist, was drawing away all the time from Surtees," stated Autosport, "and was changing gear by judging r.p.m., his car being completely clutchless."

The magazine had entitled their article "The Magic of Moss" and the magician lapped all but Surtees and Graham Hill in second and third places respectively.

July

Stirling Moss Scrapbook

1961

Dan	4.01.5
Joe	4.03.1
Hans	4.04.3
Taylor T	4.05.9
Bruce	4.06.1
Jim	4.06.5
Barth	4.07.3
Jack B	4.07.4
SM	4.07.6

"Took about 15 laps to learn circuit."

Saturday: "Up late and shopped. Practice. Gears better. 2nd a fraction too high. 3rd too low. Later to Gunther Molter's party. Bed at 12.30am."

Gurney	4.01.5
Bonnier	4.01.5
McLaren	4.02.0
Ireland	4.02.6
SM	4.03.7
Hans	4.03.8
Jack B	4.04.4
Clark	4.04.4

The crowd on Sunday was enormous. "300,000 people. Race. Had a fair start from 2nd row. Then jammed in 2nd. Lay 7th then 8th. Finally transmission broke (Hell). Did 4.01. Couldn't slipstream due to gearbox. Get 7,600. Prize giving after food with Inge Max and her friends. Left at 10.20pm. Stopped at Limberg at 12.15. Bed at 1.45am."

SM was up at 7.30am next morning and set off for "Bonn/Koln airport. Caught 11.50 to LAP via Amsterdam. Norm to Milano. Met by Val. Work and later to food with Freddy and met JC. Bed at 1.30am."

On Tuesday, he worked all day till 11pm! During the day, he lunched with Ronnie Riley to discuss a film for BP. He also saw someone from Ackles and Pollock, the tubing company who became part of Tube Investments. This was to do with the new house. Ironically, he then went to Ken Gregory's "new place and then at 11.30 food with Judy and Janet. Bed at 1.30am."

Stirling did an interview with CBS on Wednesday. "Lunch with Peter Easton. Later met man re. seat belts. Work till 8pm. Jenny's for cocktails and then met Dave and Karen and later Jean Long. Food at the Village and on to Blue Angel. Bed at 3.45am."

Stirling's social life continued apace. On Thursday he saw Veronica and Val Tetley. After a BRP directors' meeting on Friday he took Carolann and Jane Coles to the Candlelight Room, retiring at 3.15am. On Saturday, Ken's birthday, he took Judy to see "Peggy Lee G. She was drunkish. Bed at 3.30." Sunday saw him working on drawings, presumably for the new house, and a Pony Autoplane, whatever that may be!

Silverstone GT Race

In the GT race, Stirling came up against the brand new E-types for the first time. They had won first time out at Oulton Park and were generally beating the Ferraris and Astons. However, it was a different matter when the Jaguars came up against 'the genius' in the very latest competition 250GT Ferrari. Moss took the lead from the start and the as-yet undeveloped E-types had an off day with Graham Hill retiring and Roy Salvadori slowing. Bruce McLaren upheld Coventry honours by finishing second ahead of the Davison Aston Martin and Whitehead Ferrari.

What a handsome car the big Cooper looks in these shots and how different Stirling's season might have been if the Championship had not changed to the smaller-engined, less demanding 'roller-skates'!

Re-united at Silverstone with the unique Fangio - great team mates in 1955, great rivals until the Argentinian's retirement and always great friends based on tremendous mutual respect

THE MOTOR July 12 1961

Ferodo First

British Empire Trophy – Silverstone

1st Cooper Stirling Moss

2nd Cooper J. Surtees **3rd B.R.M.** G. Hill

And first in every other race

Results subject to official confirmation

fit race-proved
FERODO
Anti-Fade Brake Linings
Disc Brake Pads

FERODO LIMITED · CHAPEL-EN-LE-FRITH · *A Member of the Turner & Newall Organisation*

'Secret Weapon'

For the British Empire Trophy race at Silverstone, Rob Walker had a 'secret weapon' according to George Bishop writing in one of the British newspapers. "Rob Walker, the Scotch whisky millionaire who owns the cars Moss drives, used a walkie-talkie radio to get instructions to Moss from the pits.

"Moss was thus able to keep his eyes on the track and concentrate on his driving as he took Woodcote Corner at well over 100mph instead of having to look for pit signals."

July — Stirling Moss Scrapbook

1961
Stirling Moss Scrapbook

On the last day of July, he was up early because Shirlee called. After much work, he took Jenny to see a Danny Kaye film, had food at the Village and was in bed at 2.30.

The new E-types had been doing rather well in their first few races ... until they came up against a certain S. Moss who broke his own GT lap record by 11.2 secs. Salvadori, in the Coombs E-type BUY 1, which is actually shielded by the Moss Ferrari in the start photo above, led the E-type charge until he had problems and slowed up

Stirling Moss Arrives

Stirling Moss, his arms loaded with luggage, leaves a Starways plane to-day at Liverpool Airport on his arrival for the British Grand Prix at Aintree on Saturday.

Liverpool Echo 13.7.61

Reader's Letter

In mid-July a letter appeared in the pages of *Autosport* from a Mr. B.W.M. Harris. Seemingly, people had been comparing Moss and Brabham, the reigning World Champion. After a variety of comments, Mr. Harris concluded with: "Stirling Moss has proved beyond all doubt that he is at home in practically 'any' type of car, on 'any' type of circuit and in 'any' type of weather; this cannot be claimed on behalf of Brabham. Moss has even come second in the Monte Carlo Rally and has one of the only two Coupes des Alpes en Or – his versatility and ability may not be questioned.

"No-one denies Jack Brabham his Championships, but surely no one would claim that he is 'the' World's road-racing driver; this honour 'must' fall to Stirling Moss."

MOSS LOSES CHANCE TO BE WORLD CHAMP

By TOM WISDOM

STIRLING MOSS has been robbed of his chance of winning the world championship this year because other countries are cancelling races they agreed to run.

Moss, four times second in the world championship, leads the new Intercontinental Formula championship this year following his brilliant victory in the British Empire Trophy race at Silverstone on Saturday.

CANCELLED

But Moss relies on the big-car races. And the International Automobile Clubs which runs the championship insists there must be at least FIVE big-car races to decide the champion.

Britain, Italy, Belgium and the U.S.A. agreed to organise these Intercontinental races.

Now Italy's Ferrari team says it is not interested and the two races planned for Monza and Turin have been cancelled.

The United States has dropped its event. And the Belgium race is unlikely to be held.

So although Moss has won the first two Intercontinental Grand Prix events—at Silverstone in May and on Saturday—the requisite five races will not be held.

Moss will be robbed of the first Intercontinental championship, but it was a moral world champion's day on Saturday.

He drove his Cooper to victory without using the clutch, which failed at the start.

This is part of any racing driver's skill—changing gear without the clutch. But none can do it better than Moss.

RESULTS. — British Empire Trophy: 1, Moss, Cooper, 104.58 m.p.h.; 2, John Surtees, Cooper; 3, G. Hill, BRM; 4, B. McLaren, Cooper; 5, J. Clark, Lotus;

Daily Herald 10.7.61

HOW TO COPE WITHOUT A CLUTCH...
by STIRLING MOSS
in an interview with JOHN HALL

I HOPE that the news of my winning the British Empire Trophy at Silverstone will not encourage young enthusiasts to try clutchless driving in their family saloons.

If they do there will be a lot of churned-up gearboxes around. And there are few more expensive noises in motoring than the stripping of gears.

However, if your clutch does pack up while you are driving, here is what you do. Take it gently; delicacy of touch and a sympathetic feeling for your engine are essential.

Say you are driving along when the clutch goes and you want to change down. Ease the gear lever into neutral. Rev the engine up until you hear the note that you judge it would make at that speed in the gear you want to engage. Then firmly but smoothly ease into the next gear.

Wait for it

Changing up, you pause in neutral until the engine revs die down to the corresponding speed.

Learning to recognise the exact pitch of the engine at which to engage the next gear is something that cannot be taught. The driver has to learn from experience.

The technique is part of a racing driver's stock-in-trade and this is not the first race I've won without a clutch.

But in day-to-day motoring I use my clutch all the time.

Daily Mail 10.7.61

Stirling Moss ...

FREDDY ROSS

"Freddy Ross was very much into show business. She was not my type but a very good friend. I'd go to first nights with her. She later married Tony Hancock [the great comedian]. We still see her and she is our son's godmother."

BRITISH GRAND PRIX
STARTING GRID
(First 7 rows)

P. HILL (Ferrari) 1:58.8	GINTHER (Ferrari) 1:58.8	BONNIER (Porsche) 1:58.8
VON TRIPS (Ferrari) 1:58.9		MOSS (Lotus) 1:59.0
BROOKS (BRM) 1:59.0	IRELAND (Lotus) 1:59.2	CLARK (Lotus) 1:59.2
BRABHAM (Cooper) 1:59.4		
G. HILL (BRM) 2:00.0	GURNEY (Porsche) 2:00.2	SURTEES (Cooper) 1:59.6
		SALVADORI (Cooper) 2:00.8
MC LAREN (Cooper) 2:01.0		LEWIS (Cooper) 2:01.0
GREGORY (Cooper) 2:01.4	H. TAYLOR (Lotus) 2:01.8	DE BEAUFORT (Porsche) 2:02.0

July — Stirling Moss Scrapbook

1961

Ferguson car races into history with Moss at the wheel

By TOM WISDOM

THE revolutionary Ferguson four-wheel drive car with non-skid brakes made motor history yesterday when it returned the fastest time during practice for today's British Grand Prix at Aintree.

With Stirling Moss at the wheel, it lapped at 88.82 m p h on a wet track.

None of the other competitors could match this time.

Yet they included the four-man Italian Ferrari team, new star John Surtees and the world champion Jack Brabham, all of whom were faster in the dry conditions on Thursday.

So the Ferguson, brain child of the late Freddy Dixon, race-driver and engineer, has at last proved itself.

Its four-wheel drive system and the advanced non-skid brakes showed to tremendous advantage on the Aintree course.

STIRLING MOSS
Big chance today

Orthodox

But, despite its outstanding performance, Moss has decided to drive his more orthodox Lotus in today's 225-mile race — sponsored by the *Daily Mirror* — which is the fifth round of the world championship. The Ferguson will be driven by Jack Fairman.

On the front row at the start today will be two Ferraris, driven by championship leaders Phil Hill, of America, and Count Von Trips, of Germany, and a German Porsche with Swedish champion Jo Bonnier

Moss is on the second row. This race is vitally important to him as he is lying equal third in the world championship and a win today could put him in the lead.

If it rains, his mastery of a slow car on a wet track could defeat the all-conquering Ferraris

Daily Herald 15.7.61

Circuits

Moss on: AINTREE

"Aintree is quite hard on the brakes. Aintree is actually a lot more difficult than it might first appear. But not difficult in the way Spa was, because there are not many high speed corners, but it was the brakes. It was so hard on the brakes and so you had to try and scrub off as much speed as you could."

To say it was wet for the British GP at Aintree is a rather pointless statement! The conditions suited Stirling, though, and as can be seen he is already amongst the Ferraris and Bonnier's Porsche as they leave the line

British Grand Prix

The Ferraris of Phil Hill and Ritchie Ginther occupied the front row with the Porsche of Jo Bonnier. Second row consisted of Wolfgang von Trips and Stirling, who was in the Walker Lotus but had tried the Ferguson in practice. In one wet session, in the Ferguson he was four seconds faster than the next quickest.

The race began in appalling conditions which suited SM. Gregor Grant, writing an amusing account in Autosport, stated that "Lewis's stores in Liverpool completely sold out of plastic macs. John Bolster looked as if he was going sailing instead of doing a B.B.C. motor race commentary from the pits. I thought of asking him to write the report for Watersport, our sister journal."

The three Ferraris took up their customary position with Stirling in pursuit. "On the sixth lap, Moss splashed passed Ginther to take third place." Four laps later and showing his consummate class, SM took second from Phil Hill. He closed up on von Trips and the two pulled away from Hill and Ginther. "Programmes were waved and the crowd cheered like mad as Moss tried everything he knew to take von Trips." Stirling was closing under braking but the power of the V6 Ferrari kept the German just out of reach. Fairman was going steadily in the Ferguson but was suffering from misfiring. He pitted and had to be push-started to get going again.

"Stirling Moss was showing sheer genius, and time and again came up to von Trips's rear wheels, to the great excitement of the crowd. It was very definitely Moss versus the Ferraris... Stirling definitely had Ferrari bothered, for he was continually snapping at the heels of von Trips. He must have been driving by radar, for he couldn't have been able to see anything at all in the clouds of spray produced by the flying Ferrari."

Then SM made a rare mistake. He spun 360° on a deep puddle but held it brilliantly to continue without contact and a loss of just 10 seconds. Then the rain stopped and the track dried, allowing the Ferraris to exert their superior power. Gradually they relegated Stirling to fourth and then sadly he pulled in to retire with the left rear calliper bridge brake pipe broken.

While the stewards were debating whether the Ferguson should be disqualified for its push-start, Stirling took it over and began to circulate rapidly. Cooper and Ferrari protested the car and SM was brought in, his race run. A DNF (Did Not Finish) was rotten luck after all that hard work.

In the appalling conditions, Stirling sailed passed the Ferraris of first Ginther and then Hill, in whose wash he is seen above!

1961

Stirling Moss Scrapbook

Drivers

Moss on: TAFFY von TRIPPS
SM: "I always think of Taffy more really doing things with Porsche. He was another good, but nondescript driver."
PP: "Adequate rather than inspired?"
SM: "Yes."

SOLITUDE

July — **Stirling Moss Scrapbook**

Drivers

Moss on: DAN GURNEY

"Dan Gurney was, I think, was one of the best Americans we have ever seen over here. Dan had a great rapport with the car, a great understanding, he was easy on the car, he was very fast and very fit. I co-drove with him because he was that good. There weren't many other people who I would have liked to go with who were as fast as him. You see, apart from being fast, he was also reasonably light on the car – he was good."

The non-Championship F1 race at Solitude was a triumph for Stirling's mate, Innes Ireland who fought off the two works Porsches to win by a tenth of a second. Interestingly, he gambled on using the new 'Green Spot' wet weather tyres in the dry. For Stirling, it was not a good event. After a very average practice, he had transmission problems before retiring while in midfield. The body language in this shot says it all!

Ferrari withdraw from Grand Prix

Moss driving Lotus

STUTTGART (West Germany).— The Italian Ferrari firm have withdrawn from the German Grand Prix formula one event here on Sunday. The firm gave no reason for the withdrawal, but sources said Ferrari were saving their fast rear-engined machines and drivers for the Grand Prix of Europe at Nürburgring on August 6.

The Ferrari decision means that Wolfgang von Trips, who leads the world championship placings, and the American driver, Phil Hill, will not take part in Sunday's race. The event does not count towards the world championship.

Stirling Moss will drive a four-cylinder Lotus of the private U.T.D. Laystall racing team.

COOPERS ENTERED

Two other top competitors are Jack Brabham, of Australia, and Bruce McLaren, of New Zealand. They will drive Coopers entered by the English factory.

Another British factory team, Lotus, will enter three rear-engined cars, with some minor modifications on last year's models. The drivers are the two Scots, Innes Ireland and Jim Clark and Trevor Taylor.—A.P.

The Scotsman 22.7.61

AUGUST

Calendar

- **6** European GP (German GP), Nürburgring, Germany – 1st in Lotus-Climax 18/21
- **7** Brands Hatch, Kent, UK – Peco Trophy – 1st in Ferrari 250GT SWB; Guards Trophy - (InterContinental race) – ret'd in 2.5 Cooper-Climax T53P
- **19** RAC Tourist Trophy, Goodwood, UK – 1st in Ferrari 250GT SWB
- **20** Karlskoga Kannonloppet, Sweden – 1st in 1.5 UDT/Laystall Lotus 18/21
- **26/27** Danish GP, Roskilde, Denmark – 1st in three heats and 1st on overall aggregate in UDT/Laystall 1.5 Lotus-Climax 18/21

The first weekend in August was to be a hectic one but rather successful. The German Grand Prix was to take place on the Sunday and, as it was a Bank Holiday in the UK, there was a major race meeting at Brands Hatch on the Monday.

As a consequence, Stirling was at Brands practising on Wednesday with the Inter-Continental Cooper and 2735, the Wilkins/Walker 250GT Ferrari. "Used I.C. Cooper with 35/38 lbs. Get 6,600, 6,700. FTD Also Ferrari. I get 6,750rpm, not 7,500!. Understeer and gears way off. Office and work. Saw joiner and then to food with Herb." The joiner was presumably seen in connection with the house project.

SM	1.37.4
Bruce	1.38.8
Surtees	1.38.8
Hill	1.38.2 Etc.

| Ferrari SM | 1.52.8 |
| Roy | 1.53.8 |

Stirling awoke Thursday morning, after a bad night, suffering from neck ache. Late afternoon he flew to Cologne, picked up the Facel and drove to Altencher. Up early next morning, he began the day sketching. Whether this was still life or plans for the

Huschke von Hanstein

Baron Huschke von Hanstein was Rennleiter and Public Relations Director of Porsche. He raced pre- and post-war, joining Porsche in the early fifties and selling examples to his aristocratic friends. He built the PR department and was particularly effective at getting the Porsche name into the media, often with the famous. He created the image that Porsche ownership made one special by association.

Evi Butz Gurney (she married Dan in 1969) was his PA and later head of the Porsche Press Dept. She wrote in a biography, "The elegant parties he and Ursula [his wife] gave before the Solitude Race every July became legendary. From Stirling Moss to Sir Jack Brabham, from Gunther Sachs to the King of Spain, from David E. Davis to Bernard Cahier, everybody who was anybody in the motor racing world gathered to sip Camparis on hot summer nights at the Kraeherwald."

Stirling goes filming at the Ring. Slightly different from the size of cameras today!

DUNCAN MEASOR previews the German Grand Prix

Britain's chances slim in Battle of the Ring

SWALLOW'S Tail and Fox's Throat ... Schwalbenschwanz and Fuchsrohre. The sorcery of Macbeth seems to have a rhythmic bond with the witchery of the Nurburgring where what may be the greatest Grand Prix of the year will be fought on Sunday.

It will attract the biggest crowd of the season—up to 500,000 are anticipated—and the most bitter struggle the new formula has produced will rage around the colourful spots I named above.

For the "Ring, winding for 14 tortuous miles through the Eifel mountains, demands real mastery at the wheel to stay in front when the suspension is dancing a cha-cha and a driver must spin the steering wheel like a lifeboat helmsman in a hurricane.

It is a track where drivers started using a ditch to save split seconds at one corner. Now the ditch has been cemented to make the "ear-holing" less perilous.

It is a track where an error can send a car plunging into a ravine or through a dense forest.

BUT in German eyes this week it is the familiar battle-scarred arena in which a new German champion could win for the first time since Caracciola blasted round in a Mercedes-Benz at 75.18 m.p.h. in 1939. A car from this same works did win in 1954 (at 82.77 m.p.h.), but the driver was the great Argentinian, Juan Fangio.

Now Count Wolfgang von Trips leads the world championship; two of the season's classic races have fallen to him and his Ferrari. There is no race he would rather win than the German Grand Prix.

It will be no lonely journey far ahead of the howling pack. The silver bullets of the German Porsche team are as suitable for the "Ring" as are their brilliant drivers, Dan Gurney and Joakim Bonnier.

There is, unfortunately for the British cars, a straight of about a mile and plenty of other sections where superior power will leave them behind.

Is there then any hope for a British victory?

As with any Grand Prix so far this year, the answer must be a regrettably faint pinning of faith on skill over power—with a chance that the new Climax V8 engine in Jack Brabham's car will be the answer to the Ferrari and Porsche machines.

On this circuit we could see Tony Brooks doing well in the B.R.M., Brabham given a chance to "hang out" his Cooper's tail, and Innes Ireland perhaps demonstrating as he did at Solitude how a Lotus can keep the Porsches at bay.

BUT, as always, our brightest prospect of all must be Stirling Moss in the Lotus. In sports and Grand Prix cars he has driven so fast on this circuit that he has been untroubled when pit stops have left him swamped by the passing traffic.

In the last Grand Prix at Nurburgring (in 1958) he came past with such a lead after the first lap that as the seconds ticked by a suspicion grew in the pits that everyone else had retired.

That race was won by Tony Brooks in a Vanwall at 90.35 m.p.h., which was a race record. The fastest lap, which is still the record, was put up by Moss with 92.9 m.p.h. (9min. 9.2sec.).

On that day the leading Ferrari (and first foreign car) was in fourth place. Its driver? Wolfgang von Trips.

Stirling Moss and the Lotus — Britain's best hope for the German Grand Prix. Our picture shows the 2½-litre car.

Manchester Eve. News 4.8.61

Moss shatters lap record

Stirling Moss broke world champion Jack Brabham's lap record of 94.82 mph at Brands Hatch, Kent, yesterday when he went round the circuit at 97.94 mph while practising for Monday's race.

Daily Herald 3.8.61

1961

house, we cannot now be sure! "...then to circuit. 1st practice. Car feels fair, engine not good. 7,000 rpm. Changed axle and 2nd period. Got 7,500 (129) (BRMs 137mph!) Car shaky and loose. Did 9.10 standing lap. Reckon 9.06 is max. Took Innes round for a lap in Porsche and then BP cocktails. Hotel and food with Li and bed at 1am."

P Hill	8.55.2
Jo	9.04.8
Dan	9.06.6
Clark	9.08.1
SM	9.10.5
Brooks	9.10.5
Jack	9.10.6
Surtees	9.11.2

Saturday: "Up earlyish and circuit practice. Used D12. Got 7,600 (131mph) Did BP TV film. Only did one flying lap. Stooged around. Huske [sic] not polite re Carla as passenger for practice run. He had the track 3 – 4pm. Later to hotel and food and drawings and bed at 1.15am. Friends of Walt came. Helen and Ingrid." The Huschke referred to is Huschke von Hanstein, the Porsche PR chief. Walt was an old American friend called Walt Monaco.

Jack	9.01.4	8 cyl
SM	9.01.7	D12
Hill	9.07.0	

Sunday was to be a special day in Stirling's remarkable career. "To circuit by 1pm. 500,000 people! !X! Race. I had a good start but Jack's 8 passed me, I tried to pass, he chopped me and then went off the road. Drama over Dunlop D12s. Told 8 laps max and danger of burst. Anyway I lead till end and had 1 mm left. Really drove hard. Flat out all over the place. Trips 2nd – 22 secs, then Phil. Prize giving at 9.35 and finished at 10.10pm. Off to Düsseldorf by 1.15. Waited 40 mins on an Autobahn and no move. Bed at 2am." Just as with Monaco, Stirling had held off the might of Ferrari through sheer driving skill on this most challenging of circuits.

He was up again after just five hours sleep and flew back to London. "Dad collected me at LAP at 11.00 and to Brands via 36. Race for G.T. 1st and LR [lap record]. Flc. Had a fair start and lay 2nd to Surtees. Could go faster. Jack passed so I speeded up and took lead. Later when + 6 secs, 4th gear broke. Later out and Dave and Karen and Judy."

Next morning Stirling was up early and went to London Airport. "Collected Shirlee. Home and work. Later we saw *Stop the World* (EX). Met Tommy, Jack and Cicely Sears. Food at 55 and bed at 2.30am." On same page, he wrote, "Had a press 'do' re Katy. Took delivery of the NSU."

On Wednesday, he worked till 8pm and then took

Moss on: NURBURGRING

"The Nürburgring is, I suppose, the greatest man-made circuit of all. There is something for everybody and that is the great thing about it. And the secret to the Ring is really that you do not need much in the way of brakes. You are relatively easy on the brakes, because there are so many places where you come over a brow and just roll back the throttle and then you accelerate again. There are 176 corners, of which you only probably take 100 because you roll one through to another. So a very rewarding circuit because of what you can do with a car."

 Circuits

No Television

The Germans had banned any live television transmission so those who could receive it had to rely on the BBC Light Programme, as it was called in those days, for live coverage of the race.

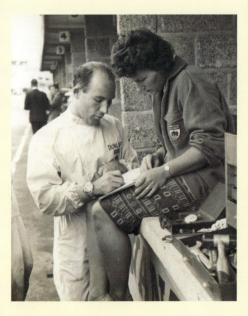

Tyre Choice

Innes Ireland had managed to brilliantly win the non-Championship Solitude GP in late July on Dunlop's new rain tyres and this may have been Stirling's inspiration to attempt the same. Also, the weather in the Eifel mountains was notoriously changeable and often inclement. Stirling had set his practice time on the super-sticky 'Green Spot' Dunlop D12s.

However, Alf Francis had cunningly painted out the green spots that identified them as the rain tyres so the other teams were unaware of their ruse. Indeed, not even the Dunlop technicians knew until Vic Barlow went round the pits the night before the race, checking all the cars.

"After he had okayed ours," Rob Walker once wrote, "Stirling said, 'What, with Green Spot?' and showed him how we had blacked this out. The Dunlop people were furious – their Sporting Director, Dick Jeffries, said it was a waste of time and money sending a specialist team to races if they were to be ignored."

Dunlop were worried about the temperatures building up and the tyres blowing out.

"Stirling had been very reluctant to tell me what he and Alf were up to because he knew I would worry about it, and he was right."

Stirling and Rob dined that night at the Hotel Lochmuhle and Walker tried to persuade SM that he already took enough risks without adding to them. However, Stirling felt it was "a calculated risk worth taking". He felt the Ferraris had a 15mph advantage on maximum speed and this was worth four seconds per lap on the main straight alone.

Even though there was a shower during the supporting GT race, Dunlop advised Ferrari to run with their dry tyres. Meanwhile, Cooper had been frantically trying to find a set of wets for Brabham's car but could only obtain suitable fronts. He, thus, started with a combination which was hardly ideal.

The story of the German GP in Stirling's diary makes fascinating reading and it was rare for him to write about a race in such detail. Once again, we see, "Really drove hard. Flat out all over the place". Is Stirling pointing at Jack's tyres in this shot (left)? Is he winding him up before the start?

1961

Shirlee to Tiddy Dolls. This was a delightful restaurant that occupied a whole block at one end of Shepherd Street. At the time of writing (2006) it was semi-derelict and presumably awaiting redevelopment, though its restaurant licence had just been renewed. "Work and bed at 2.30am."

Next day he had lunch with Sunday Times motoring correspondent and photographer Maxwell Boyd and worked on an article. He called at the Building Centre, no doubt doing a spot of research for the house design. In the evening he "took SA to see *No My Darling Daughter* (G). On to Candlelight Room. Bed at 1.15am."

On Friday SM took SA to Harrods and dined at the Savoy in the evening. Next day he was testing at Brands. "Tested BRP 1500 F1. Short circuit 52.8 (wet tyres) both cars. 61 suspension too high geared and Lacey engine. 6,900. 60 car 7,200 same revs. Also Ferrari. Town via Phipps and then saw *Ladies Man* (F). Food and bed at 3am." Clearly Stirling was comparing the 1960 Lotus 18 and the Lotus 18/21 with the 21's 1961 suspension.

On Monday Stirling was rudely awakened "due to road drilling. They also started doing the tanking at 42. Work till 7.30. Out and saw *One Over The Eight* (G). Food at Village plus Dave and Karen. Bed at 2am."

On Tuesday, August 15, "Called on Dad. E-type arrived. Work till 7.30 and then out with HJ and SA to Rib Room, on to Starlight Room and saw *Prince and the Showgirl* (F). Bed at 2.45am."

Next day SM called on Plyglass, in connection with the house, and then went to the White Elephant with SA.

That Thursday he took Shirlee to the airport and he headed "off to Goodwood in the E-type at 1.10. Arrived at 2.30. Practice [Ferrari]. Car is much better on 15" wheels x 700 and 15 x 600 than 16" and wear is a bit better, 22 laps to 20. Get 7,200 and 7,400. 45lbs f & r. Off and home. Packed, bath and took Jean to food at Beachcomber. Bed at 2am."

SM   1.34.8
Parkes   1.35.2
Roy S   1.36.2 etc.

The following day he went out in Jaguar's sensational new sports car which he had been loaned by the company. It is ironic that he would be racing against Coventry's finest in Italy's finest that weekend at the Tourist Trophy which he had so far won no less than six times, beginning with two victories in Jaguars (XK 120 and C-type).

"Off in E-type and then to Goodwood. Practice. 1.34.5 FTD when I left. Later Parkes did 1.34.4 (Both times on 15" wheels) Off + Ken by Aztec to Blackpool. Bill Palfrey met us in a Police Mk 9. Good

European Grand Prix

Centre of interest in practice was the new V8 Climax engine, which had finally come to fruition. Only one had so far been built and that was given to the current World Champion, namely Jack Brabham, rather than the man most likely to beat the Ferraris. Stirling was not particularly impressed.

Brabham had a traumatic time in practice but finally managed to record the second quickest lap to Phil Hill's first ever sub-nine minute revolution of the fiendish 14.165-mile Nordschliefe. SM was third fastest and they shared the front row with Bonnier's Porsche.

Brabham's new V8 provided the grunt to get him into an immediate lead, with Stirling and the three Porsches on his heels. Halfway round Brabham's tyre combination of wet fronts and unscrubbed dry rears caught him out and he understeered wide on a damp patch and departed the scene through a hedge, allowing Stirling into first spot.

Phil Hill briefly took the lead at the Adenau crossing but Stirling had it back by the famous Karussel. At the end of the first of 15 laps, he led by just two seconds. "Moss," stated Autosport, "driving with matchless artistry, was getting away from Phil Hill." Taffy von Trips was now third. At the conclusion of the next lap, Stirling's lead was 8.5 seconds. Over the next laps this increased to 14 seconds and then fluctuated by a matter of a couple (two seconds equals 0.37% of nine minutes) either way with von Trips catching his team mate.

After eight laps SM led von Trips, who had taken Hill and was now fronting the Ferrari challenge, by 12½ seconds but the German was going faster and faster. The track had been completely dry for a while and surely there was no way Stirling could hold on. After nine, it was down to 9.4 secs. On the 10th, Stirling recorded nine minutes dead. Trips shaved a tenth off this but Hill gouged 2.2 secs. out of it. The red cars were wheel to wheel and just 8.7 secs. behind. Could Stirling's tyres last out?

After 11, it was down to 6.9 secs. Then the rain came, a drizzle at first and then more serious stuff. But, wet weather or no, did Stirling's tyres have any or sufficient tread left?

The answer was 1mm but it was enough and indeed 'SUPERMOSS', as Autosport headed one of their articles, stretched his lead and took another absolutely brilliant win.

"When Stirling won at Monaco," Walker was quoted as saying in his eponymous book by Michael Cooper-Evans, "I thought that neither he nor anyone else could possibly drive a finer race; then at the Nürburgring I thought he had."

Another superb Michael Turner painting graphically illustrates the circuit set amongst the Eifel mountains and the strong Ferrari and Porsche challenge to the sole Walker Lotus as David once again takes on Goliath. *Reproduced by kind permission of Michael Turner*

1961

ride and bell, etc. to Morecambe in 50mins. Rain. Reception Good and I switched on the illuminations. Tower and bed at 12.30am." To translate and elaborate, SM flew in a Piper Aztec up to the northern seaside town of Blackpool, to which he was driven in a police Jaguar Mark IX with its bell ringing (before days of sirens!), to switch on the famous Blackpool illuminations. It sounds as though he then went to Blackpool Tower.

August was to be a month of frantic weekends. This Saturday he had the classic Tourist Trophy race at Goodwood before taking a trip to Scandinavia, which commenced with a single-seater race in Sweden next day and one in Denmark a week later.

Saturday morning thus saw him heading back down south for the TT at the Sussex circuit. "Up at 9.30. Off at 10.30. Plane at 11.30. Goodwood at 1pm. Race at 3. Bad start. Lay 2nd to Parkes. (His car is a bit quicker) Then lead. He changed wheels at 19 laps, SM 25. Later I had two more stops – he 3. Others 4 & 5 all told. Won by 1 lap. Given cake for 7th TT win. Off + Innes and Jim at 6.30. LAP 7.00 food and off BEA at 9.30. Gottenburg at 10am. Hotel and bed at 2.30am."

There was little time for relaxing on Sunday. "Up at 8.45 and off at 9.15. To Karlskoga by 1.15pm. Many people (70,000) No practice. Started at back. 5 rows behind. 1st on lap 3! Car fab 5.0.1 and 7,900 odd. Missed a little sometimes but later OK. All on wet tyres. I did 1.30.5 FTD and record race speed. Joe 2nd - 14 secs. 3rd Surtees. Lacey engine. Colotti 'box, 61 suspension. Hotel, food and 'do'. Bed at 2am."

On Monday: "Up at 8.30. Off + Jim, Dad and Eric (BP) at 10.30. Broma at 1pm. Brunch and collected Pat at 2.30. Met Erik Carlsson. Castle Hotel. Stooged around. Later met Jim, Gunella Hanson, Olf, Joe and Co. Food and night club and bed at 4.30am."

Tuesday was spent shopping. "Later met Jimmy and Gunella and Lilian Aperlund for food and to Strand. Bed at 3.30am." Another early night! Next day he travelled to Copenhagen with Pat and Gunella. On Thursday, "Up earlyish and shopped. Bought a sideboard £51 in teak. Later food and we all saw *One Night's Work* (G). Martin & McLaine."

After a press reception, Stirling was out practising for that weekend's Danish GP at Roskilde in which he was again driving a UDT/Laystall Lotus. "I used '60 car. Mk1/2 engine. Get 7,400 in 4th with 5.3 axle. Use 3rd/4th only. Later town and bought eight chairs at £13 each in teak and leather. Food plus Ken, Nym, Gunella and Tiny (Nadine) Olinchoff."

    SM   42.2
    Jack 42.9

Saturday August 26: "Up early after bad night. Shopped then to circuit. Wet race. I had a good start

STIRLING THE TRIUMPHANT

Stirling Moss ...

EUROPEAN GP

SM: "At the Nürburgring, I knew I had to make a good start. Jack had the eight cylinder, which I couldn't get. I still had the four cylinder. I remember the start quite well. Jack took the lead and I followed him and then I knew I had to get some sort of lead on him and the Ferraris before we got to the straight and so I pushed Jack as hard as I could.

"I had managed to convince him to change his Green Spots, so that he had two Green Spots on the fronts but he didn't have them all round which I didn't know at the time.

"Anyway, I pushed him as hard as I could and at one point he went wide and I managed to take the lead and then I went as hard as I could, pushing hard through the Fuchsröhre, round all the corners, all the way up the back hill and everything else, as hard as I possibly could and then came on to the straight. I couldn't see the Ferraris behind me and I remember crouching down and looking in the mirrors and then I could see them about 250 or 350 yards, or whatever, behind. Thank God, I got to the end of the straight still in the lead but they were closing up. However, then we got to a couple of fast curves and I managed to hold it through that lot and came through the pits in the lead and again got to the start of the downhill section and made some more up. Eventually, I was saved really by the slight rain, because my tyres were getting very worn because they were not supposed to be driven that hard in the dry. Thank God, I had got sufficient tread left, you know, and so it was all over."

PP: "And you painted out the green spots so people wouldn't know you were using them."

SM: "Dunlop didn't want us to use them. Vic Barlow came up to me and said it was dangerous because they are just going to explode. They would blow out. And they would blow out at high speed, not in a slow corner but on a straight. He really tried to put the s***s up me, but I had to go for it."

PP: "You just had to gamble?"

SM: "Yes. If I had gone on ordinary tyres, I wouldn't have been in contention at all."

PP: "How much was it the advantage the tyres gave you and how much was it your skill that brought you victory?"

SM: "I think my skill certainly helped, but my skill with ordinary tyres wouldn't have been enough to beat them."

PP: "Were you as flat out as you were at Monaco?"

SM: "Yes, I would say so. Certainly for the first few laps. You see the Ring is a lot easier. At Monaco you go round and round 100 times, whereas at the Ring you are only doing 13/14 laps. Because of that it is an easier challenge to face, really. Certainly, it is a different set of circumstances."

PP: "At Monaco you have all the walls and railings…"

SM: "And everything to hit, but of course with the hairpins you could see the opposition behind you. At the Nürburgring I would look in the mirror and I really wouldn't have a clue who was behind me. It was just a red car, obviously a Ferrari, but I didn't know which one."

PP: "But one small mistake at Monaco could put you out if you hit a curb or something."

SM: "Yes, that's true. But at the Ring you would be much more likely to hurt yourself seriously than at Monaco. The great thing about Monaco is that really your maximum speed was relatively slow, say 120mph, whereas at Nurburg you were up to, say, 160."

PP: "And the Ring was a lot more challenging in that there were far more bends, hills, dips, cambers and brows on this exceptionally long circuit."

SM: "I knew it well. The point is at the Nürburgring you could get into a rhythm. You could get into fantastic rhythm at Nurburg. Monaco is not so easy because it is shorter and, you are on it, off it, on it…you had over a thousand gearchanges."

Drivers

Moss on: JOHN SURTEES

PP: "Pretty wild to start with?"

SM: "Surtees was very wild at the start. Tremendous amount of talent and very fast. I think hard on the machine early on. I think that he learnt a tremendous amount very quickly, because as he slowed up he went just as fast, and then he became World Champion. It showed that he had enormous car control."

PP: "Is there any relationship between two and four wheels, do you think?"

SM: "I think with strategy and that type of thing, yes, I think there probably is."

PP: "And balance is very important, isn't it?"

SM: "I would say so. I don't know that much about him, but I remember saying to John Surtees, 'Which is safer – a car or a bike?' and he said. 'A bike, miles so.' I asked why? He said, 'If [on a bike] I see an accident about to happen I get off it, I just leave it behind!' I said, 'Well Masten Gregory is a bit like that...!'

"John was a very tough competitor."

InterContinental Cooper at Brands for Guards Trophy race

Guards Trophy Race

Stirling's pole position time for the InterContinental race at Brands Hatch was so quick that it only just appeared on the speed chart provided in the programme! He was no less than 1.4 secs. quicker than McLaren in second spot. When Nick Syrett briefed the drivers on the grid there were some weary types after their dash from a strenuous day's work at the Nürburgring. Apparently, Moss commented, "Let's cut the race to 50 laps and all go home to bed!" Sounds apocryphal.

Surtees made the best start and took the lead from Stirling. Brabham made a disastrous getaway, almost stalling, and lay ninth. With grim determination, Black Jack carved through the field and, to their surprise, even overtook the two leaders. "Moss wasn't having this, however," wrote the late-Chris Nixon in Autosport, "and slashed past the Australian to the hysterical roar of the crowd." Stirling led comfortably until lap 23 when he was forced to retire with gearbox gremlins.

> **Moss takes lead and lap record**
>
> After his weekend in Germany, Stirling Moss was in fine form at the international meeting at Brands Hatch, Kent, today.
> Driving a Ferrari, he took an early lead in the Grand Touring Car race and broke the lap record on his first time round.
> On the the master's heels were Roy Salvadori, Graham Hill and Bruse McLaren, all driving "E" type Jaguars.
>
> *Darlington Eve. Despatch 7.8.61*

A little oversteer in the Ferrari 250GT at Brands

1961

and JB on my tail all the race. Won by a length. He waved his fist. Reminded me of Silverstone in reverse !X!. Lotus is bad in the wet. Hotel and food with Eric C, Gunella, Henry T and Tiny."

That was the first of three heats. The second and third were run on the Sunday. "Sunny. 1st heat I was 4th then 1st after two laps. Won by 30 secs from Innes. 2nd heat I led with seven to go. Innes 2nd. Car is a little slower than the 61 Lotus but Lacey engine might be better. Jack broke his gearbox, Surtees a tappet (8200 on clock!). Hotel, party and dance. Bed at 3am."

Stirling flew back to London next day. "Office and worked. VP on holiday, Stella stand-in. At 8.00 met Dave, Karen and Jane Cole and saw Sammy Davis Jr. (EX). Food and bed at 2am."

"Stella was a friend of mine," states Val Pirie.

Next day he saw "Pat G. for food at Village. Discussion with Vasca Lazlo." He went to the Daily Mail Ideal Home Exhibition on Wednesday, did a radio show at 8.30 and ate later with Judy Carne.

Thursday, the last day of the month, was a solid day of work. "No food. At 7.30 tux and collected Jean Long and saw premiere of *Victim* (G). Food. Saw Judy and bed at 2.15am."

Though the single-seater race at Brands Hatch saw Stirling retire while leading, the Peco Trophy brought another win to add to the tally

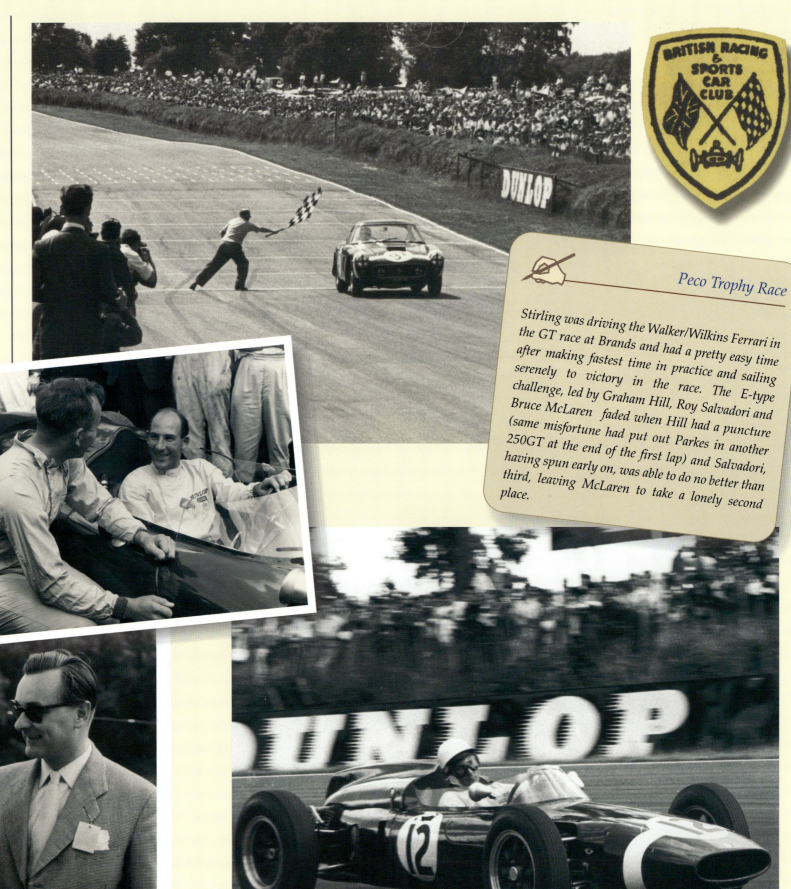

Peco Trophy Race

Stirling was driving the Walker/Wilkins Ferrari in the GT race at Brands and had a pretty easy time after making fastest time in practice and sailing serenely to victory in the race. The E-type challenge, led by Graham Hill, Roy Salvadori and Bruce McLaren faded when Hill had a puncture (same misfortune had put out Parkes in another 250GT at the end of the first lap) and Salvadori, having spun early on, was able to do no better than third, leaving McLaren to take a lonely second place.

BRANDS HATCH

RACE TALK was between (left to right) Jack Brabham (world champion), Innes Ireland, Stirling Moss and Colin Chapman. Moss was happy with his terrific win in Germany over the Italian Ferraris in the German Grand Prix. ("K.I." Photo H 5295)

DAY OF CRASHES AND BREAKDOWNS

The first-ever world championship race at Brands Hatch turned out to be a field day for the mechanics on Monday. Of 17 starters only six finished the 200-miles course; the rest either piled up their cars, or retired with mechanical trouble. The Italian Lorenzo Bandini (Maserati) was credited with seventh place, but he completed only 34 laps between pit stops.

In the absence of competition, however, Brabham's win was not to be sneered at. He did not achieve his lead when others in front dropped out—he was already where others started retiring. In fact the reigning world champion drove as brilliantly as ever, and for Stirling Moss's Rob Walker Cooper was gone, there was no-one left to touch him.

Almost half-a-mile behind, young Jimmy Clark, in a Lotus Climax, was equally comfortable. Soon after half-distance the race developed into something of a procession, the only contest being between Graham Hill (B.R.M.) and Bruce McLaren (Works Cooper) for third place.

Though McLaren established a new course record lap of 95.20 m.p.h., he could not catch the wily Hill. Four more laps and it would have been a different story.

ENDURANCE POWERS

The race counted towards the Inter-continental Manufacturers' world championship, though what the manufacturers are thinking after seeing so many of their cars break down is anybody's guess. Perhaps they will concentrate their efforts in future on producing racing cars not necessarily super-fast, but capable of enduring 200 miles without mechanical failure.

Other items on the programme included a John Davy Trophy race, closely fought between Peter Arundell, Mike Parkes and Tony Maggs, the Peco Trophy event, in which was seen again the sight of two E-type Jaguars trailing behind a Ferrari Berlinetta.

ALL THE RESULTS

John Davy Trophy race for International Formula Junior cars (20 laps): 1 Peter Arundell (Lotus Ford), 36 m. 17.6 s., 87.62 m.p.h.; 2 Mike Parkes (Gemini Ford); 3 Tony Maggs (Cooper B.M.C.). **Peco Trophy race for Grand Touring cars (20 laps):** 1 Stirling Moss (Ferrari Berlinetta), 38.33.6 s., 82.47 m.p.h.; 2 Bruce McLaren (E-type Jaguar); 3 Roy Salvadori (E-type Jaguar). **Guards Trophy race for Inter-continental Formula cars (76 laps):** 1 Jack Brabham (Cooper Climax), 2 hrs. 10m. 53.6 s., 92. 32 m.p.h.; 2 Jim Clark (Lotus Climax); 3 Graham Hill (B.R.M.); 4 Bruce McLaren (Cooper Climax). **Redex Trophy race for Touring Cars (20 laps):** 1 Mike Parkes (Jaguar 3.8) 40 m. 54.8 s., 77.73 m.p.h.; 2 Roy Salvadori (Jaguar 3.8); 3 Jack Sears (Jaguar 3.8).

Kentish Independent 11.2.61

> ### NSU
> The origins of NSU (originally Neckarsulmer Strickmaschinefabrik) can be traced back to 1873 when the company made knitting machines, followed by bicycles, motorcycles and, from 1905, cars. However, production of cars ceased in 1931 but resumed in 1958 with the introduction of the Prinz, a small rear-engined car with a 20bhp ohc air-cooled vertical twin engine of 598cc. With the launch, NSU built a holiday camp near Venice, called the Lido solely for Prinz purchasers. "Drive your Prinz to the Lido" ran the slogan! In 1961 the Prinz 4 was introduced. The NSU PR man in London was very keen for Stirling to be seen driving one of their cars and no doubt it was financially worthwhile for him so to do. It was certainly not the sort of car you would associate with a jet-setting international sporting superstar, or vice versa!

★

Stirling Moss watches the rest of the field go by. His luck has deserted him. His car is in the pits for good.

★

But how dull it all was

IT was the most important race of the year, with the world's top drivers taking part before the biggest crowd ever to pack Brands Hatch. But, oh what a dreadful disappointment Monday's main event turned out to be.

Pre-race fever was running at an all-time high as the drivers took up their grid positions for the 200-mile inter-continental Guards Trophy race. More than 70,000 fans—the highest attendance at any circuit in the country this year—were tense with the greatest of expectations.

A deafening roar, a scintillating start and it looked as if all was set for a humdinger of a race. Then it started. After a few fantastically exciting laps, one star name after another dropped from the running.

The race developed into rather a dismal procession and only four completed the full 76 laps, with three others finishing.

At the start all eyes were on Stirling Moss, fresh from his magnificent win in the European Grand Prix the day before, who set up the best practice time at Brands last week with a record breaking 97.94 m.p.h. lap speed.

But it was John Surtees who first took the lead in his Yeoman Credit Cooper with Moss second, Graham Hill in a BRM third and Masten Gregory, the American, fourth.

A great battle

On lap five Gregory spun off at Druids, crashed through two advertising hoardings and hit the bank, shocking everybody when he walked away unhurt.

World Champion Jack Brabham, who has had such a poor season, moved up into fourth spot and then the lead was snatched and regained by Brabham, Moss and Surtees fought out a brilliant battle. But the brilliance was soon to fade.

Tony Marsh dropped out and then John Surtees skidded off at Clearways. Moss, the motor racing maestro himself, was next to go when on lap 24 he completely lost fourth gear. Others followed in quick succession. It was mechanical slaughter.

Brabham increased his lead and soon looked uncatchable. With the remaining drivers he had a few narrow escapes when one of the two Italian centro-Sud Maseratis started to leak oil in a treacherous trail round the track.

The Maseratis retired and then one driven by ace Lorenzo Bandini made spasmodic appearances throughout the rest of the race.

After 76 laps and two hours, 10 minutes racing Brabham's Cooper flashed over the winning line with Scotsman Jimmy Clark (Lotus) second, Graham Hill

by Harry Nye

(BRM) third and Bruce McLaren in a Cooper fourth.

Brabham averaged 92.32 m.p.h. and the fastest lap was set up by Bruce McLaren with a record breaking speed of 95.20 m.p.h.

Punctured

In the Peco Trophy race an incredible piece of bad luck struck team mates Graham Hill and Mike Parkes. Parkes had to retire his Ferrari in lap one because of a puncture and on lap eight Hill's E-type Jaguar was also in the pits...with a puncture.

Stirling Moss won the race in his Ferrari Berlinetta and broke the Grand Touring car class record with a fastest lap of 83.53 m.p.h. Bruce McLaren (E-type) was second and Roy Salvadori (E-type) was third. This was the second time a Ferrari had mastered the new E-type Jaguar at Brands.

Peter Arundell in a Lotus Ford won the John Davy Trophy race for international Formula Junior machinery and Mike Parkes (Gemini) was second.

Parkes had his share of the honours later however when he carried off the Redex Trophy event for touring cars with a fine win in his Jaguar 3.8.

Kentish Mercury 11.8.61

No My Darling Daughter

'No My Darling Daughter' starred Michael Redgrave with Juliet Mills, Michael Craig, Roger Livesey, Terry Scott and Joan Sims. The film theme was written by Herbert Kretzmer.

August — Stirling Moss Scrapbook

1961

Stirling Moss Scrapbook

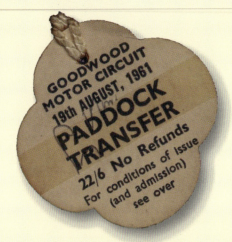

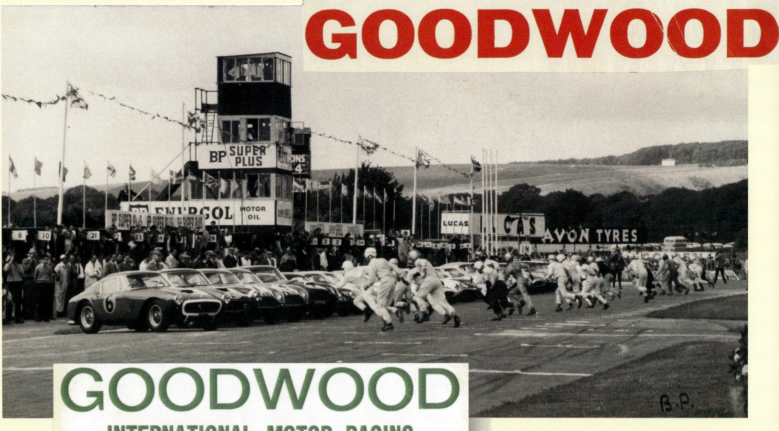

Tourist Trophy - Practice

Having been first run before the Targa Florio, the TT claimed to be the oldest race in the world. Sadly, Britain's main sports car race, coming at the end of the season, did not receive the international support it deserved and Ferrari, having clinched the World Sports Car Championship, found no reason to make the journey. The 1961 TT thus turned into a fine domestic contest, principally between the Ferraris of Moss and Parkes, and the Astons of Salvadori, Clark and Ireland. The E-types, being so new, were not considered ready for a serious competition of three hours' duration and the Wicken and Coombs entries were withdrawn.

Tyre wear was going to be a major factor and during Thursday's practice, Stirling had experienced a puncture which put him off the track. The Dunlop technicians were continually monitoring the tyre temperatures which alarmed the Walkers' small son. "Look, Mummy, that man is sticking a needle into our tyre!"

Stirling was quickest on both Thursday and Friday and left during the day for his engagement in Blackpool, confident that he had pole. While SM was flying north, Parkes in the Maranello Concessionaires 250GT pipped him by a tenth.

The Ladies Man

This 1961 comedy was written by, produced by and starred Jerry Lewis. The plot consists of the main character going to work, after his girlfriend leaves him, in a house occupied by a large number of females. Stirling assessment of 'Fair' sounds fair!

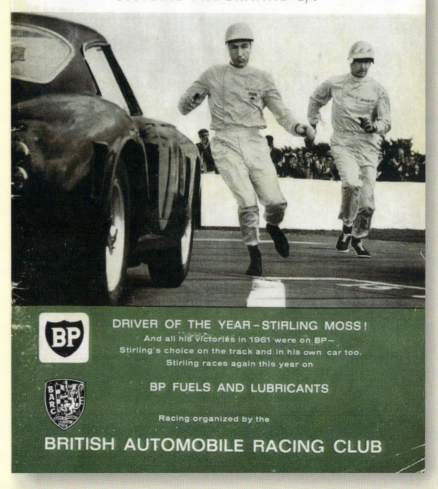

Guess who is ahead above? Goodwood programme from 1962 (left) shows 1961 start

MOSS SKILL AVERTS DISASTER

STIRLING MOSS came near to disaster yesterday when a rear tyre of his Ferrari 250 Berlinetta burst during practice for to-morrow's race at Goodwood.

An official observer said: "There was a cloud of smoke and a loud bang, and the Ferrari spun round in the centre of the track. Moss controlled the car with magnificent skill and pulled up on the grass verge."

He estimated Moss's speed at more than 100 m.p.h.

Questioned by reporters later, Moss said: "Oh, that's nothing! I just wore a tyre through and went round in circles."

Then he went out for a second spell on the track—and set the fastest lap of the day, at 91.14 m.p.h.

Aberdeen Journal 18.8.61

Though Stirling still looks ahead of Parkes (above), the less agile Parkes was actually first away

Drivers

Moss on: MIKE PARKES

SM: "Mike Parkes was a good competitor; he was quick, but not [then] a Formula 1 driver. Later on he did some F1 but was more on the development side, plus sports cars. He was a very big man and so had a weight disadvantage and found it difficult to get in the cars."

PP: "He went particularly well in the 250 Berlinetta against you in the TT."

SM: "Yes, he was very good. Fast!"

1961 — Stirling Moss Scrapbook

Superb study of car control as the master leads the pupil

Tourist Trophy - Race

Not only was he not on pole for the Le Mans start but, most unusually, Stirling was not first away. Parkes, Clark and Salvadori headed him, though he quickly disposed of the Astons and set off after the sister Ferrari. On lap eight, Stirling took Parkes but they continued to have a thrilling dice, split by less than a second. What a magnificent sight – two examples of, arguably, the most beautiful Ferrari ever built, being hurled round the fast and challenging Goodwood circuit by the best driver in the world and a worthy competitor. As Parkes was now working for Ferrari as both an engineer and a driver, one wonders if his car had benefited from any special developments.

Parkes was undoubtedly quick but it was at a heavy cost – to his tyres. After just 17 laps, the tall Englishman had to stop for rear tyres, a stop which cost him 40 secs. It dropped him to third behind Salvadori. Crucially, Stirling did not need to stop until lap 24. He was stationary for 35 secs.

Parkes was pressing hard to get back on terms with Stirling and in doing so broke the lap record. After an hour the difference between them was 7.2 secs. Once again, Parkes's pace was costly. He pitted on lap 37 for four tyres, taking no less than 96.4 secs over the process. Then, attempting to overtake Jimmy Clark, Parkes went wide at Woodcote, taking to the grass and hitting something which deranged his sump-guard. He was black-flagged to have it removed which took another 70 secs.

By half distance, Stirling led second-placed `Salvadori by a lap and "whilst others were resurfacing Goodwood with a layer of rubber," as Autosport put it, "the master was going on without stopping at all". At 58 laps, he finally stopped for four new boots and fuel. Parkes stopped for four more at 62 laps and they both stopped for rears at lap 85.

Stirling's seventh TT win was a fine birthday present and he was presented with a cake with seven candles by the Duchess of Richmond and Gordon.

In taking his seventh TT win, Stirling showed not only outright speed but the ability to conserve his tyres, thereby demonstrating his supreme class. He can be seen assisting his mechanics

Drivers

Moss on: JO BONNIER

"Jo Bonnier was most like Graham Hill. You know, good, steady, solid – he wouldn't do anything stupid. Probably not as good as Graham Hill, actually. He was a man that, if you had a car, you could give it to him and then, no matter how long you were gone, he would bring it back in good condition. He wasn't hard on the machine. Yes, I had quite a lot of respect for his ability, but he was not fast enough."

Alan Fearnley's wonderful painting captures all the drama and atmosphere of the dog-fight between the old pro and the young charger. We are fortunate indeed to have in this book paintings by the two of the fine and best known motor racing artists in the world. *Reproduced by kind permission of Alan Fearnley*

BARC GAZETTE — OCTOBER 1961

Seven-Times Winner. Stirling M... once again receivi... classic rac... and Majo...

The Br...

FOR PRIVATE CIRCULATION

BP

ROYAL COUPLE AT GOODWOOD

THE Duke and Duchess of Kent arrived at Goodwood's 26th Tourist Trophy races today in time for luncheon with the Duke and Duchess of Richmond and Gordon.

They were accompanied at lunch in the restaurant beside the starting grid by the Dowager Duchess of Richmond and Gordon, Brig. H. N. Williamson, of West Wittering, and his novelist wife Eve Orme.

The Royal couple arrived in the Duke's green 3.4 Jaguar a

Driving a Lola-Ford he came 12th in the second heat after lying fourth in the early laps.

Dibley, a B.O.A.C. pilot, only returned from New York in the early hours of this morning. He rushed to the track with little time for sleep.

Gavin Youl, the driver who rebuilt his car after it burnt out in practice, took fourth place in the heat.

Driving his M.R.D. Ford, he stayed in fourth place from the second to the last lap.

For Stirling Moss the Tourist Trophy race was the highlight of a busy week-end.

Stirling was in high spirits when interviewed by an Evening News reporter after a few practice laps.

CAR A BEAUTY

"This is my favourite race, and this car is a beauty," he said. Stirling exuded confidence but would say nothing about his chances in the race, in which he drove a Ferrari Berlinetta for Rob Walker's stable.

After winning the race on six occasions, he was definitely the favourite today.

His mechanics counted on making four, maybe five, tyre changes during the three-hour test of speed and endurance, guarding against a recurrence of his 100 m.p.h. tyre burst on Thursday.

"When the tyre burst I corrected the steering immediately and the car responded magnificently. I am very relieved the car was not bent," he said.

Four cars left the track in the first lap of the Formula Junior Championship. One car overturned and the driver was believed to be hurt.

Portsmouth Eve. News 19.8.61

Driving Lesson for Parkes

Mike Parkes was quoted as saying, "I learned more about race driving from following Moss that afternoon than on any other occasion…". Stirling once wrote of the Rob Walker Berlinettas and concluded with Parkes's quote and the following comment. "It did not seem long ago that I had been the young newcomer, learning my trade by following Fangio in a similar car. Now I was the bald-headed old schoolmaster with the talented newcomer following in my wheel tracks…how time had flown."

Though the 1961 season brought disappointment, yet again, in the World Championship for the world's pre-eminent driver, nevertheless, he clocked up his usual clutch of wins in almost every form of racing around the world, proving he was not only the fastest driver in F1 but the quickest in every category

August — **Stirling Moss Scrapbook**

1961

Stirling Moss Scrapbook

Victim

When a young homosexual, 'Boy' Barrett, commits suicide in his police cell, barrister Melville Carr, motivated by his own guilt, risks his successful career and his marriage to break a sinister blackmail ring. One of a series of social problem films made by the director/producer duo of Basil Dearden and Michael Relph. Starred Dirk Bogarde and Sylvia Syms.

TÄTDUON VANN IGEN MOSS MOTORSUVERÄN

Segerns sötma: Stirling Moss har vunnit "Kanonloppet" i Karlskoga och hyllas inför 33 000 åskådare av kranskullan Ulla-Britt Lagergren som gratulerar den engelske fabriksföraren.

Tour de France Preparations

During August it was being stated in the press that Stirling would be driving the Walker/Wilkins 250GT in the Tour de France. SM certainly noted in his diary that he had entered with Norm Solomon of Nassau as his co-driver.

A rather interesting list was drawn up of "items to be effected on the Ferrari Berlinetta before the Tour de France". These included: glove pockets either side of the passenger's legs, a mapboard to be fitted to the facia panel, map light, a biscuit tin (!) "to contain food and drinks", a detachable torch, two safety belts, one ashtray, one cigarette lighter (shades of Peter Ustinov's Grand Prix of Gibraltar!), two Speed Pilots, set of tools including jack "which we do not appear to have", one "set of 15" wheels for Stirling Moss' personal service van, together with one set of 16" wheels." A meeting had been arranged with Mr. Bizzarini on September 1 to discuss with SM any further requirements.

The car was to be flown from Hurn to Cherbourg "and Mr. Bizzarini, who is driving it, hopes to arrive at Modena either late Thursday evening 24th August or early Friday…"

Dear Ronnie

On August 30th, Stirling wrote to Ronnie Hoare at Maranello Concessionaires, saying he "was very pleased for the success the two cars had at Goodwood, particularly as Mike had that extra unscheduled stop. I do hope we will be able to co-operate again in the not too distant future at some other race." Ferrari charged 74,772 Lire to prepare the car for the TT.

Apart from being a brilliant racing driver, Stirling has always been a very fine ambassador for Britain and for motor sport. He represented the very epitome of sportsmanship and was loved the world over

Krock i 200 km – vann

Stirling MOSS mästerlig

● Inför 40.000 motorentusiaster vann världsmästaren Stirling Moss elegant racerklassen i Karlskogas kanonlopp. Jocke Bonnier visade dock sin höga klass genom att bjuda Moss en hård sekundstrid över hela banan, men med iskall behärskning höll engelsmannen undan trots att han en gång i 200 km fart krockade med en motståndare. C. G. Hammarlund var för grön i racerdebuten mot de båda storåkarna men var som vanligt suverän i turistklassen.

Stirling Moss pratar efter segern med Ulf Norinder.

August — Stirling Moss Scrapbook

1961
Stirling Moss Scrapbook

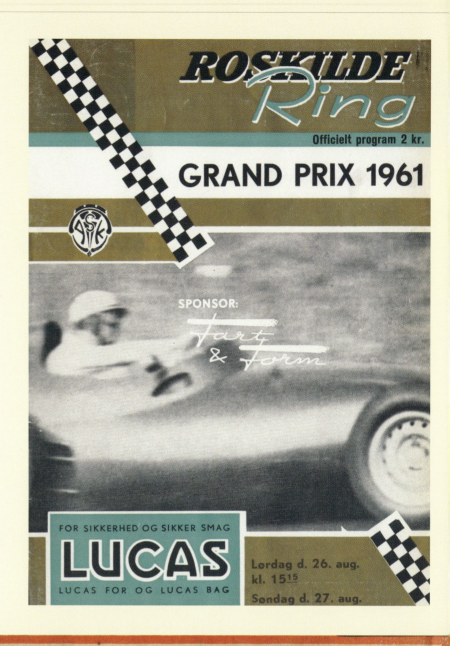
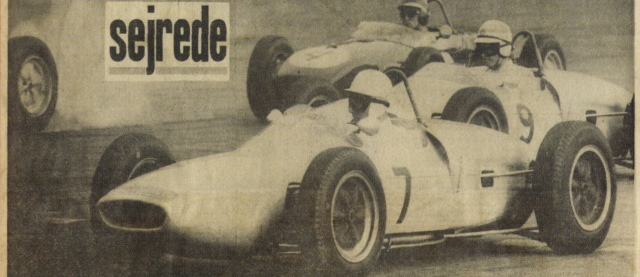

One Over The Eight

This revue starred Kenneth Williams, Sheila Hancock and Lance Percival. It was written by the incomparable Peter Cook, with additional material by John Mortimer, John Bird, Lionel Bart, N.F. Simpson and Carl Davis, with musical content by composer Lance Mulcahy and lyricist John Law. Opening at the Duke of York's Theatre in April, 1961, it was the follow-up to 'Pieces of Eight' and ran for 415 performances. Probably the best known sketch was 'Hand Up Your Sticks', a play on 'stick up your hands'. Cook revived 'Interesting Facts' for the first 'Secret Policeman's Ball' in 1979.

The visit to Scandinavia brought victories in both Sweden and Denmark (above).

Stop The World, I Want To Get Off

Written by Anthony Newley, together with Leslie Bricusse, and starring Newley (who later married Joan Collins in 1963), the show was a great success in London's West End and later on Broadway. Newley had made his name as the 'Artful Dodger' in David Lean's 1948 film Oliver Twist, and Stop The World was an ideal showcase for his prodigious talents. Hit song from this musical was 'What Kind Of Fool Am I'. Original production ran for 485 performances at the Queen's Theatre in Shaftsbury Avenue.

August — Stirling Moss Scrapbook

September

Calendar

3	Modena GP, Italy – 1st in 1.5 Lotus-Climax 18/21
10	Italian GP, Monza, Italy – ret'd in Team Lotus Works Lotus-Climax 21
23	Oulton Park Gold Cup, Cheshire, UK – 1st in Ferguson-Climax P99
30	Canadian GP, Mosport Park – 3rd in Lotus-Climax 19

The evening of the first day of September, "Drove to LAP and stayed at lousy International Hotel. No breakfast in room, rude and wrong call." The next day did not start too well either. "Up at 7.45. Bad night. Fog delayed take-off. Milano and Alfa 2 litre and to Modena. Practice. When I arrived no-one had done better than 60 secs+. Later food with Rob, Betty, Mum and Dad."

SM	58.6
Jo	59.3
Dan	59.2
G. Hill	59.3
Clark	59.6
Gregory	59.7
Brabham	59.8
Bandini	59.8
Surtees	59.8
Brooks	1.00.1
Taylor	1.00.1

The non-Championship Modena GP was to take place on the Sunday, but first SM went to a "Church 'do' for kids' school. Met Francesca and circuit. Hot. D12 [tyres]. Fair start, lay 2nd and followed Dan, then took lead at 90 laps odd [to go] and won by seven secs. Eased off at the end. Ran over broken engine and broken wheel. Hotel and chat and bath and food and Milano. Bed at 3am. Jack passed out at the end of the race."

After just three hours sleep, Stirling was up again. He and Alf Francis flew back to London in an "AL Caravelle. Office and work. Felt bloody, a cold and tired." Proving that perhaps he was human after all, SM was still tired next day but nevertheless met "Dave, Karen and Jean and we saw *East of Eden* (VG).

 "Unsatisfied Customer"

Under this heading, Autosport printed a letter on September 1st from a Mr. Gowan of Southampton. He wrote: "After reading your reports of Formula 1 racing this year, I am rather fed up with reading how wonderful Moss has driven and very little about the wonderful drives by the Ferrari team drivers who, in my opinion, are as good as, if not better than, Moss." He went on to state that the drivers were not being given credit for having faster cars and that Autosport was biased!

A week later a Drummond Bone (!) wrote in response, asking: "…is there really any doubt that Moss has been the outstanding driver of the season?"

Old friends together again. The great Fangio was at Modena to start the race. As the Argentinian did not speak a word of English, they used to communicate in Italian

Stirling's parents remained enthusiastic supporters throughout his career and here we see Alfred and Aileen Moss in the pits at Modena with Betty Walker in the middle

The Modena Grand Prix was a pretty relaxed affair in that it was a non-Championship race but nevertheless Stirling would never give less than 100%, and that included his social life!

Third time lucky for the Ferguson?

Manchester Eve. News 1.9.61

By DUNCAN MEASOR

STIRLING MOSS will drive the Ferguson Grand Prix car in the 165-mile Gold Cup race at Oulton Park on September 23.

This is a significant choice of car by the British champion, for it shows that he and the people behind it believe the revolutionary machine is ready to win a big race.

As a professional driver Moss races to win, and always picks his cars with care. Last year he picked a Lotus for the 150-mile race—and won. The year before he decided a Cooper was the horse for the course —and again he won.

And as there is a great deal of money involved for the winner there is no doubt this time that the Ferguson is being entered in its third race with the object of winning.

Modena GP

Jack Brabham, writing in his regular piece in Motor Racing, stated that 30 drivers had turned up for this event to find that "the organisers only intended having 14 starters, and three of these had to be Italian." The result was that a lot of cars were worn out before the race as the remainder fought over just 11 places.

In the race, on a circuit Brabham described as "a square box with a little wriggle in it", Bonnier led initially in a works Porsche, then team mate Gurney passed him but on lap 12 Stirling took the lead. For the next 88 laps he controlled the race and maintained sufficient margin to the squabbling Porsches. The Ferrari team had chosen to keep their powder dry for Monza.

September

Stirling Moss Scrapbook

1961

Blue Angel and bed at 4am." However, casting doubt on whether he was actually human, after that late night he was up again four hours later. "Up at 8am! Work. Lunch with Kinney, Mai-Ling and Mr Lall. Work and later to Terry's Cocktails. Work and Collected JC. Food. Herb came down. Bed at 2.30am."

After a generous six hours sleep and almost a full day's work, he headed back to Italy for his second visit within a week, this time for the Italian GP. He flew again by Air Alitalia Caravelle with Max Boyd, Denis Jenkinson and L. Lee to Milan. "Met by Francesca. Audrey's for food. Bed at 2am."

On Friday, "Up at 9. Collected Francesca and [to] Monza. Did two laps in the GT Ferrari and then its oil overflowed. (Works car). Town, food and then F1 practice. 4 cyl very slow. 6,600 (137) with 650 tyres. Also 8 slow 8,200 (4.7 axle 138mph) 1.06. On banking, 4 cyl. 1.09 and Ferrari 1.02.7. Clark 1.04.7, etc. GPDA [Grand Prix Drivers' Association] meeting and then hotel. Changed and food with Mum and Dad."

Saturday saw Stirling shopping with Francesca. "Circuit and tried new GT Ferrari (works prototype) 1.49 in 2 laps 245 kph. F1 practice and I did not get one good lap due to overheating of V8. Wasted all practice messing around with the water system."

Innes Ireland and Stirling were good mates and SM had helped Innes on several occasions. On Sunday Innes repaid that kindness with a noble gesture of his own. "Innes gave me his Lotus and I started miles back. Only 2 abreast on grid (no slip-streaming for Ferrari). Poor Taffy was killed in accident and I lay 2nd/3rd with Dan G behind Phil for ages and then seven laps to go the wheel bearing broke! Town and Francesca broke down. Real love for Taffy! Food and bed at 2am."

In his role as President of the GPDA, Stirling issued a statement, saying Wolfgang von Trips would be "sorely missed". He concluded, "He got to where he was in motor racing by his ability, hard work and interest in it. Above all, he was a gentleman in the widest sense of the word. We shall all miss him."

Possibly saddened or troubled by Sunday's tragedy, Stirling had a bad night. "Called Alfas and met Dir. General and Guidotti. BEA to LAP and met by VP. Office, two TV shows and work. At 8pm met Steve McQueen, Ritz Room and 'Wheel' and then to Sammy Davis dressing room. Met JC and bed at 2am!" From hereon, Stirling adds, on occasions, an exclamation mark in his diary after the time of his retiring. Readers are left to ponder upon the significance, if any, of this possible code!

L. Lee

Leonard Lee, later Lord Lee, was the Managing Director of Coventry Climax, a company founded by his father H. Pelham Lee in 1903. The company provided engines for tractor and car manufacturers but during the Depression, Leonard shrewdly and successfully diversified into fire pump engines. Famously, post-WW2 Ministry of Defence requirements for a faster and lighter pump led Lee to hire Walter Hassan and the resulting power unit found its way into all manner of racing cars, beginning with Stirling's old mount, the Kieft. Stirling scored the company's first GP win with a Cooper in 1958 at the Argentine GP.

Without Ferrari present at Modena, it was all too easy for Stirling

East of Eden

East of Eden was a 1955 film based on the novel by Steinbeck. It starred Raymond Massey, James Dean, Julie Harris, Burl Ives and Jo Van Fleet who won an Oscar for Best Supporting Actress. Based on the WW1 period, Cal Trask, played by Dean, feels he has to compete against overwhelming odds with his brother Aron for the love of their father Adam. Directed by Elia Kazan, it was said to be one of the finest movies to come out of Hollywood. Amusingly, the film is set in 1917 but a band plays Avalon which was not published until 1920!

Moss wins

MODENA, Italy, Sunday.—Stirling Moss today won the seventh Grand Prix of Modena Formula-One race in his Lotus. It was his 15th win this season. Joachim Bonnier (Sweden) and Daniel Gurney (U.S.), both driving Porsche cars, were second and third.—A.P.

Daily Mail 4.9.61

Stirling sampled the prototype 250 GTO while at Monza. The rudiments of the classic shape are here but the car would evolve before next season, especially at the rear

A classic shot of Stirling on the infamous banking at Monza. The British works teams had boycotted the event the previous year but the Italians had the last laugh in 1961

Ferrari Test at Monza

Early in his career, Stirling had had a falling out with Enzo Ferrari and steadfastly refused to race for the factory team thereafter. However, time is a great healer, as they say, and Enzo was actively courting SM during 1961 with a view to a F1 liaison in 1962. To this end, Stirling was invited to try the prototype of what would become the legendary 250 GTO at Monza in September.

The 250 GT was a thing of beauty but not sufficiently aerodynamic to achieve its potential top speed. A better shape was needed and Ferrari had secretly commissioned Giotto Bizzarrini to develop a new car with better penetrative capabilities. When Stirling tried the car, known as the Papero (fool), it had the usual wet sump oil system which led to cavitation on the corners, resulting in large clouds of smoke being emitted from the exhaust pipes on the exit of the Parabolica. However, Stirling was still able to record 1.46 and 1.47 against the 250 SWB's time of 1.50 and 1.51. It was a taste of things to come. "It really impressed me," says Stirling.

Enzo is quoted as saying on one occasion that he considered Tazio Nuvolari and Stirling Moss as the two greatest racing drivers of all time, and Stirling as the single greatest.

1961

Stirling Moss Scrapbook

After working till early evening, Stirling, "met Dave, Karen and Jean and to Taggs Island. Home … and bed at 3.45 am!"

On Wednesday he "took Mai-Ling to Beachcomber. Saw JC and bed at 2.15am!" Thursday saw him invited to the "premiere of *Fanny* (VG). Food and on to Woodlands 'do'. Bed at 2.30am." Friday was a long day. "Up at 10 and work till 10.30pm. Janet called… Met Judy. 55 and bed at 3am!" He saw Sammy Davis Jr on Saturday, ate at Sir Harry's Bar and called at the Cabaret. He took to his bed at 4.30am that night. In his diary, he noted "Voted one of the 7 best dressed men of the year!"

Sunday was spent relaxing at Tring. "Herb gave me some tapes, a shirt and a P38 plane We flew it! Ha ha. Got dizzy. Food. Town at 8.30 and DH and met Karen and Jean. Bed at 2am!"

On Monday September 18, SM met "Mr Howard, Mr Christiansen and Pat Mennem for Goodwill lunch. Work and at 8.00 took Pat and Pete G and Sonya C. to Harry's Bar. Chatted and bed at 2am." On Tuesday, he worked until 11.30pm, but during the day saw his father professionally for a new steel plate to be fitted (Stirling had lost a couple of front teeth in his earlier days) and then, "Saw JC. Bed at 1.45am!" He also noted, "Louis Stanley called and apologised re. his book!"

Wednesday concluded with Pat Scott, presumably a female, calling and "we saw Fred Astaire film. G. Food at Angel. Chat and bed at 3.30am!"

Stirling was entered in the Gold Cup race at Oulton Park that coming weekend. He had won the first Gold Cup events back in 1954 and 1955. Val took him to the airport where he met Rob Walker and flew up to Manchester where they rendezvoused with Alf Francis who drove them to Chester. They ate with Tony Rolt, who had himself been a most successful driver and team mate to Stirling in the Jaguar team and was now heavily involved in the Ferguson company. Indeed, Stirling was to drive the revolutionary P99 four-wheel-drive single-seater in the main race.

Practice was on Friday. "Up at 8.00 and practice, car fairly good. 1.44.8. Bruce 1.44.6, etc. We tried odd things."

Bruce	1.44.6
SM	1.44.8
Graham	1.45.0
Brooks	1.45.2
Clark	1.45.2
Brab	1.45.4
Surtees	1.45.6

Saturday dawned. "Up early because I woke at 8.00. Looked at shops. Circuit. Rain. Parade lap. Start and I couldn't get 1st. Used 2nd. Dropped back to about 8th. Took lead in six laps odd and pulled away. It dried

Circuits

Moss on: MONZA

SM: *"The great thing about Monza is that you have the enthusiasm of the Italians. Monza was enjoyable because of the fans, really, you know."*

PP: *"And you had the banking."*

SM: *"Well, the banking was really bad to start with. The first corner after the pits, the Grande Curve, was really quite difficult. It was quite difficult to get round there flat."*

Italian Grand Prix

With the Constructors' World Championship at stake, SEFAC Ferrari turned up at Monza with no less than six cars, two being the 90°-engined machines, of which one was a spare and the other was to be piloted by young Ricardo Rodriguez. They exhibited total domination in practice, occupying the first two rows of the grid with Rodriguez sensationally recording a time which was only a tenth slower than poleman von Trips.

At the start of the second lap tragedy occurred when von Trips appeared to lose control and hit Clark's Lotus. The German was flung out of the Ferrari and killed instantly as the car caused havoc in the crowd, killing several and injuring others.

Later, Ferrari lost two more cars as Rodriguez and Baghetti retired with engine trouble, and then Ginther dropped out to leave Phil Hill as the sole representative. Initially, Brabham had managed to dice with the Ferraris but the new Coventry-Climax V8 was still under-developed and gave up the fight. Stirling, who had had so much trouble with his new V8 in practice that he had decided to race the old four cylinder, was now enjoying a dice with Gurney in a Porsche for second place. That fizzled on lap 36 when a wheel-bearing failed on the Lotus. Hill went on to win and take an unassailable lead in the World Championship. Though not in Stirling's league, he was a worthy World Champion and it was excellent for the sport to have an American win the crown.

Drivers

Moss on: PHIL HILL

SM: "Phil Hill, I think, was a versatile, adaptable driver who was good in sports cars and Formula 1, the lot. A number of drivers were not, but he was good in both categories and fast! Phil was one of the better drivers."
PP: "But not in the very top league?"
SM: "No, just one down."

The '8' appears to have dropped off which is ironic as the (V) 8 gave so much trouble in practice that SM used the 4 (cylinder)!

1961

and I got ftd. Car is not easy to drive, but holds road well. Is hot. Big crowd. Left at 5.30 + Celia in 220 SE Coupe and to 36 in 3hrs 5. At 11.30 David and I collected JC (last night) [presumably a theatrical 'last night'] and food. Bed at 2.15am!"

The workaholic Moss was at it till 7.00pm on Sunday. Then, "Collected Mai-Ling and to Ronnie and Leo's for food. Home, packed, saw JC and bed at 2am."

Next evening he "took Judy to see *Beyond the Fringe*. (G). Food at Candlelight and bed at 2.30am!"

On Tuesday SM saw Cecil Lewis, of the Daily Mail, Pete Murray (not the disc jockey) and, "At 6.00 Helen called around. Later met Jane Cole and to Lotus Ho. [House] Bed at 1.30am."

Midweek, "At 8.30pm JC came and cooked me a fat shepherds' pie. Packed and bed at 2am!" It would be their last evening together for a few weeks because Stirling was departing next day for a North American tour and races in Canada and the USA. Indeed, next morning Val drove him to London Airport where he "met Vandervell and Miss Moore. Flew BOAC to Toronto. Arrived late. TV etc and bed at 11.30pm (UK 4.30am)."

His team mate was to be Belgian Olivier Gendebien, occasional Grand Prix driver and sports car specialist. It was not a happy weekend, or at least not on the race track.

"Up at 9.00 and to circuit and hotel. Practice car is awful, engine rough, brakes bad, gearbox lousy and windscreen windy! Tyres 38. Get 7,500, 6,800 and on Oliver's car! Qualified in his as mine had its bonnet fly off. Hotel and food, bed at 12pm!"

As to Saturday, "Up at 8.30 after little sleep. Joan called early! Circuit in BP 'copter. Race. Olivier and I lead switching. Easy. A 1.46, 1.39. Then a rod hit rad, also 3rd gear jammed in twice. Lost 3/4 laps. Did 1.34.5 but still 3rd to Ryan & Ricardo [Rodriguez]. Car rough. Olivier broke axle. Hotel. Food and 'do' Saw Joan. Bed at 4am!"

Stirling Moss ...

FATAL ACCIDENTS

PP: "*Did any fatal accidents really affect you? Did any one fatality upset you more than the others? Was there anybody you were close to?*"

SM: "No, not like [the death of] Marimon affected Fangio. No! One knew, obviously, all the people who died, but one didn't, or I didn't, particularly have, or make, my closest friends in Formula 1. You know I was pretty close to Innes, because I liked the guy, but not as close as I was to someone like David Haynes, for instance. Yeah, it did affect me, but the one thing that you could say, that made it easier to continue, was that they were doing what you knew they liked doing. At least they were killed doing what they liked, but that is a pretty poor reason, actually, you know.

"You grab at straws when you are in that situation. I, personally, couldn't quantify why. I never really thought of giving up. I am too selfish. I got too much of a kick out of racing, I suppose, and what success means and brings. It was the respect of drivers, the adulation of fans, the benefit of the money, the pleasure of your mechanics and all those things come together. It is a package and the package of winning is pretty strong and addictive. I think if I hadn't have been as successful as I was, it would have been a lot easier to get out."

In spite of Innes's fine gesture of lending SM his works Lotus, it let him down in his final quest for the Championship

MOSS WARNED ABOUT MONZA

JUST a year ago Stirling Moss warned of the dangers of the Monza circuit, a warning that was tragically fulfilled yesterday — although ironically the crash was on a "safe" section. "Of course we are scared of the dangers," said Moss, "I am frightened by any chance of mechanical failure. Modern Grand Prix cars are built for road circuits, not this sort of banking. We are not speedway riders."

And it was at Monza, near the point of yesterday's disaster, that Moss, driving at nearly 180 m.p.h., had his closest brush with death three years ago. His steering buckled and only his consummate skill and nerve saved him from disaster. "The bumps there shake you so much you need straps to keep you in the car," he said.

Other famous drivers, including the incomparable Fangio himself, had foreseen that this moment of horror would come to Monza.

It is a high-speed, winding road circuit. Six years ago the Italians decided to extend it. To do so they added the wall of death, a high-banked, sweeping bend reminiscent of the old Brooklands race track.

The extensions turned Monza into the most frightening circuit in the world.

Moss and other leading race drivers protested and boycotted last year's race. The Italians replied that the drivers were afraid. Even at this meeting the official Italian programme repeated the jibe at "frightened" drivers. "In reality the English feared the come-back of our Ferraris on the ideal track for their power..."

Wolfgang von Trips was driving a Ferrari when he died at Monza yesterday.

Denis Holmes

Death of the man who worshipped Stirling Moss

Three British aces in 4-car pile up with Germany's champion

VON TRIPS DIES

Daily Mail 11.9.61

Taggs Island

Taggs Island was a small island in the River Thames just upstream from Hampton Court. In the late 19thC, the Angler's Retreat had been transformed into a hotel and was a Mecca for the rich and famous. The island was ringed with houseboats which were used for covert liaisons! JM Barrie wrote many of his plays on the houseboat he rented. By the beginning of the next century, the popularity of the Taggs Island Hotel had waned and it fell into disrepair. Fred Karno, of circus fame, had begun his career busking at a nearby lock. Having made his fortune, he was persuaded to take on the lease.

Karno demolished the existing hotel and built the Karsino. It flourished for a while but then went through a number of unsuccessful phases. In an extraordinary change of use, AC Cars took over the island, built a bridge from the Middlesex bank and converted the hotel into a factory. Later AC built their infamous invalid carriages there. There were further attempts to re-open the hotel but in 1971 it was demolished. Today it is inhabited by houseboats and wildlife, as opposed to a wild life on the houseboats!

Stirling Moss …

STEVE McQUEEN

"I remember meeting Steve, because I knew him reasonably well. We raced in the same team at Sebring. He was very keen on cars, very keen and very cool - the most cool guy I ever knew, because I wasn't into that sort of thing, you know, jeans and wild man. He was very laid back. Very nice. Would drive me mad I am sure because I am not that laid back, but I liked him."

Stirling Moss probes Monza death crash
From DENIS HOLMES: Milan, Monday.

STIRLING MOSS turned crash detective today to make a secret investigation into the death of his friend, Count Wolfgang von Trips, and spectators in Sunday's Italian Grand Prix at Monza.

Fourteen spectators have now died and 20 were seriously injured in the 140-mile-an-hour crash.

Moss delayed his return to London to take action as chairman of the newly formed Grand Prix Drivers' Association to which all top international drivers belong.

The association was formed this season to make improvements in safety for drivers and spectators.

Moss decided to make an immediate investigation in the interest of motor sport and will report to the 17-member association, probably in the United States, next month.

STIRLING MOSS
Checks skid marks

circuit. It was, in fact, on the south curve of the road track and nowhere near the speed banking.

2. British driver Jimmy Clark, whose car and that of Von Trips collided, could not have been in any way to blame.

3. Some unknown factor caused the disaster and made Von Trips swerve suddenly across the path of Clark's car and then charge into the spectators.

Moss told me: "Although we have been warning about the dangers of Monza for over a year now, I must be fair and say that I believe that no blame can be attached to the race organisers. There could be no possible connection with the banking, either…"

Daily Mail 12.9.61

Stirling Moss …

THE FERRARI DRIVERS

PP: "Who would you say was the best of the Ferrari drivers - Ginther, Von Trips or Phil Hill?"
SM: "I think Phil."
PP: "So the right man won the Championship?"
SM: "Yes, I think so. He is a very nice guy. He was a good, constant, steady driver. He was not wild. I mean, Taffy and Richie were much the same. I think that they had a fairly balanced team there. I think Ferrari always had an extremely good car. I can't think of a driver ever dying because Ferrari caused it. I can't think of any mechanical failure that happened, with one possible exception to that, which is Ascari. It is possible that he went to get fifth and it may have gone into the wrong gear but, in principle, Ferrari was a very, very safe car."

"He did pick drivers who, I think, were pretty well matched, you know. For example, he had Hawthorn and Collins together."

PP: "And Brooks…"
SM: "Brooks, of course, was terrific. I think Ferrari picked up pretty good people actually."

1961 SUNDAY 10TH SEPTEMBER
15th after Trinity

Up at 9.00. Later to circuit. Innes gave me his Lotus & I started with Vad on 2 abreast grid. (No slip-streaming for Ferrari). Poor Taffy was killed in accident. I lay 2nd/3rd with Dan G behind Phil for ages & then 7 laps to go the wheel bearing broke! Jim & Francesca broke down. Real loss for Taffy! Ford & bed at…

Dan

Beyond The Fringe

'Beyond the Fringe' was one of the most significant theatrical productions since the war. It has been dubbed the beginning of satire and starred four multi-talented writers and performers who would become giants in their respective fields – Peter Cook, Dudley Moore, Jonathan Miller and Alan Bennett. Born out of the Cambridge Footlights, the show enjoyed huge success in London before transferring to Broadway.

SM Pulls Out Of Tour de France

At the last minute, Stirling pulled out of the Tour de France so he could race the Ferguson at Oulton Park. Originally, he had planned to take a helicopter from Corsica to Nice on the day before the Tour ended, flying during the day to London and that evening to Manchester to compete at Oulton on the day the Tour was due to finish.

Peter Garnier, pointing out that Stirling had finished second in France in 1956 and fourth the following year when Garnier had accompanied him, wrote, "This is a great pity, for Moss could well have won the Tour in this car…"

1961

Fanny
Based on the Marseilles Trilogy by Pagnol and a Broadway musical of 1954, this bittersweet story of romance and regret starred Leslie Caron, Charles Boyer and Maurice Chevalier. Nominated for five Oscars, including best picture.

Though a front-engined car in what had become a rear-engined era, the Ferguson had the unique advantage of four-wheel-drive

But only Stirling Moss is hoping for rain

MORE than 40,000 people are hoping for fine weather on Saturday for the International Gold Cup motor racing meeting at Oulton Park, Cheshire.
But one man is hoping it will rain.
He is Stirling Moss, who drives the revolutionary four-wheel drive Ferguson in the race. the right ratio.
Stirling's mechanic, Alf Francis, has tuned the engine until it almost sings.
Advance bookings are higher for this meeting than any other since the race began.
Mr. Foster estimates that given fine weather a 40,000 gate is fairly certain.
But a 40,000 gate could mean that Stirling's car won't be first past the checkered flag.

Daily Herald 21.9.61

Stirling Moss ...

THE FERGUSON P99

SM: "I was quite involved with the Ferguson because I knew Tony Rolt, of course. The Ferguson was quite a unique car. I have never driven a car that did things so well but was so difficult to cope with.

"Take an ordinary car - you usually want it to slightly oversteer or understeer or whatever. The Ferguson didn't. The Ferguson was a very neutral steer. You might think that must be fantastic but, because you are trained to take a car that isn't as good as it could be, you begin to benefit from its failings. You know, you find with a car that, when you go into a corner and then you put it into an oversteer and OK that scrubs off some speed, that when you've got round the corner you can then press on without any problems. In the Ferguson, you didn't do that. With the Ferguson you go straight into a bend and you drove it round. Although that sounds like that should be the absolute epitome of perfection, for whatever reason, it didn't work out as easily as that. It was a difficult car to get to grips with, because if you tried to drive it as you would a conventional car, it just didn't respond correctly that way.

PP: "If it was more glued to the road, perhaps there was the concern that, when it did break away, it would be more dramatic."

SM: "No, I don't think so. I think that it was just that it… It was very difficult to even know what it was. With the Ferguson, as long as you were precise, it would do precisely what you wanted it to do. But it was very difficult to be precise when your upbringing has been one where you thought, 'Well, I better just tweak it here to get the back end out, or I will back-off here to stop the understeer or whatever. You have to ignore all…"

PP: "Your conditioned responses?"

SM: "Yes! You had just got to say, 'Well, this is a clean sheet of paper. This car is going to do what it should do without me damn well making it do it.' Of course, I was so used to making it, that was a bad thing."

PP: "Could you put it into a four-wheel drift in a conventional way?"

SM: "If you are talking of a four-wheel slide, no. You see, you balance a normal car on the throttle, but the Ferguson, when you were going round [a bend] you were putting the power on and just driving it. You had just got to hold it in."

"You see all of us, to a greater or lesser extent at that time, were used to a car that one would knock into shape the way you wanted it by doing whatever you needed to do to get the best out of it. If I drove Jack Brabham's car and he drove mine, we would be completely lost and would not be the best, but with the Fergy you drove it the way it was."

"In the wet the car was unbeatable. I mean, I was passing cars on the outside. I mean, literally, going around the outside and saying, 'Thank you!' – absolutely ridiculous. Whereas in an ordinary car you'd be fearing things, this thing was terrific."

Outon Park Gold Cup

Stirling, who was second fastest in the revolutionary four-wheel-drive Ferguson, shared the front row with McLaren, Clark and Graham Hill. At the start, it was Clark who took the lead and Stirling, taking care with his gear selection, was down in fourth. However, on lap four Hill and Stirling overtook Clark and two laps later SM took the lead on the drying but still slippery track. He dominated from thereon, even when the track dried completely, setting the fastest lap and winning by over a minute from Brabham.

Louis Stanley

Louis Stanley was married to Sir Alfred Owen's sister, Jean, a most delightful lady, and thus became involved with running the BRM team towards the end of its days. He was a prodigious author of books, his specialities including motor racing and golf. He became known in the 1970s for his considerable efforts to improve medical facilities and created a mobile unit that attended Grand Prix races. He ran the struggling BRM team from 1974 to 1977, the last two years under the name of Stanley BRM. Unfortunately, 'Big Lou', as he was latterly known, became something of a figure of fun in the motoring press.

MOSS ROCKS OULTON IN NEW FERGUSON

Above: Stirling uses the Ferguson's advantage of four-wheel-drive to overtake on the outside in spite of the slippery conditions. Right: Stirling follows Graham Hill in the works BRM, a combination that would take the Championship in 1962

Stirling Moss ...

BEST DRESSED MEN OF THE YEAR

SM: *"Extraordinary. I suppose I dressed alright."* Stirling finds the recollection very amusing!
PP: *"You have always liked dressing well."*
SM: *"I am sure there were people out there who were a lot more dapper – a red carnation [in their lapel] each day and all that sort of stuff. I think it was because I had been to Vegas and gone into a fashion place and got a couple of upmarket, with-it jackets. I never dressed in jeans as they weren't the thing then. I was always reasonably well turned out. It was all good PR!"*

1961

Stirling Moss Scrapbook

Above right: Stirling holds the 'bonnet'. No wonder. Ironically, it flew off in practice at Mosport

5. Moss and Gendebien leave the BP helicopter which brought them to the track at Mosport.

Canadian GP, Mosport Park

In practice for this race for sports cars in which Stirling was driving a Lotus Monte Carlo (otherwise known as a 19), he broke the lap record by almost five seconds! SM's team mate, Gendebien in another UDT/Laystall Lotus 19 led initially until supplanted by Stirling. Opposition came from the Rodriguez brothers, Pedro and Ricardo in Ferraris, and local man Peter Ryan in a third Lotus 19. They filled the next three places. All was going swimmingly until lap 70 when Stirling had to pit. The gearbox was stuck in third and a punctured radiator had to be repaired. He lost about 10 minutes and, although he set a new lap record in a fine display of inspired driving, had no chance of catching Ryan who had taken the lead when Gendebien had retired.

Why sit in traffic when you can arrive by helicopter, courtesy of BP? Commonplace at major races today, it was pretty unusual in 1961

Drivers

Moss on: OLIVIER GENDEBIEN

"Olivier was terrific on sports cars but never really made it in Formula 1. A charming man. I rather doubt that he would have been as fast as Phil Hill. I think he would be very similar, but a little bit slower. But again a man that you could give a car to and he could drive for 12 hours and wouldn't take anything off it."

Stirling particularly enjoyed the new Mosport circuit and was going well, heading for yet another win when the gearbox stuck in third and a punctured rad ruined the party

IN MOSPORT WARM-UP TIME TRIALS
Moss Best -- Even in Borrowed Car

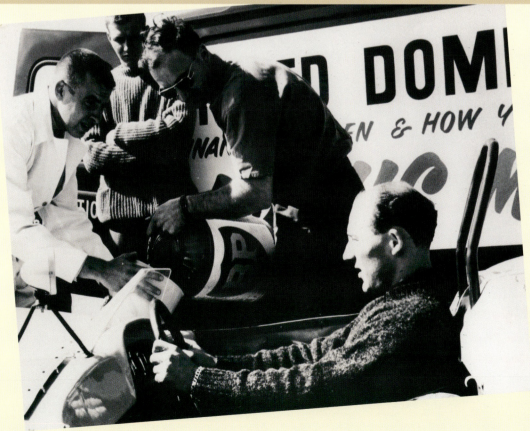

September — Stirling Moss Scrapbook

1961

Stirling Moss Scrapbook

Moss again or Gendebien?

Here's why we're rooting for both!

STIRLING MOSS

OLIVIER GENDEBIEN

Stirling Moss and Olivier Gendebien will have more in common than their well-earned reputations as crack racing drivers when they compete in Canada's first Grand Prix at Mosport Sept. 30.

This time they'll both be driving Lotus Mk 19 Monte Carlos (the car in which Moss won the Players 200.) As sponsors of both cars, we find it difficult to choose between these two men, so we're wishing them both the best of luck.

For you, the choice is much easier when it comes to selecting the finance company which can help you get the most mileage out of your purchase credit.

As a member of the worldwide United Dominions group, we offer you the benefits of more than 40 years of experience in business and industrial financing in every part of the globe.

Whether you require financing to take advantage of a special opportunity, to meet an emergency, or as a sound basis for preservation of working capital, United Dominions has the experience in your field to quickly set up a plan that works best for you.

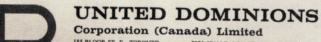

UNITED DOMINIONS
Corporation (Canada) Limited
185 BLOOR ST. E., TORONTO   3901 JEAN TALON ST. W., MONTREAL
448, 42ND. AVE. S.E., CALGARY   10006, 107TH ST., EDMONTON

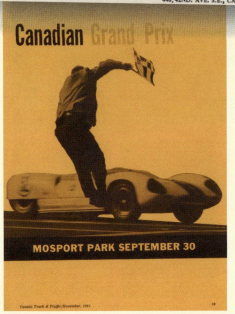

OCTOBER

Calendar

8	United States GP, Watkins Glen – ret'd in Lotus-Climax 18/21 (4-cyl)
13-15	'LA Times' GP, Riverside, USA – 16th in Lotus-Climax 19; 3-Hour production car race – 3rd overall & 1st in class in Sunbeam Alpine (sharing with Jack Brabham)
22	Pacific GP, Laguna Seca, USA – 1st in heat 1, 1st in heat 2 & 1st overall on aggregate in Lotus-Climax 19

On Sunday, October 1st, Stirling flew to Detroit where he visited Waterford Park, a 1.5 mile (2.4 km) circuit in Michigan, and did a few laps in a Lotus Elite. He then went on to a press reception where he spoke for 1¼ hours. "Another 'do' and hotel. Park Plaza Motor Hotel. Met Adele. Bed at 4am!"

Next morning he was doing radio and TV interviews. That evening he gave a three-hour talk, commencing at 8.30pm. "Then met Susan Sherl. Chatted and bed at 2.45 am!"

Tuesday he flew by Caravelle to IDL (known as JFK Airport today). "Dee Thorpe was the stewardess. Met by Harold Jason in Caddy limo. St. Morritz and fab suite. Meeting & on to BRDC 'do'. Food at Sardi's. Later Harold Loes & Dee to dance. Bed at 5.45am." He was working next day before meeting Shelley. "TV and bed at 1am!" On Thursday, he had lunch with Louise Collins before flying from La Guardia to Elmeira.

Next day he went up to the Watkins Glen circuit, venue of that weekend's US GP. He made a TV film for which he was paid $500. "Practice. V8 doesn't handle well due to suspension set-up? 130mph. Misses after a few laps. Feels good when OK. 4 too low geared 128mph. Chassis and brakes good. Hotel and on to cocktail 'do'. Film, TV and bed at 1.30 am."

JB	1.17.3
SM	1.18.7 V8 & 4 cyl
Bruce	1.18.7
G. Hill	1.18.8 etc

He continued practising on Saturday. "8 handles better but misses after 4-5 laps, even then it's quicker

 Stirling Moss ...

LOUISE COLLINS

"I managed to pinch her off Donald Healey in the Bahamas in 1955. She was an actress and her husband was one of the male singers on A Street Where you Live from My Fair Lady. They got divorced and she was having a holiday in the Bahamas and we went out together. Ultimately, she married Pete Collins. Her show business name was Louise King, but her real name was Cordier.

"We went out again in 1961 – a little romance!"

She had married Peter Collins on February 11th, 1957 in Coconut Grove Miami. Collins tragically died in 1958. Eva Marie Saint, a character in the John Frankenheimer move Grand Prix, was based on Louise King.

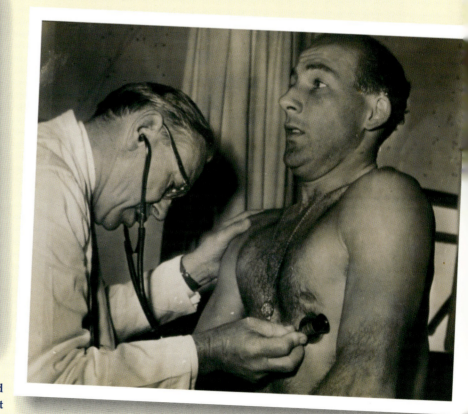

Further investigations took place in the USA to try and determine whether Moss was human or a robot

Hill, Moss Arrive for U.S. Grand Prix

By KENT NIXON

The two champions of world road racing arrived at the Chemung County Airport early Thursday night prior to the start of the United States Grand Prix at Watkins Glen at 2 p. m. Sunday.

Phil Hill, world's champion; and Stirling Moss, hailed internationally as the "uncrowned champion," arrived at the airport seconds apart Thursday night.

Moss arrived by private plane just ahead of the commercial craft carrying Hill, which landed at 6:18 p.m.

Hill, first American to hold the world's title, will not race Sunday but will serve as honorary steward.

Moss, a tremendous favorite at the Glen, will again be the driver to catch, even though — as an independent driver — he will be driving without benefit of some of the latest racing innovations.

Twenty drivers are entered in the 230-mile, 100-lap race over the 2.3 mile course.

Warm Greeting

Hill and Moss greeted each other warmly and joined Moss' manager, Rob Walker, for a brief at Watkins Sunday.

The manufacturer was greatly upset after the Monza tragedy—as was Hill.

Since former two-time champion Jack Brabham had acquitted himself well in finishing ninth in this year's "Indianapolis 500" did Hill have any wish to enter the race?

"I haven't really considered it," he said, but in the next breath added, "if I were in the race I'd have to have the right car and I've never had any difficulty with Ferrari cars."

Did Mr. Ferrari ever express any hopes of entering one of his cars in the "500?"

"None that I know of," Hill said.

Moss seemed cool to the idea of racing in the "500."

"Frankly, I don't think there is very much interest in it back home" the Englishman said.

"He was a wonderful fellow. A happy-go-lucky individual," Hill paid tribute to his former teammate.

"I have no plans right now," Hill said after it was mentioned there had been wide-spread speculation he might consider retirement.

"Yes, I'm still under contract to (Enzo) Ferrari," he added.

It is because of the wish of Ferrari, manufacturer of the famed Italian racing car bearing his name, that Hill will not race

DRIVERS CHAT—Two of the world's top road racing drivers arrived at the Chemung County Airport Thursday night, en route to Watkins Glen for Sunday's U.S. Grand Prix. From left, Rob Walker, manager of Stirling Moss (center) and Phil Hill, world's champion driver who will be honorary steward at the race.

Circuits

Moss on: WATKINS GLEN

"Tremendous amount of changes there. Quite a good road circuit, you know. Not the best, but quite a good one."

"One year we had hailstones the size of moth balls!"

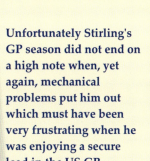

Unfortunately Stirling's GP season did not end on a high note when, yet again, mechanical problems put him out which must have been very frustrating when he was enjoying a secure lead in the US GP

Stirling Moss seemed not a happy man at the 'Glen. 'Twas one thing, then another. Here, during practice, he personally looks over front suspension of Rob Walker's Lotus "4," chosen over Lotus V-8 for big race.

Stirling Moss ...

SUNBEAM ALPINE

"The Alpine was quite a nice, if rather effeminate-looking car, but it was never a sports car in a real performance sense, although this outing made it feel a lot worse than it really was!"

October — Stirling Moss Scrapbook

1961

Stirling Moss Scrapbook

than 4. 35lbs. Oil 85°, oil and water. Later GPDA meeting and special [discussion] re. thoughtlessness, etc. Met Louise & Lynne."

JB	1.17.1	8
SM	1.17.2	8
Hill	1.18.1	
SM	1.18.2	4
Bruce	1.18.2	
Brooks	1.18.3	
Clark	1.18.3	

Sunday was race day. "Many people. Race. I had a good start. Switched round with Jack for lead. He then lost water. Also skirted retainer wall, but held it. Jack out and I had 58 secs [lead] at 59th lap. Car OK. Suddenly the oil pressure lowered and big end went. Out and H²O OK before. Got 7700 alone. Car felt good. Innes 1st, Dan 2nd. Flag Marshals slow on oil flag. Blue good. Hotel, food & bed at 3am."

On Monday he flew to New York and then on to Los Angeles. Here he met up with Shirlee Adams. Next day, he shopped, picked up an "airconditioned Rolls" and called on Mary and Rita. As Shirlee was working next day, he ate with Mary and Rita at the Plush Horse. "Bed at 2am!" On Thursday he gave a 30-minute talk at the Sportscasters' Lunch. Friday saw him at Riverside, a circuit in Southern California, where he was taking part in two races that weekend. He would be driving a Lotus 19 again and, rather curiously, a Sunbeam Alpine. The Rootes team had drafted in Stirling and Jack Brabham to share an Alpine in the three-hour production car race. On Friday SM concentrated on the Lotus. "Up at 8 and to circuit. Practice. 40/40lbs, 155mph. 2.01.3. No brakes. Oil 40-45 at end of straight! Hot day. H²O 85°. Oil 98°. Home and cocktails. Food and bed. Party on and on till sleep at 4.00am."

Jack:	2.01.0	2.7
SM	2.01.3	
Bruce	2.01.5	2.7
Dan	2.01.5	
Jim Hall	2.01.7	Chaparral

Saturday October 14th: "Up at 7.20 and out to track. Practised Alpine 2 laps and big ends fell out! Lousily prepared by US. Later shared other car with Jack and we won class and 3rd overall. Jack 2.35. SM 2.33. Car fair 6000 in 4th. Only used 3rd/4th."

Sunday was a day of frustration. "Hot 115°. Had a fabulous start and got to +12 [seconds] then rear brake seal went! Pit stop for 16mins. Then gearbox up the slot. Finished 9th OA. Ease at 6800. No brakes turn 1, 2 or 3. Brake before 5 on str. Jack used rain tyres! To do and then LA. TV and bed at 3am!"

Monday was spent 'stooging around' (one of Stirling's favourite phrases at this time) and later he went to see *Splendour in the Grass*. (G). On Tuesday he

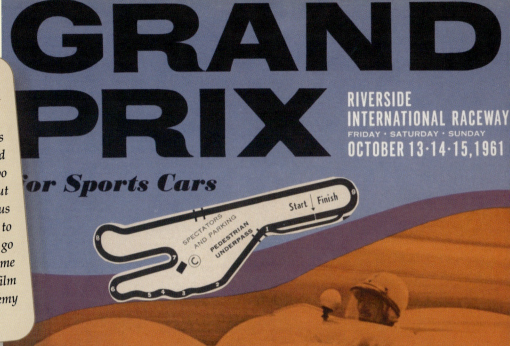

Splendour in the Grass

Starring Warren Beatty and Natalie Wood, this American film was written by William Inge and directed by Elia Kazan. The plot involves two Kansas high school sweethearts who fall in love but parental pressure, social correctness and class, plus the stockmarket crash of 1929, all conspire to frustrate the relationship and cause the girl to go insane. The title, taken from a poem of the same name by William Wordsworth, is recited during the film by Wood who was nominated for an Academy Award for her performance.

Brabham, Sunbeam No. 1, took third in enduro.

Stirling Moss Arrives, Eager for Grand Prix
'Uncrowned Champion' of Road Racing Plans Full Rest Before Riverside Event

Mimi Hines

Mimi Hines's career as a singer and comedienne started in 1958, initially in partnership with Phil Ford. After playing in all the leading nightclubs in the USA, she took the lead role, replacing Barbara Streisand, in Funny Girl on Broadway in 1966/7. She still lives in Las Vegas when not on tour.

FINAL PLACINGS — **RIVERSIDE**

1	Jack Brabham	Cooper Monaco	2:9:33.8	94.06 mph
2	Bruce McLaren	Cooper Monaco	2:9:44.8	
3	Jim Hall	Chaparral Chevrolet	2:10:55.8	
4	Roger Penske	Cooper Monaco	1 lap behind	
5	Bob Drake	Old Yaller III	3 laps	
6	Olivier Gendebien	Lotus Monte Carlo	3 laps	
7	Ken Miles	Porsche RS-61	3 laps	
8	Jack McAfee	Porsche RSK	3 laps	
9	Dan Gurney	Lotus Monte Carlo	4 laps	
10	Bob Donner	Porsche RS-61	4 laps	

Fastest lap: Jack Brabham, Cooper Monaco, 2:01.0, 97.416 mph.

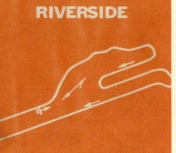

Patti Page

Born Clara Ann Fowler with a father who worked on the railroad and a mother who picked cotton, Patti Page has been a top American singing star for over 50 years. Her big hits were 'Tennessee Waltz' and '(How Much Is) That Doggie In the Window'. In October 2005, she was inducted into the Casino Legends Hall of Fame. Apart from still performing around 35 concerts a year, she has a business producing maple syrup products at Hilltop Farm, Bath, New Hampshire. When unscrewed, the bottle tops play a Page song!

Talking with Ryan, Moss tries out Nassau hat.

Sticking to the straight and narrow is not always a prudent policy as the unfortunate driver in the background appears to to be proving. Meanwhile, Stirling proves the merit of negotiating the bend instead!

Drivers

Moss on: INNES IRELAND

SM "I think Innes was very talented. He had a lot of car control. He was like a forerunner of Jean Alesi. Jean Alesi, even in later times had enormous talent, but he couldn't get it strung together to take a big win. Innes was much the same, I think. He had a lot of talent and he was as quick as Jimmy [Clark] in a similar car. I think his biggest problem was Colin [Chapman] was not as keen on him as he was on Jimmy. I think that he could see that Innes was a bit of a loose cannon by comparison and he did what most people would do, he settled for the guy that was more reliable."

PP: "Was he tremendous fun? Pretty wild?"

SM: "Yes he was. Half of him was good fun to be with; the other half you would try and ignore. You know he was one of those people who was a bit of a Jekyll and Hyde. Peter Collins was another good friend of mine, but he was a lot more realistic."

PP: "During 1961 you and Innes helped each other. He lent you the works car for Monza. On another occasion he followed you around because he was struggling to even qualify. You were clearly good pals and very supportive of each other?"

SM: "Yes, and he beat me twice with the latest Lotus, at Goodwood in 1960, which just showed that he was right up there when he had a distinct advantage. The Lotus, when it came out, was quite ahead of other cars and he didn't need that much advantage to be able to win."

PP: "He had quite a lot of accidents!"

SM: "Yes, but don't forget he was driving for Lotus! That is the point."

$20,000 Pacific Grand Prix

OPEN TO DRIVERS AND CARS REGISTERED AND IN GOOD STANDING WITH THE UNITED STATES AUTO CLUB

FIRST OVERALL — $3,000

	HEAT No. 1		HEAT No. 2	
	Over 2 Litres	Under 2 Litres	Over 2 Litres	Under 2 Litres
FIRST	$2,000	$1,250	$2,000	$1,250
SECOND	1,000	700	1,000	700
THIRD	700	400	700	400
FOURTH	400	200	400	200
FIFTH	200	100	200	100
SIXTH	100	—	100	—

Plus $50.00 for each car starting the first heat but not in the prize money for that heat and $50.00 for each car added from the non-qualifiers to complete the starting field for the second heat but not participating in prize money.

1961

flew to Las Vegas. That evening, "Food and then saw Patti Page and Mimi Hines. Fab. Gambled – blackjack and won $165 from Patti !X! Snack and bed at 3.30am!" Wednesday was not too stressful either. He sunbathed and swam before seeing, "Juliet Prowse in *Irma* and then Della Reece. Lost $120. Bed at 4.30am!" Della Reece was a singer and actress.

On Thursday, he flew back to LA and drove for five and half hours to Laguna Seca where he would be racing the Lotus 19 in the Pacific GP that Sunday. Friday was spent practising. "4.6 axle 38lbs f & r. Get 6700 (118mph) 60° oil. Later to pancake house with Olivier and MC and SA. Hotel and bath. Cocktail, party and food. Called at hospital to have something taken from my left eye. Bed at 12.45am."

SM	1.15.9
Penske	1.17.0
Ryan	1.17.8
McL	1.18.7
Olivier	1.18.5

A radio interview and a visit to the movies to see *C. English* (NG) was about all Stirling did on Saturday. Sunday was a contrast. "Up at 9.45 and to circuit. 65,000. 1st heat. Good start. Later throttle springs broke and brakes bad. Dan and I diced. He left road 2 x. I won by about 10 secs. 2nd Heat, I lead to finish but lost all brakes with 15 laps to go. Dan also 2nd again. Jack and Bruce lost oil. 'Do' and off to San F. Check in Hilton Hotel and bed at 3am!"

Stirling was up six hours later and flew back to London, via New York,. "No bed. Landed at 11.00. Met by VP. Office. What a mess. Work all day till 7.00. Met Judy. Food and to EC Rd. Mess !X! Sold Lotus XIX to Donald Miles of Texas. Bed at 1am!" Next morning: "Up at 7.45. Took JC and VP to breakfast at Cumberland [hotel]. Work all day. Row with Ken. Later to Cunard cocktail 'do'. JC cooked a fab meal. Called on David and bed at 1.30am."

This new habit of early mornings continued with Stirling rising at 7.30am on Thursday morning. VP cooked him breakfast and he worked all day, seeing Andrew Hedges and Bill McCowen during the day. "On to Bob Ball and JC. Bed at 3.45am!" Next day he worked, did a press interview in Italian and, from 6pm, had a four-hour BRP directors' meeting. "'Wheel' for food and to JC and bed at 1am.

He was at the Steering Wheel Club again next day for "J. Webb's wedding 'do'. To see JC and then met David and Jean and to Churchill's for food." Next day, a Sunday, he visited Bert Rees at Harefield Hospital, en route to his parents' place at Tring.

On the concluding day of the month, he worked from 7.30am until 8.00pm. "Collected Sheilagh Poulter-Marron. To Village. On to Satire (dragged). Lousy daiquiri. 51 & bed at 2am!"

McLaren Reflects

In his column in Motor Racing in October, Bruce wrote of his two outings in the new E-type, on both occasions having the 'misfortune' to be up against Stirling. "So far I've had two drives for Peter Berry, and on both occasions I've finished second after seeing Stirling Moss disappear into the distance with the Walker/Wilkins Ferrari Berlinetta. The Italian car has a tremendous amount of steam in a straight line, but already I think the Jag is faster through the twisty bits…and as I've said, there's more to come!"

Stirling has always been very popular and well known in the USA and continues to be which, in spite of his great modesty, is a source of great pride to him

Sheilagh Poulter-Marron

Sheilagh Poulter-Marron is remembered by Stirling and Val Pirie as a stunning dark-haired girl with a very deep voice. A friend of Caroline Nuttall's, she was a "top quality model" but sadly committed suicide many years later.

It's All Moss at Monterey

 Guild of Muttering Rotters

Stirling was voted Driver of the Year by the Guild of Motoring Writers and was the first driver to receive the accolade for the second time.

The October issue of Motor Racing had a nice cover shot of Stirling in a Cooper single-seater. In their caption, they stated that he was already the winner of 15 international races that year "but still unable to capture the Championship".

 'Satire'

This is a puzzler. With the popularity of 'Beyond the Fringe', satire was in vogue. It sounds as though Stirling is referring to a club but the private members' club formed by Peter Cook and dedicated to satire, and which did open in 1961, was known as The Establishment. It seems likely this is what Stirling is referring to. The mention of a daiquiri cocktail is also mysterious as Stirling did not drink such concoctions at that time.

Moss Winner Without Brakes

MONTEREY, Calif., Oct. 22 (UPI). — Stirling Moss of England, running the final 15 laps without brakes, took both heats in winning top honors in the Laguna Seca Pacific Grand Prix Sunday.

The lead-footed Englishman shot his green Lotus Climax across the finish line only five seconds ahead of Don Gurney, Riverside, Calif., in the second heat after beating the same driver by seven seconds in the opening heat.

In both 100-mile heats the order of finish was the same for first four places, with Jack Brabham of Australia finishing third and Bruce McLaren, a speedster from New Zealand, fourth.

Moss said that his brakes gave out with 15 laps to go in the last heat. He slowed his car for the curves only by gearing down.

Philadelphia Inquirer 23.10.61

STIRLING MOSS here leads Ken Miles (9) and Jack McAfee at Riverside Oct. 15. Moss led for 27 laps, was forced out but re-entered to finish 16th. Miles edged McAfee for 7th after race-long duel. (MOTORACING photo by Gus V. Vignolle)

NOVEMBER

1961 Calendar

No racing events this month

November was a very different month for Stirling. There was no racing and films dominated the early part of the month with much filming and much film-going. The first day began with two hours recording for BP with the doyen of motor racing commentators, Raymond Baxter. That evening he dined with old friend David Haynes at Simpson's in the Strand. Next day he was buying furniture. "Helped Lotus on publicity deal and Innes, Graham & Jimmy." Later he went to the "premiere of *Bachelor in Paradise*. Bob Hope made an appearance. Food at Angel. Bed at 4am."

Friday was a day of work before changing into tails, attending a BARC dinner (alone unusually) at the Grosvenor House, making a speech and receiving the BARC Gold Medal for 1961. "On to Saddle Room with a crowd and Sheilagh. Home and bed at 4am!" The BARC Gold Medal was awarded to British subjects in recognition of outstanding achievements in motor racing.

Next day he collected Diana from LAP and later saw "*The Lord Chamberlain Regrets* (G). Food at Angel and bed at 4am." On Sunday, he "Saw *Two Women* B. LAP & Diana off. Food with Herb & met Sheilagh. Bed at 2am!" Monday saw him, "Up at 8. B'fast & off to Shepperton for BP film with S. Filmed all day. Work and then ATAS meeting at 51. Work & at 9.30 took Jean Lochwood to 36. Home and bed at 2.30am!"

On Tuesday a day of work was relieved by a more light-hearted evening. He was a Miss World judge! "At 7.15 home & tux & to Talk of Town. Met Miss Germany Romy März and Miss NZ, etc. home and bed at 2.30am." Romy Marz was a semi-finalist and Miss New Zealand, Leone Mary Main, a finalist.

A couple of days later he was filming at Madame Tussauds, the famous waxworks before seeing *Two Laps of Honour* (G) in the evening. This motor racing film was based upon his two momentous 1961 victories. Friday, he attended the "Sportsman of the

Two photos of Inge from Stirling's albums

The Lord Chamberlain Regrets

The Lord Chamberlain Regrets was the revue guru Peter Myers's last big West End success. It starred Ronnie Stevens, Millicent Martin and Joan Sims, opening at the Saville Theatre in August 1961. Most notable song was the 'Ballad of Basher Green'.

Bachelor in Paradise

Starring Bob Hope and Lana Turner, this comedy features Hope as bachelor author A.J. Niles who moves into an American suburb called Paradise Cove. One bachelor plus lonely housewives apparently equalled many angry husbands!

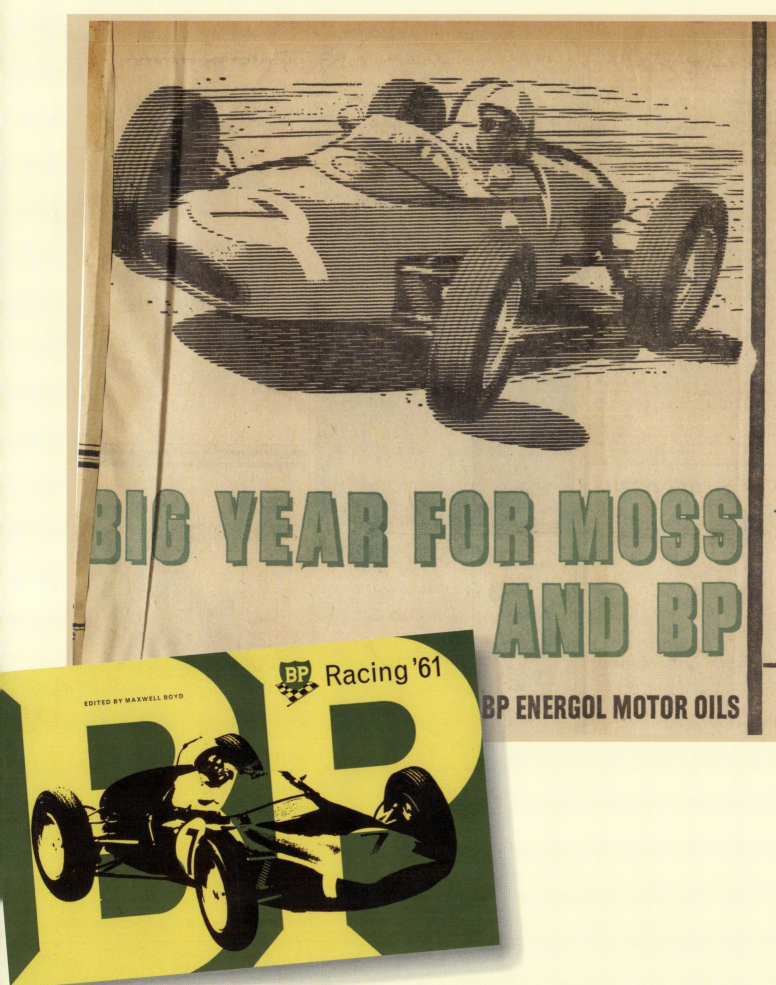

MOSS'S OUTSTANDING 1961 SUCCESSES

JANUARY:	101 MILE INTERNATIONAL RACE, SYDNEY (AUSTRALIA) (LOTUS)	1st
APRIL:	LAVANT CUP, GOODWOOD (GREAT BRITAIN) (COOPER)	1st
MAY:	B.R.D.C. INTERNATIONAL TROPHY, SILVERSTONE (GREAT BRITAIN) (COOPER)	1st
	MONACO GRAND PRIX (MONACO) (LOTUS)	1st
	NÜRBURGRING 1,000 KM. (GERMANY) UP TO 2000 CC. CLASS (PORSCHE)	1st
JUNE:	SILVER CITY TROPHY RACE, BRANDS HATCH (GREAT BRITAIN) (LOTUS)	1st
	200-MILE INTERNATIONAL SPORTS CAR RACE, ONTARIO (CANADA) (LOTUS)	1st
JULY:	BRITISH EMPIRE TROPHY RACE, SILVERSTONE (GREAT BRITAIN) (COOPER)	1st
AUGUST:	EUROPEAN GRAND PRIX, NÜRBURGRING (GERMANY) (LOTUS)	1st
	G.T. BRITISH RACING & SPORTS CAR CLUB EVENTS, BRANDS HATCH (GREAT BRITAIN) (FERRARI)	1st overall
	SWEDISH GRAND PRIX, KARLSKOGA (SWEDEN) (LOTUS)	1st
	DANISH GRAND PRIX, ROSKILDRING (DENMARK) (LOTUS)	1st
	R.A.C. TOURIST TROPHY RACE, GOODWOOD (GREAT BRITAIN) (FERRARI)	1st
SEPTEMBER:	7th MODENA GRAND PRIX (ITALY) (LOTUS)	1st
	INTERNATIONAL GOLD CUP, OULTON PARK (GREAT BRITAIN) (FERGUSON)	1st
	PACIFIC GRAND PRIX, MONTEREY (U.S.A.) (LOTUS)	1st

JOHANNESBURG NEWS

NINE HOURS ENDURANCE RACE

1st DAWIE GOUS and JOHN LOVE driving a PORSCHE SPYDER
2nd BRUCE JOHNSTONE and NICK KINGWILL driving an ALFA ROMEO T1

BOTH CARS USED BP SUPER

Stirling Moss ...

1½ LITRE FORMULA

PP: *"Did you enjoy the smaller 1½ litre formula?"*

SM: *"No, No. The 1½ litre 1500cc [formula] was to my mind a stupid way for the FIA to go. The one benefit was that it made a driver consider everything. In other words, every time you turn the steering wheel you slow the car, therefore, you do less steering – the less you can do the better. But having power is quite often, if you know how to use it, a help to get out of trouble."*

1961

Year (D. Express) 'do'. Got medal for 4th & Pat for 6th." Later that evening, "Leone Main (Miss N.Z.) to Elephant & on to Angel. Bed at 3.30am." Saturday saw Stirling and VP off "to BBC TV Trial at [near] Tring. On to farm. Snacks & later to Jane Estel Cole's 21st via Sue in hospital. Party VG. Met Jenny Burgoyne. Blonde 5'5" - 34.22.36 - Size 10. 51 & bed at 5.00am!" He was spectating at the Trial and *Autosport* had a photo of him presenting the winners' trophy to the captain of the Northern team, rally driver Eric Jackson.

Sunday was a day of stooging, before taking Judy Carne to the "Lotus House. Bed at 12pm!" Early evening on the Monday, he had a two-hour UDT meeting before taking JC to Ken Gregory's. "Home & bed at 2am!" Tuesday was busy. "Up at 8.00. Work all day. Rushed around. Heard our Lotii not exactly as factory cars! Ordered Elite also for Herb. Later called on Pete Garnier who had an accident at MIRA. He looks OK but has lost some teeth & has 40 stitches in his face! On to food with JC and David and Leone. Home and bed at 2.30am!"

He was up again a few hours later as he had a boat to catch. "Up at 8am. Office and then off to Southampton with JC and DH in Jag at 10.15. Boarded. Food & met Kim Cutting. Stooged round. Cabin A116. Bed at 2.00am. Up at 8.30 when KC woke me! Cinema, gym, swim, Turkish bath, etc. Later to Tourist Class & met Sarah Ross. Danced till 3.30. Bed at 5.30am!! Up at 8.30. Pool, gym, etc. Films, Turkish bath. Danced, bingo & bed at 2.30! Up at 9.00. Same as yesterday's routine. Saw *Parent Trap* (EX). Bed at 3.00am! Up at 9.30. Same as yesterday. Saw Nikki G. film. Bed at 3.00am!"

On Monday Stirling arrived, presumably in New York, having packed and paid his tips. He dropped off his baggage, plus that of Kim and Sarah. "Later met Shirlee and to Persian Room and saw Diahann Carroll. Bed at 2.00am." American singer and actress, Diahann Carroll has enjoyed a prolific career, commencing with Carmen Jones in 1954, and starred in many films and US TV series, and more recently *Dynasty* and *The Colbys*.

Next morning, Stirling flew off to Miami. "Met by Bill France, Jr. & flew to Daytona in Beach Twin. Saw track, talked and back to Miami. Met Joan Morris & food. Bed at 1am." Also on this page of his diary, Stirling wrote, "Saw missile shot up from Cape Canaveral". "It was impressive to me," recalls Stirling today, "to see how slow it was."

Wednesday, November 22: "Up at 9.00 and a ghastly day. Did tickets and then to Joan's and Bev's. Plane delayed until 4.15 from 1pm (Gust). Good flight to Mexico. Met by Rootes Chief. Mr. Freshney

THE TELEVISION TROPHY TRIAL. Stirling Moss holds the trophy with Raymond Baxter looking on, just before the trophy was presented to Eric Jackson of the Northern team.

Stirling Moss permanently flameproof overalls

Cut a smart figure with the new Stirling Moss-designed permanently flameproof overalls that never need reproofing. You can wash or dry-clean them as often as you like—they'll retain their stylish appearance and flame-proof properties. Each suit bears Stirling Moss's signature and has concealed double-ended diagonal zip, pleated back, elasticated wrists and waist. Lightweight poplin, flameproof to B.S.I. No. 3120.

COLOUR: STIRLING BLUE
When ordering, state height and chest measurement.

£7. 15. 0 (p/p 2/3d.)

Send 6d. stamp for bright little catalogue

LES LESTON LTD (Dept. A.14) 314 HIGH HOLBORN LONDON, W.C.1
Trade and export enquiries invited CHAncery 8655

GPDA

The Grand Prix Drivers' Association was formed in 1961 and Stirling was the first President and Chairman. In an interview with John Blunsden for Motor Racing magazine, he was quick to point out that it was not "some sort of racing drivers' trade union". The aim of the GPDA was "to make motor racing safer for everyone – drivers, officials, spectators, the lot. As I said just now, this is no drivers' union, and discussion on entries, contracts or anything to do with finance does not take place at our meetings. I can't stress this too strongly. You know, even now one or two people are inferring that our 'safety' theme is a shield for a campaign to gain a better deal for ourselves. This just isn't true!"

Among his other comments, Stirling talked of marshals at certain circuits. "The standard of marshalling at times is not good; I don't think some of the people who are given flags realise what a vital job they are supposed to be doing. Some of the blighters seem far more interested in taking photographs than waving flags; maybe they think that by hiding the oil flag they may get the action shot of the year!"

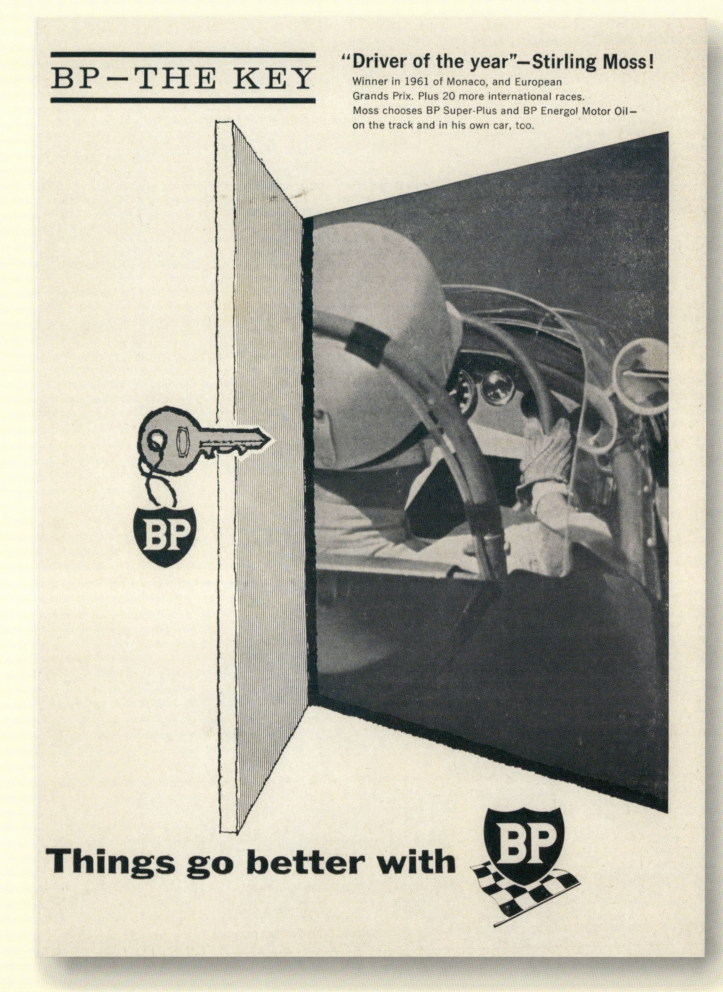

with Minx. Off at 7.30. Had petrol pipe troubles and then the big ends went! at 12pm. Rented taxi for Acapulco, 400 pesos. Took 5¼ hours. Bed at 6am." Deservedly, Thursday was a day of relaxation with a selection of swimming, sunbathing and looking around. He went to bed early – at midnight. On Friday he went deep sea fishing, water skied, swam, shopped, wrote cards and "Saw La Perla divers, bed at 1am!" After rising late on Saturday, he did a photo shoot for Hertz before more water skiing.

Unfortunately, something had disagreed with him. "Felt lousy. Checked out and flew to Mexico and on to Houston. Bed at 1.30am. Up latish and Joan flew to Miami, self to NY. Harold & Lou met me. Took Dory out. Bed at 2.15am! Up at 9 and off to Roosevelt Raceway. Laid out circuit. Later town and called on Anita. Bed at 3.30am." The Roosevelt Raceway was originally and briefly the site, in Westbury, Long Island, of the Vanderbilt Cup auto races, the facility was developed for harness (horse) racing through the fifties and sixties.

Next day Stirling had a medical for All Star Insurance, followed by lunch with Rob and Betty Walker. They then went to Idelwild (JFK) and flew by BOAC to Nassau. "Met by Norm and to NB Lodge. Food, cocktails and then met KM, drinks and bed at 3am." KM would be Katie Moss, his first wife.

On the final day of the month, Stirling called on Katie and together they ate at Margot's. Margot Beaubien, like Katie, a Canadian lady, was Maid of Honour at their wedding, at which she met her future husband, Sir Gawaine Baillie, Bt, amateur racer and one of the pre-eminent stamp collectors of the twentieth century. That night, Stirling and Margot "Chatted till late…"

Eric Jackson

Eric Jackson ran the Polar Motor Company, a Ford dealership in his native Barnsley, and was a successful international Ford works rally driver. He would be British Rally Champion in 1964 and Trials Champion in 1965. He was also known as the Marathon Man and loved a challenge. They included breaking the London to Cape Town record in a Ford Corsair, driving round the world in 43 days (possibly unbeaten to this day?), racing the Windsor Castle ocean liner from Cape Town to Southampton (beating it by 1hr 3mins!), attempting to drive to Timbuktu and back in a fortnight for a bet and driving a Ford Cortina down the bobsleigh run at Cortina in Italy in company with Jim Clark. Today he and his lovely wife, Kathy, are active members of the International Jaguar XK Club, whose Patron is one Sir Stirling Moss!

1961

DECEMBER

Calendar

3-12	Nassau Tourist Trophy, Bahamas – 1st in heat, 1st in final in Ferrari 250GT SWB
8	Governor's Trophy – ret'd in heat in Team Rosebud Lotus-Climax 19
10	Nassau Trophy – ret'd in Lotus-Climax 19
17	Natal GP, Westmead, Durban, South Africa – 2nd in UDT/Laystall 1.5 Lotus-Climax 18/21
26	South African GP, East London – 2nd in UDT/Laystall 1.5 Lotus-Climax 18/21

Stirling spent the early part of December in Nassau and the second half in South Africa. The month began, as the previous one had ended, in relaxed fashion with much socialising. However, the weather was not too good and he could only sunbathe for a while as it was too cold. "Called on Diane, Ileana & Norm who has flu. Later to Margot's and met Morag. Food and to Rum Keg. Bed at 3.30am." On Saturday, he had breakfast with Katie before going to the local circuit where he would be racing next day and the following weekend. "Later cocktails at PG, food with crew at Blackbeard's and called at Sun and bed at 12.30am." He was in bed comparatively early for Sunday was a day of action with 2735 GT, the Walker Ferrari 250 SWB.

Next morning Bill France called, he had breakfast with Norm and "met Dorothea Mimms and Beverley. Circuit 3 laps practice. The heat – 1st. Wet. Final 1st by 80 secs and wet. Snack and drink. Bed at 2 am. Had a visitor (female) at 6am!"

"Stirling's victory was a popular one," stated Car and Driver. "Island residents cheered him enthusiastically. He is well known there, maintaining a vacation home in Nassau, and when he breezed over the finish line, a large crowd of small boys rushed across the track. Officials forced them back, since other cars were approaching at high speed, but as Moss entered the winner's circle, he was mobbed by admirers."

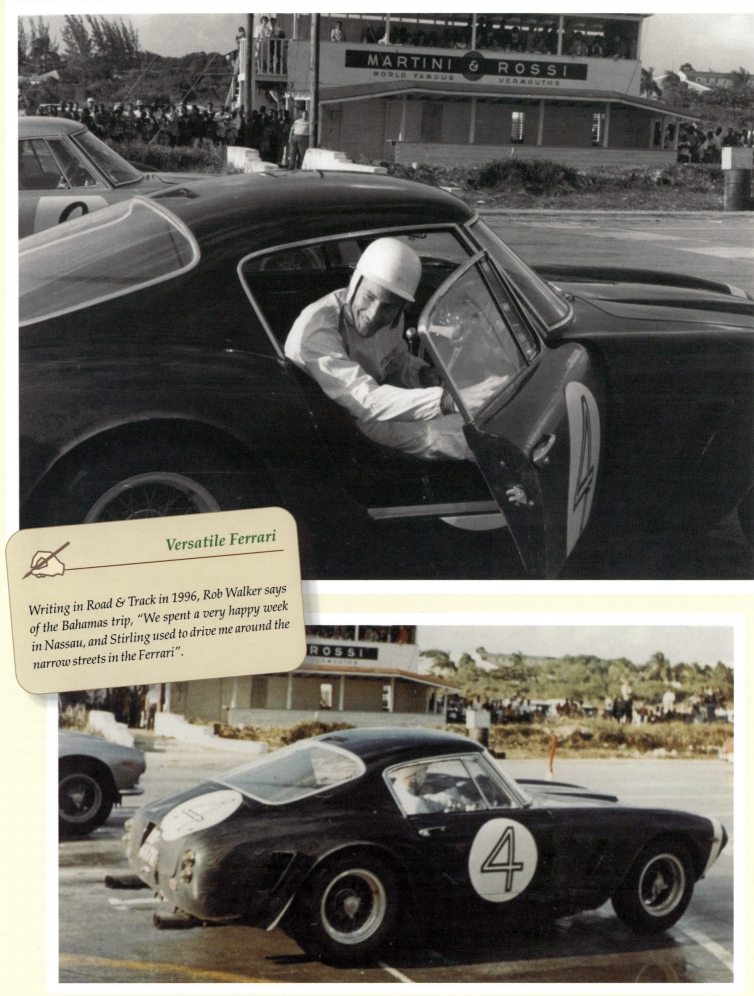

Versatile Ferrari

Writing in Road & Track in 1996, Rob Walker says of the Bahamas trip, "We spent a very happy week in Nassau, and Stirling used to drive me around the narrow streets in the Ferrari".

Stirling powers off the line in 2735GT in pretty miserable conditions

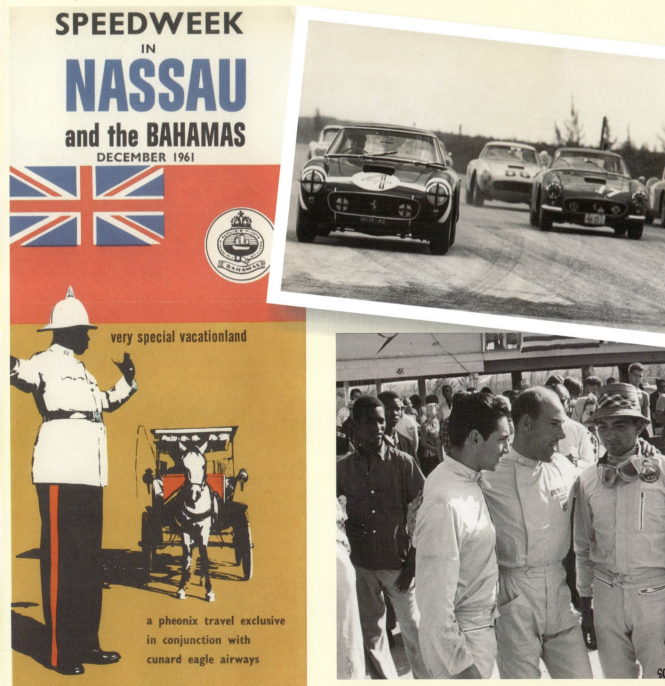

Stirling with two young rising stars, Ricardo and Pedro Rodriguez

Nassau Tourist Trophy

"Splattering through tropical rain showers and buffeted by high winds, Stirling Moss returned to his vacation home here today (Dec 3)," ran a bulletin put out by the Bahamas News Bureau, "and scored a repeat victory in the Nassau Tourist Trophy race at Oakes Field Course."

As the rain came down but the sun shone on parts of the track, a large rainbow hung in the sky as Stirling easily won a five-lap heat in the Walker-Wilkins Ferrari Berlinetta from American Bob Grossman in a similar machine and two more 250 GTs.

The TT was to have been of 25 laps but the weather would intervene. "At the start…, Nassau skies had cleared considerably and the sun, dropping lower in the west, made a golden mirror of the still-wet asphalt track." Grossman took the lead with SM in pursuit. At the end of the first lap the American lead by a length and a half. "Great plumes of water rooster-tailed on Emerald Beach Pass behind the sleek speedsters," continued the rather flowery local report.

Stirling took the lead on the second lap and, as the track dried a little, increased his speed and his advantage over Grossman. By the fifth circuit, he started lapping the field. "Completing his eighth lap Moss passed three competitors going by the viewing stands, bringing the promenade spectators to their feet.

"On the basis of elapsed time for the first 10 laps…, officials anticipated that the full race distance could not be covered, since … only 19 minutes separated the drivers from the automatic 5pm cut-off time."

By the 17th lap, Stirling had lapped all but three of the field and at the end of his 21st lap received the chequered flag as 5pm had arrived and most cars had their headlamps blazing as darkness settled over the tropical island. He won from Grossman by 83 seconds and averaged 80.118mph over the 12-turn 4½ mile course.

"Greeting Moss in the victory circle was his car owner, R.R.C. Walker, scion of the British whisky family, and Lady Symonette, wife of Sir Roland Symonette of Nassau, who presented the gigantic silver trophy as the crowd pressed in."

1961

It seems Stirling got up twice on Monday morning as he recorded, "Up at 9am and 11am" in his diary! "Usual windy day. Stooged around. Later to circuit. Used Ferrari GT. Cocktails at Junkanoo [a club in Nassau]. Met Pat Kennedy and to BC. Bed at 2am. Up at 10am. Looked around. Cocktails at Pilot House. Then took Dorothea to Buena Vista and Goombay. Bed at 4.30 am."

Unfortunately the rather miserable weather impacted on Wednesday. Stirling went up to the circuit but there was no practice so he just had to fall back on socialising again! "Later cocktails at Be-Ma. Met Helen Gizzi and Sheila McRoberts. Food at Sun and on to Junkanoo and Cat & Fiddle. Chatted till late. Bed at 6.30am."

Stirling was up four-and-a-half hours later and driving the Lotus 19. "Nice Day. Breakfast and circuit with Helen, Sheila and Norm. Practice. 2.57.0, brakes fade, tyres are normal and fair and oil down to 40lbs! Get 6800 3-times with 4.1 and 650. 40lbs f & r hot, tyre wear OK. Could use speeds; no tyres. Home and cocktails at Montague. Food at Buena Vista. Bed at 3am."

Dan	2.53.9
Penske	2.55.3
Hall	2.55.5

Friday was not to be a good day. "Up at 10. Town and circuit. Race. Car awful. Slides a lot. 40/40psi. Oil 40lbs! Ease at 6800 3x, Penske passed, couldn't stay. Laying 3rd from 32nd start place, then back rt hub carrier broke - also damper. Found bits in Lauderdale. Cocktails. Food with Norm and Graham. Party. Collected Helen. Bed at 4.30am."

Stirling's friend, Norm Solomon, was racing next day but had an accident. After collecting parts for the Lotus 19 from Dan Publicher in Lauderdale, SM gave Norm a lesson. Sunday's race with the Lotus started better for Stirling. "Good start and lead for 26 laps. Dan very fast. Wishbone broke. Tyre wear quite reasonable. Hotel. Later took Helen and Sheila to Oakes Field. Collected Dixie Boatright. Cocktails and food and Norm and Beverley. Then danced 'Meringue' and 'Twist' until 5am. Bed at 6am."

Monday saw him heading back to London. "Up at 9.30. Packed. Saw Donald Healey and Don Miles and Co. To airport and Dixie. Saw KM and Rob and Betty and Graham. Latter 3 to NY. Off at 6pm. Met Doug Smith at NY. Off at 10.30 to LAP. No sleep. Crowded and how. No bed."

As to Tuesday, "Up all night. Met at 10.15am by VP. Office and work all day till 9.15pm! To JC and food. Bed at 12pm!"

Wednesday was a very mixed day, starting badly and ending in triumph. "Up at 10 after an awful

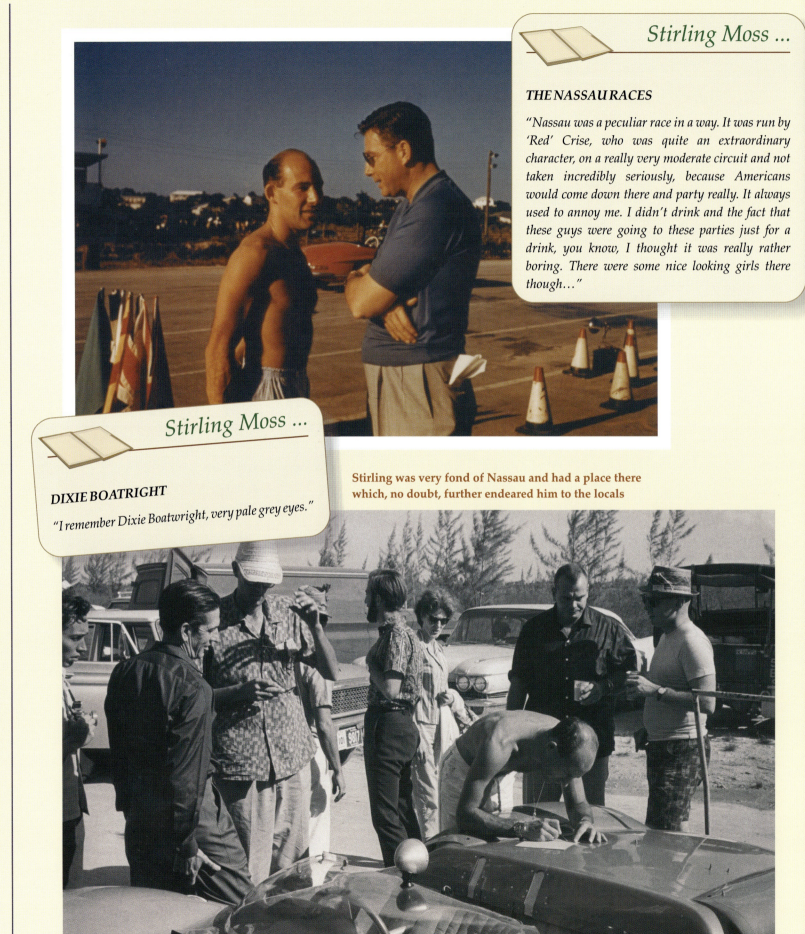

Stirling Moss ...

THE NASSAU RACES

"Nassau was a peculiar race in a way. It was run by 'Red' Crise, who was quite an extraordinary character, on a really very moderate circuit and not taken incredibly seriously, because Americans would come down there and party really. It always used to annoy me. I didn't drink and the fact that these guys were going to these parties just for a drink, you know, I thought it was really rather boring. There were some nice looking girls there though…"

Stirling Moss ...

DIXIE BOATRIGHT

"I remember Dixie Boatright, very pale grey eyes."

Stirling was very fond of Nassau and had a place there which, no doubt, further endeared him to the locals

Moss Wheels Car To Nassau Title

NASSAU, Bahamas — (AP) — Stirling Moss of London opened the car portion of the eighth annual Bahamas International Speed Weeks Sunday with an 83-second victory in the Nassau Tourist Race.

Driving through occasional tropical showers, Moss wheeled his Ferrari Berlinetta to the finish nearly two miles ahead of Bob Grossman of West Nyack, N.Y., in an identical model.

The wet track held Moss speed to 80.113 mph compared to his 83.559 mph record.

Miami Herald 4.12.61

Rob Walker's Reflections In The Wet

Rob Walker wrote up the Nassau Speed Week for Autosport who described him as "our special (very) correspondent". He commented that the untypical un-tropical conditions of heavy showers "did not suit the many American drivers, who on the whole do not race in the wet, but, of course there was one driver it did suit – S. Moss Esq., O.B.E to give him his full title, but he did not need any advantages and would have preferred the rain to have saved itself for the following Sunday, the day of the big race."

As to the first heat of the TT, "All the cars were lined up with our mechanic Stan Collier sitting in our car as Stirling had got held up on the other side of the course, and the starter was just about to send them off when I pointed out that we had no driver. Fortunately, at this point Stirling appeared, wearing lilac trousers, an olive paisley pattern shirt and sandals, in keeping with the surroundings, which he did not have time to change before the start of the heat."

When Hayes in the third-placed Berlinetta spun off, Walker wrote, "…even Stirling said it was extremely slippery and anybody could be excused for going off, although I doubt if he would have excused himself".

After explaining that "Nassau racing is somewhat less serious than European racing", Walker stated, "The whole organisation has for some years rested on a colourful character by the name of Captain Sherman (Red) Crise, who goes about wearing a yachting cap, and I doubt if there is anybody who can take the wind out of his sails. The starter, Arch James, wears a wonderful uniform, comprising a black and white striped cap and shirt , white 'plus four' trousers and black stockings with white shoes."

As for the final, "The circuit was still very wet and Stirling found he was shipping a lot of water, being behind Bob Grossman, and this was getting on his plugs and making the car miss down the straight; the only kind of miss that Stirling does not like!

"Suddenly at 5pm, after 21 laps had been completed, the chequered flag fell. This surprised everybody but apparently they never race after 5pm as it gets too dark very quickly, and whatever the state of the race, they drop the flag and results stand as at that time. Stirling came in and said I did not know what I was doing and I had been giving him the wrong number of laps to go, and it was not until I explained to him what had happened that he realised he had not completed the full 25 laps, because he had set his mileometer at the start of the race and it so happened that it was reading the exact full distance when the flag dropped, but it was incorrect owing to axle ratio and wheel sizes.

"The general opinion of the populace was that 'dat Moss man sure can drive'."

1961

night. Helen Gizzi called, she has left her husband! Chatted for 20 mins plus! Work all day. Feel awful. At 8pm to TV Sportsview Sporting Personality of the Year 'do'. I was it! Nervous. On to see JC. She is ill. On to Colony and DH. HJ, Pat & Eric and Jean and Nina. Sandra joined us. Bed at 4am."

After a full day's work, Stirling and Herb flew from London Airport to Paris and from there to South Africa. On the plane, he met a lady called Christina Rice. He had no sleep and arrived at Johannesburg at 2.30 local time. From there he flew on to Durban where he was met by "Jill Margery and Co. Food, Party and bed at 12.00."

Next day was Saturday, December 16th. "Up at 10. To garage. Photo. Circuit. 7 laps. About 1.29.0. I did not do a flying lap on purpose. Track in bad condition due to 6 inches of rain. Car feels twitchy and won't rev over 7400 without valve float feeling! Brakes heavy. Home. Changed. Chinese food and bed at 12.00pm."

With scarcely any time to recover, Stirling was racing on Sunday. "Up at 10.00. Nice day and to circuit. Race, and I was made to start last! Difficult to pass. Got to 2nd behind Clark but couldn't make any way on him. I had D9, he D12. Got 7450 with 4.4. Jim 7500 with 4.2! Track slippery. Other drivers 11, 20, 25 very bad to pass. Hotel, bath and food. Bed at 1.30am."

Monday was a well-deserved lazy day and mainly spent on the beach. Prize-giving took place that evening.

After visiting a snake farm and doing a radio recording, Stirling flew back to Jo'burg and then drove for five hours. After getting to bed at midnight, he was up at 5.30am and in the Kruger Park half-an-hour later. "Saw all types of animals. Elephants, Giraffes, Zebras, Lions, Leopards, chameleons, etc, etc. 20 varieties !X! To Park Hotel. Bed after barbecue at 10pm. Up at 6.30am. Off into bush at 7.45. Saw a few animals. To Bushman's Rock Hotel and swim and snack. Off at 2.30 to Jo'burg. I drove a bit. Checked in Carlton Hotel. Food and bed at 11pm."

Friday saw him flying to East London where he was to drive the UDT/Laystall Lotus 18/21. "Arrived at 12.30pm. Dials Hotel and practice. My car is not ready cos valve springs not here. Used Masten's. Good engine. Get 7700 1 lap and 1.34.5 then car away. Windy. Hotel. Food. Saw *Last Sunset* (F). Bed at 12.00pm." Masten Gregory was driving the team's second Lotus 18/21.

Jim	1.33.9	
Masten	1.34.5	Masten's car 1 lap
Masten	1.35.5	

Unfortunately Team Rosebud preparation during this period appeared to leave a lot to be desired and this impacted on Stirling's performances in the Governor's Trophy and Nassau Trophy races with the Lotus 19

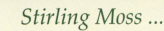

DOROTHEA & BEVERLEY

"Dorothea Mimms used to drive in pink and Beverley would be Beverley Wheeler, who was with Cunard Airlines."

Spectators got a good view!

Sartorial Sensation

"Moss, incidentally," stated the Bahamas News Bureau, "was the sartorial sensation of Sunday's race. He wore skin-tight lilac trousers, an olive, paisley-pattern shirt open at the throat revealing a large gold medal hanging from his neck, and thong slippers.

"His only concessions to racing apparel were his familiar scuffed crash helmet and leather driving gloves."

Stirling and Lady Symonette are dwarfed by the Nassau Tourist Trophy

B.B.C. Sportsview Personality of the Year

PP: "Did you consider it a great honour?"
SM: "Oh yes, most certainly because motor racing is not the first choice of the public. Really they normally preferred football."

Autosport's editorial was devoted to Stirling's triumph and noted it was the first time a racing driver had won the award, which is decided by votes from the viewers. "The title of Champion of the World many have eluded Stirling Moss so far, but there is little doubt that his many stirring performances have gained for him one of the largest followings of fans that any single sportsman has today."

Stirling met both Helen Gizzi (left) and Dixie Boatwright (right) in Nassau

1961

Stirling Moss Scrapbook

Saturday December 23rd: "Up at 8.30. Shopped,. 1½ hours sun. Am now pretty tanned. Lunch. Practice. Little wind. My car has lousy brakes (small callipers) is twitchy. Faster with Masten's. He offered me his car. Hotel and bath. Mayor's 'do'. On to Club and danced. Bed at 1am."

Clark	1.34.1
SM	1.34.2 Masten's car
	1.35.1 SM car
Trevor	1.34.5
Bonnier	1.34.6
Masten	1.34.5
Maggs	1.36.4 etc

"2 fast corners just on flat. 1st ease, 2nd flat."

Christmas Eve was spent relaxing as the race was to be on Boxing Day. Stirling spent the day water skiing. "Taught Jimmy Clark. Snack, trampoline and roller skated. Tea and then dinner. Party at Alco Whitefield's place. On to another one. VG. Bed at 2.30am." Unfortunately, Christmas Day was not so pleasant for the hyper-active Moss. Not only was he bored but he was also under the weather. "Up at 10. Lousy day. Wet, nothing to do all day. Food and bed at 12pm. Lousy night, sick."

Boxing Day was not a lot better but he stoically made the best of it. "Up late because I feel lousy. Circuit. Warmish and fine. Race. Had a good start. But Trevor and Jim out accelerated me. Later Jim spun and I had a lead of 14 odd secs. Couldn't keep him off. Too quick. My car OK but too slow. Other drivers really bad at getting out of the way! Felt lousy still. Hotel and bath. On to do, made speech. Bed at 2.30am."

By Wednesday, things were improving. "Beach. Sun tan. Thousands of autographs on beach. Circle of people looking all the time! Hotel (off to Jo'burg). Met by Evelyn Langley and Annette Ford and to Club. Kept changing partners !X! Bed at 2.30." Most unfortunately, the hotel sounded a bit like Fawlty Towers! "Victoria Hotel. Awful. Woken at 4am by mistake. 6.30 by tea arriving and 7.00 by church bells. 8 by maids!"

Next afternoon, Stirling was on his way back to London, via "Salisbury and Brazzaville. No Bed." Saturday: "Up at no time due to no bed. Paris and LAP. Met by Ken and to office. Work till 7.00. Met Helen and then Herb & Pat and to Candlelight Room."

Demonstrating his incredible stamina and energy right up to the end of the year, "Up at 8. Work till 6.00. Party with Val and Sprinzel, Herb and Pat, and Jane Cole."

Though the year may not have ended on a high note, it had been one of his very best. With few

When he arrived at Louis Botha Airport in South Africa, Stirling was greeted by 30 members of the Durban Vespa Club who formed a 'guard of honour' to welcome him, under the leadership of Club Chairman Frank Billing! Stirling has always favoured scooters and in 2006 was still riding a variation on the theme around London - with a large sticker on the side saying "Speedy Deliveries"!

MRS. MARGARET BUNN, a Durban racing enthusiast, was thrilled last night to receive the autograph of world-famous racing ace Stirling Moss (top picture) when he arrived at Louis Botha Airport for the Natal Grand Prix at Westmead, Pinetown, tomorrow.

Natal Grand Prix

Describing Jimmy Clark as a "Berwickshire farmer", which indeed he was, the Natal Daily News stated, "Stirling Moss, the driver most people came to see, was given a place right at the back of the starting grid. In a spectacular bid to cut the starters apart, Moss weaved through the first nine cars through Club Corner." Within 14 laps, SM had moved from 22nd to fifth place. The Motor stated that he was "indicating his displeasure with a little fist waving at slower drivers who would not co-operate on his signal to pass". Clark, who had already won the first race in the Springbok series at Kyalami, then speeded up and actually began to pull away from Moss who was up to second by lap 30. The Scot finished 30 seconds ahead of Stirling and the two were a couple of laps clear of the rest.

December

Second win for Clark in Grand Prix series

JIM CLARK, Berwickshire farmer, came home at Westmead yesterday in one of the most spectacular Grand Prix races in South Africa in 2hr. 13min. 58sec. for the 200 miles, making an average speed of 89.5 miles an hour.

Clark chalked up his second victory in South Africa in the present Springbok Grand Prix series. His first win was with Trevor Taylor (his team-mate) at Kyalami last week.

Stirling Moss, the driver most people came to see was given a place right at the back of the starting grid.

First away with Clark were Trevor Taylor (Lotus) and Jo Bonnier, No. 1 driver for the German Porsche team.

Then came Moss. In a spectacular bid to cut the starters apart Moss weaved through the first nine cars through Club Corner.

After one lap with Clark already in an established position, Moss steadily decreased his laps and in the 17th lap he raced into third position, but Clark had maintained his lead and if Moss was to catch him it would mean a far greater effort.

At this stage Moss was 39sec. behind Clark.

On the 23rd lap Moss was running second to Clark—but a long, long second. He had much leeway to make up and the question was—"would he?"

gained — and spectators went wild.

Coming round Devil's Leap Johnstone hit a bank and was out of the race. He was, however, unhurt.

This left the field open to South African champion Syd van der Vyver ... and it is to Syd's credit that he persevered and came home in fourth position.

On the ride of victory a spectator ran out on to the circuit and presented Syd with a can of beer in honour of his victory.

But it was Clark who stole the crowd.

YOU will not find this signal in the highway code, but it makes sense to racing drivers and the marshals. Stirling Moss of England, who came second to fellow-countryman Jim Clark in yesterday's first Natal Grand Prix held at Westmead, signals Jo Bonnier to "move over—I am about to overtake you." If Moss's hand had been clenched he would have meant the same, but in much stronger terms.

Post-Natal Observations

In their coverage of the Natal GP, the South African magazine, Car, wrote of Stirling's drive through the field from the back of the grid. "It was a great display of Moss virtuosity, for only one of the 20 places could really be said to have been a gift." This was when Trevor Taylor's offside rear suspension collapsed, but then he was driving a Lotus!

"At Devil's Leap, where the track dives steeply down, right-handed, into the straight, those privileged to stand on the edges of the deep cutting had an unparalleled opportunity to study driving techniques. The accuracy and consistency of Moss and Bonnier, who put their offside front wheels right on the edge of the track at precisely the same spot lap after lap, was fascinating to see. Clark was nearly as good, but not quite – occasionally he was as much as a foot away from the white line marking the verge."

Track ace arrives — Moss starts from scratch

Sunday Express Correspondent
DURBAN, Saturday.— Stirling Moss, British racing ace and one of the most experienced drivers in the world, undergoes a new racing experience tomorrow. For the first time in his track career he will be racing on a completely unfamiliar circuit without any practice.

"I'll just have to get used to it, that's all," Moss told me with a philosophical shrug.

"I've raced only once before without having practised but I was familiar with the track."

Meanwhile 100,000 fans are expected at the spanking new R180,000 Westmead track tomorrow to see one of the most exciting races in South African motor racing history.

Moss, in a Lotus Climax, will be driving at 160 m.p.h. in the 200-mile race to get ahead of his two main rivals—the crack drivers Jim Clark (of Britain) and Bonnier (of Sweden).

Moss—who always aims to get out in front of the field as soon as possible—will have to learn to track in the first few laps and get through the field all in one phase.

Stirling Moss steps from a plane at Jan Smuts Airport on his way to Durban.

Drivers

Moss on: JIM CLARK

SM: "Jimmy Clark was a naturally fast driver and I think the great thing about Jimmy really was that he had the right person to work with. In other words, Chapman had sufficient knowledge that he could interpret Jimmy's comments and benefit both of them from it. Jimmy was good enough that whatever car he had he could get the best that you could out of it. Above all, I think that it was his feedback to Colin that Colin could interpret correctly. They were a great team - probably two of the best driver-designers, period. Jimmy without Colin would have been, not wasted, but he wouldn't have done as well as he did and I think that Colin without him wouldn't have either. So they were a great pair."

PP: "Presumably, on pure and natural ability, he was the closest to you?"

SM: "I think so, yes."

PP: "So head and shoulders, really, above the rest?"

SM: "Yes."

PP: "But you didn't fear him? You respected him?"

SM: "I respected him... At the time I retired, I felt I could just about cope, as I did in Monaco, but I could see that he was looming up closer."

PP: "He often had better machinery than you."

SM: "Yes, he did."

PP: "But I suppose that he was still learning at this stage?"

SM: "Yes. He hadn't been competing for that long when I got out. I am sure that he hadn't reached his zenith when I retired."

1961

challenges left for Stirling in motor racing, due to his clear supremacy, the 'David and Goliath' scenario with him pitted against the more powerful Ferraris had set the stage perfectly for everyone's hero. It was pure theatre and the scripts were brilliant, especially as this David was up against not one but several Goliaths.

Once again, he had proven his all-round ability and pre-eminence with victories in sports cars and GT cars, as well as various single-seaters. He was at the height of his powers and, with rumours of a Walker-run Ferrari for 1962, would Stirling finally win the crown that he had unofficially worn since Fangio retired?

8th INTERNATIONAL R.A.C. SOUTH AFRICAN GRAND PRIX

EAST LONDON
26th DECEMBER, 1961

Stirling's autograph has always been in great demand and continues to be. It is a measure of his stature that his name is still known and revered around the world

Wherever he has gone in the world, Stirling has never been short of female company

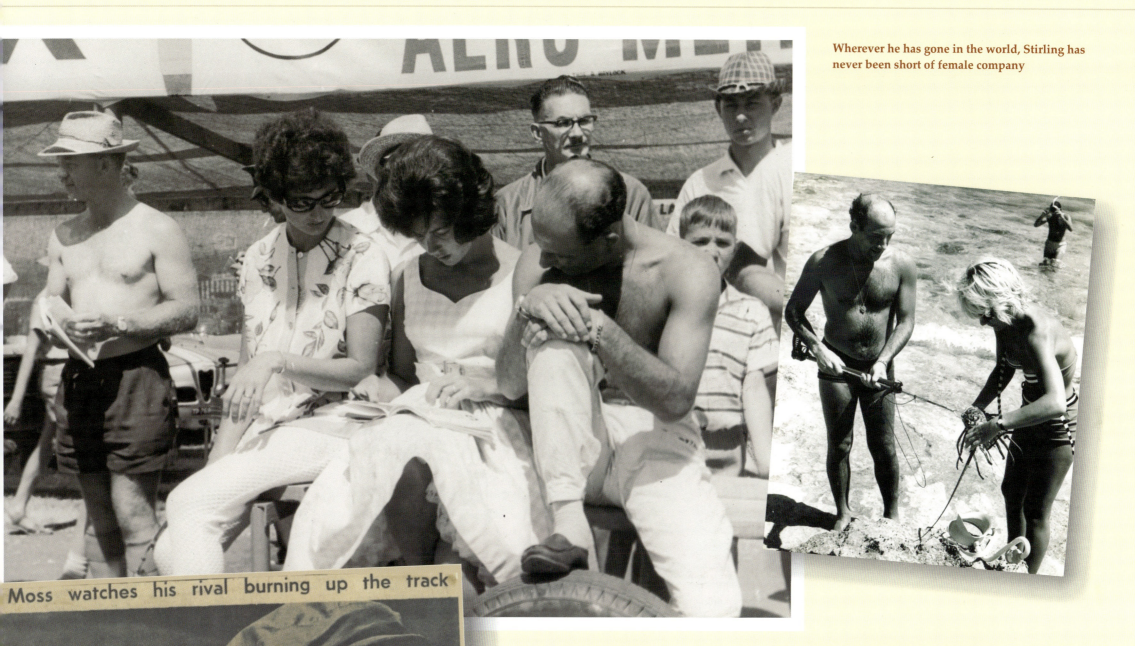

Moss watches his rival burning up the track

Team-mates STIRLING MOSS and MASTEN GREGORY look on attentively while Jim Clark sets up the fastest lap time at practice on the East London Grand Prix Circuit in his factory Lotus Climax. Clark lapped at 95.37 m.p.h. Moss lapped second fastest at 93.17 m.p.h. The U.D.T. Laystall Lotus Climaxes driven by Moss and Gregory are slower than the factory Climaxes.

Mr Moss — a prosperous man

Stirling Moss, who once described himself as a prosperous man with expensive tastes, is certainly proving the point with the new house he is building himself in Mayfair.

Though it's only three doors from the Shepherd Market home he is living in at the moment, the new house is a whole world apart in luxury fittings.

When 44-46 Shepherd Street is finished he won't get much change out of £30,000.

Stirling is designing it with the aid of an architect — and is incorporating some remarkable features.

It will have a three-car garage with radio-controlled doors. Drive up to the garage, press a button in the car, and the garage doors open automatically.

The bathrooms will be even more of a lazy man's dream.

"They will all be push-button remote control," his  secretary reveals to me. "By pressing a button in the bedroom you can run a bath to the exact depth and temperature required."

On a more utilitarian plane there will be a fully-equipped and up-to-date ground-floor office to handle Stirling's 10,000 letters a year — from fan mail to business.

Stirling, who built a house for himself in Nassau, has picked up many American ideas. It was always his ambition to build an electronic dream house.

But culture gets a look in too. He started painting about a year ago, soon after his separation from his wife Katie.

He has had lessons from Elizabeth Walker, wife of his friend Rob Walker. So there is to be a roof-top studio with patio which, incidentally, overlooks the London Hilton Hotel, now being built.

Stirling has already sold his home in Shepherd St to business man Mr Peter Werth, a wealthy hearing-aid specialist.

"I just bumped into Stirling walking down the street. He was a bit reluctant to sell his old house as the new one won't be ready for some time," said Mr Werth.

Stirling Moss Scrapbook 1961

BP welcomes the drivers

ILLUSTRATED ARE SOME OF THE DRIVERS COMPETING IN THE SOUTH AFRICAN GRANDS PRIX SEASON

STIRLING MOSS. British—(U.D.T./Laystall Team) Driving a Lotus Climax Formula 1. Named as "Driver of the Year" by the Guild of Motor Writers (first man to win this award twice). Seven times winner of the R.A.C. Tourist Trophy Race.

JO BONNIER. Swedish—(Porsche Works Team) Driving latest V-8 Formula 1 Porsche. Latest successes include 5th British Grand Prix, 6th American Grand Prix.

MASTEN GREGORY. American—(U.D.T./Laystall Team) Driving Lotus Climax Formula 1.

EDGAR BARTH. German—(Porsche Works Team). Driving latest V-8 Formula 1 Porsche.

BERNIE PODMORE. S. African—Driving Lotus 20 with modified Ford Classic 1,466 c.c. engine.

CLIVE TRUNDELL. S. African — Driving a Cooper Climax Mark II, modified.

TONY MAGGS. S. African—(Yeoman Credit Team) Driving a Mark II Type Cooper Climax Formula 1. Has just won 1961 European Formula Junior Championship.

BRUCE JOHNSTONE. S. African—(Yeoman Credit Team) Driving a Mark II Cooper Climax Formula 1. Runner-up to 1961 South African Champion Driver.

BOB van NIEKERK. S. African—Driving the Equipe Judette Lotus-Ford. Experience both in South Africa and Overseas.

REMEMBER LA...
1960 CAPE IN...
1st STIRLING MOSS (PORSCHE)

PREVIOUS WINNERS

(PRINCE GEORGE CIRCUIT, EAST LONDON)

1934	WHITNEY STRAIGHT (Maserati)	95.43 m.p.h.
1936	"MARIO" (Bugatti)	87.33 m.p.h.
1937	PAT FAIRFIELD (E.R.A.)	89.25 m.p.h.
1938	BULLER MEYER (Riley)	86.53 m.p.h.
1939	LUIGI VILLORESI (Maserati)	99.67 m.p.h.

(GRAND PRIX CIRCUIT, EAST LONDON)

1960	PAUL FRERE (Cooper-Climax)	84.88 m.p.h.
1961	STIRLING MOSS (Porsche)	89.24 m.p.h.

South African Grand Prix

With Stirling's UDT/Laystall Lotus awaiting valve springs, he was keen to set a time in first practice on the Friday with team mate Gregory's car to at least qualify. The organisers contended that he had to set a time in his own car so Stirling simply changed the numbers on Masten's car! The East London Daily Dispatch described the race as "the most exciting Grand Prix staged in South Africa since the Second World War". The front row consisted of Clark, Stirling and Trevor Taylor, the Lotus number two. Taylor led initially but Clark and Moss soon asserted themselves in the lead. When Clark spun, avoiding another spinning car, Stirling inherited a 14 second lead but Clark drove brilliantly to whittle it down and retake first place, which was the final finishing order. Autocar reported SM saying in a postcard, "Jimmy is too good to use a two-year-old car against."

The maestro and the 'young pretender' Jim Clark. What a tragedy that, with Stirling's career-ending accident in 1962, they would not enjoy future battles for years to come, in rather the same way as Senna's untimely death robbed the world of a true competitor for Schumacher

Mouse

RACING driver Stirling Moss was sporting an unusual ornament on his immaculate dark lapel when he flew from London Airport to New York yesterday.

It was a tiny golden mouse's head, its round nose peeping from his buttonhole

"It's the badge of the Mouse Club," said Stirling.

"No, it's nothing to do with racing. Just a bunch of friends." And, he added "it's like— well it's like—actually I can't think of any other club that it is like. That's why I belong to it."

Faster car was the key factor

Evening Post 27/12/

Staff Reporter

Slower Lotus

Yesterday Moss was driving a UDT-Laystall owned Lotus-Climax—but it was a 1960 model, bulkier and slower by at least five miles an hour, possibly more, than the very latest factory car of the same make driven by Clark and team-mate Trevor Taylor.

Even if Clark had not spun off, Moss would have been no more than 30 or 40 seconds behind him at the finish. When one considers that the race was over 200 miles this is no mean achievement.

Trying to keep as far ahead of Clark as possible after the spin, Moss gave a thrilling exhibition of Grand Prix driving "at the limit" — in every sense of the word.

Close thing

He braked later than any of the other drivers, cut his corners so fine that he mounted the kerb on a number of occasions. His driving through the Esses was a thrill to watch.

On one occasion he appeared to be heading for a serious accident as he tried to pass Fanie Viljoen in his Cooper-Climax. As he came up behind the slower car there was a brief "Eeee . . . ee" and Moss' car nose touched one of Viljoen's tyres.

A brief puff of smoke, a slight movement of Moss' wheel—and he was off, slicing through the field again.

The Mouse Club

"The Mouse Club was for a small number of people. The point was, if you met a girl and she was really nice and you got along with her really well, the other Mouse Club members had similar tastes and so you could say to the girl. 'Look, if you are going over to the Bahamas, there is a Mouse Club member there. Go and see him.' And he in turn would know she would be a lot of fun and good-looking. It never really went anywhere but a few of us enjoyed being members. There were two or three founder members including myself. All the guys had to have a similar outlook, enjoy going out for dinner and chatting up a girl. We had similar tastes in life at that time. We had some little gold mice made, a bit like tie pins, and if the girls were that special they would get one of those!"

*Am 20 Monte Carlo-
laps 1961
Weitmann*